Philosophers in the *Republic*

PHILOSOPHERS IN THE *REPUBLIC*

Plato's Two Paradigms

ROSLYN WEISS

CORNELL UNIVERSITY PRESS
ITHACA AND LONDON

First published 2012 by Cornell University Press

Printed in the United States of America

Library of Congress Cataloging-in-Publication Data

Weiss, Roslyn.
    Philosophers in the Republic : Plato's two paradigms / Roslyn Weiss.
        p. cm.
    Includes bibliographical references and index.
    ISBN 978-0-8014-4974-1 (cloth : alk. paper)
    1. Plato. Republic.   2. Justice (Philosophy)   3. Ethics.   I. Title.
    B395.W46 2012
    321'.07—dc23   2012015970

Cornell University Press strives to use environmentally responsible suppli-
ers and materials to the fullest extent possible in the publishing of
its books. Such materials include vegetable-based, low-VOC inks and
acid-free papers that are recycled, totally chlorine-free, or partly composed
of nonwood fibers. For further information, visit our website at
www.cornellpress.cornell.edu.

Cloth printing   10 9 8 7 6 5 4 3 2 1

For my beloved family

Excessive friendship for oneself is the cause of all of each man's wrongdoings on every occasion. . . . A man who is to attain greatness must be devoted not to himself or to what belongs to him, but to what is just.

—Plato, *Laws* 5.731e-732a

Contents

Acknowledgments   ix

Introduction: Two Paradigms   1

1. Philosophers by Nature   11

2. Philosophers by Design I: The Making of a Philosopher   49

3. Philosophers by Design II: The Making of a Ruler   85

4. Socratic Piety: The Fifth Cardinal Virtue   129

5. Justice as Moderation   164

Conclusion: "In a Healthy Way"   208

Works Cited   219

Index   227

ACKNOWLEDGMENTS

This book has been percolating for many years. Writing on the *Republic* is not a linear process. Interpretations seem right, then wrong, then better, yet still not just right. One tries again, goes back to the beginning. Finally, a book emerges—narrower in scope, more modest in ambition.

I am grateful for the many opportunities I have had to test and refine my understanding of Plato's great work. The first occasion was a conference organized by John Ferrari at the University of California, Berkeley. Other venues followed: St. Francis College, Mansfield University, the Northeastern Political Science Association, the American Philosophical Association, Marquette University, the Eastern Pennsylvania Philosophical Association, Bar-Ilan University, University of South Carolina, the Society for Ancient Greek Philosophy, University of South Florida, Case Western Reserve University, The Hebrew University of Jerusalem, University of Haifa, the International Symposium Platonicum—Tokyo, the Boston Area Colloquium in Ancient Philosophy, the Israel Society for the Promotion of Classical Studies, the Arizona Colloquium in Ancient Philosophy, and Texas Tech University. An earlier version of parts of Chapter 2 and Chapter 3 was published in the *Proceedings of the Boston Area Colloquium in Ancient Philosophy*, vol. 27, edited by Gary S. Gurtler, SJ (Leiden: Brill, 2012), under the title "The Unjust Philosophers of *Rep*. VII." It is reprinted with permission.

I appreciate the support of Lehigh University, which granted me a leave of absence for the spring of 2009 and the spring of 2010. I thank my colleague Robin Dillon for stepping in to chair the Philosophy Department for both semesters in my absence. The National Endowment for the Humanities awarded me a summer stipend in 2007 and a fellowship for 2010. (The views, findings, conclusions, or recommendations expressed in this publication do not necessarily reflect those of the National Endowment for the Humanities.) I acknowledge as well the ongoing support provided by the Clara H. Stewardson Chair.

For two hours every Tuesday afternoon for fourteen weeks, my colleagues in the Philosophy Department at Lehigh read and discussed the *Republic*, and considered what I had to say about it. They offered support—and criticism—and a variety of fresh perspectives. They are Gordon Bearn, Mark Bickhard, Robin Dillon, Steven Goldman, Michael Mendelson, Gregory Reihman, and Aladdin Yaqub. Other participants in the seminar were Robert Barnes, Bernard Dauenhauer, and Barbara Frankel.

I wish to thank the students who undertook independent studies on the *Republic* under my direction: Dave Eck, Nicole Corali, Dan Roxbury, Tom Cleary, and EJ Schuck. Together we tackled the *Republic*, reflecting on questions and problems old and new.

Two anonymous referees for Cornell University Press proved invaluable. The first persuaded me to drop the three chapters I had already written and to start the book at what was originally to be Chapter 4. The second raised a whole host of challenging questions that I have subsequently done my best to address. A special thank-you to Peter J. Potter, my editor at the Press, who read the manuscript and offered his perspicuous advice and unwavering moral support at every stage of the project's development.

I would like to acknowledge my Plato friends: William Altman, Ronna Burger, Mary Louise Gill, John Ferrari, Anthony Long, Ivor Ludlam, Gerry Mara, Mitchell Miller, Alexander Nehamas, Arlene Saxonhouse, and Alan Udoff. All had a hand in making this book better.

Donna Wagner, the Philosophy Department coordinator at Lehigh, has been helpful to me in all things. Jessica Morgan, a student at Lehigh, ably assisted me in preparing the final manuscript.

My wonderful family—my husband, Sam, and my daughters, Miriam and Dena—are my emotional mainstays.

INTRODUCTION

Two Paradigms

The modest aim of this book is to show that Plato's *Republic* contains two distinct and irreconcilable portrayals of the philosopher.[1] That this is so is something of which I am deeply confident.[2] I am less sure, however, of why this is so: it is one thing to read a text, quite another to read the mind of its author.

As I understand Plato's dialogues, particularly those in which there is animated interaction between Socrates and his interlocutors, their aim

---

1. I will of necessity pay scant attention to the *Republic*'s metaphysics—Forms, the Good, and the divided line—and to several of its central concerns: degenerate regimes, education, censorship, poetry, and the detailed workings of Callipolis and its origins in the "healthy" "city of sows." Two issues that are accorded somewhat more thorough consideration are the nature of justice and the city-soul analogy. I avoid entirely the question of whether the *Republic* is best understood as political or as psychological/moral. The books I emphasize are 6 and 7, where the two paradigms are developed.

2. The first of these two portrayals begins at 5.473c, continues on to 6.490d, and is revived and completed at 6.496a-502c; the second starts at 6.502c, runs through all of Book 7, and is summarized in the opening passage of Book 8 at 543a-c.

is to put the philosophic life on display. The characters in them, though fictionalized, are real enough: there were—are—such types. And within their respective types, the characters are each unique—as real people are. Socrates tailors his therapeutic method to the needs of his varied interlocutors, making the necessary concessions to their moral and intellectual limitations.

By presenting images of philosophy in action, Plato's dialogues speak to us, his readers. One might say that they contain two messages: one, Socrates'; the other, Plato's. Socrates' message is in the first instance for his interlocutors—not for us. It is driven by his interlocutors' moral character and by the quirks of their personalities, by their good intentions and bad, by their interests, by their desires, by the level of their understanding, and by their willingness or reluctance to inquire further. But Plato's message is for us; he invariably finds a way to remind us—by inserting some glaring peculiarity in the text[3]—that we are not Socrates' interlocutors but his.[4] It is, after all, oddities that give pause and spur thinking: in the *Phaedo* (100e-101c), what is said to rattle complacency are such puzzles as how the taller man and the shorter are taller and shorter by the very same thing ("by a head"), or how the taller man is taller by something small (a head), or how both addition and division can be the cause of two; in the *Republic* (7.523a-525a), what is said to "summon or awaken the activity of intellect" are such questions as how a finger can be simultaneously large and small, hard and soft.[5] Inconsistencies in a Platonic dialogue are therefore not to be papered over and domesticated, but acknowledged and confronted. Plato counts on his readers to disentangle Socrates' exchange with his interlocutors from

3. See Strauss (1952, 36), who lists the following as examples of "obtrusively enigmatic features" that serve as guides to the hidden truths of a text: "obscurity of the plan, contradictions, pseudonyms, inexact repetitions of earlier statements, strange expressions, etc."

4. It is occasionally objected to such a view that Plato's dialogues were not intended to be read, and hence certainly were not meant to be scrutinized for hints or clues. I am not convinced that this is so: philosophers before Plato wrote books that were read and studied. It is furthermore fairly evident that Aristotle read Plato's dialogues. Plato was meticulous in the attention he paid to detail; could he really not have intended or expected his work to be read?

5. Translated passages from the *Republic* follow Bloom's translation (1968), with occasional modifications. Translated passages from all other works by Plato rely on the translations cited in the bibliography, modified as needed. Unless otherwise noted, emphasis in quoted passages is mine.

his own address to us.[6] Although there is surely overlap between the two, there is never complete identity. We are to draw the lesson Plato intends for us by watching the interplay between Socrates and his interlocutors.

Plato's presentation in the *Republic* of two incompatible portraits of the philosopher is a case in point. Plato positions his readers to detect the deficiencies in the second philosopher by revealing—in advance—a philosopher of a different stripe. If the first philosopher can reasonably be thought to represent a Platonic ideal, then the second, a philosopher radically different from the first, cannot. If the second philosopher is thus not only second but second-rate, it is because he reflects the character and taste not of Socrates or Plato but of Socrates' interlocutors Glaucon and Adeimantus.

I. The Brothers

Glaucon and Adeimantus are Plato's brothers, and Plato's *Republic* is largely addressed to them. The more imposing of the two is Glaucon,[7] yet there are extensive and important stretches of text in which Socrates responds to the trenchant challenges posed by Adeimantus. Although the brothers are by no means interchangeable, they are not so unlike as to

---

6. I do not mean to imply, with Strauss (1952, 36), that Plato speaks to some special subset of his audience, who form an elite society of his readers: "An exoteric book contains two teachings: a popular teaching of an edifying character, which is in the foreground; and a philosophic teaching concerning the most important subject, which is indicated only between the lines. . . . Exoteric literature presupposes that there are basic truths which would not be pronounced in public by any decent man." I tend, on the contrary, to agree with J. Sachs (2004, 5) that a Platonic dialogue is *not* "a way of speaking in code to certain favored readers while screening out the rest." As I see it, all Plato's *readers* are "favored"; it is the dialogues' protagonists who often are kept in the dark. Furthermore, I doubt that Plato's "basic truths" smack of indecency. On the contrary, they are, if anything, too decent, perhaps too progressive, to be acceptable to most of Socrates' interlocutors. There is, of course, the *Republic*'s notorious proposal that the public be told lies (3.414b-415d). But, first, this directive is announced quite openly; it is in the "foreground" and hardly "between the lines." And, second, it cannot be simply assumed that Plato intends Socrates' recommendation to be taken at face value, or to be applied in any city other than Callipolis.

7. The dialogue opens with Glaucon accompanying Socrates to the Piraeus and making the decision that they must remain there instead of going home (328b). And in the *Republic*'s final scene, it is Glaucon who is Socrates' interlocutor: "And thus, Glaucon, a tale was saved and not lost" (621b).

require significantly different messages. I think it fair to say that their beliefs are alike; where they diverge is largely in their style.[8]

Adeimantus is the less refined and less inhibited of the brothers. He
will blurt out what others are perhaps too polite or too timid to say.[9] When
Glaucon defends injustice in Book 2 Adeimantus brazenly adds what
his brother left unsaid (362d). It is not that he disagrees with his brother;
he just goes further. At the beginning of Book 4 Adeimantus interrupts
Socrates' conversation with Glaucon and demands to know why the guardians are not being made happy (419a). When at the beginning of Book 5
Polemarchus has a question for Socrates he whispers it in Adeimantus's
ear, unsure whether or not to press the matter. It is Adeimantus who then
"speaks aloud": Socrates will not be let go, Adeimantus declares (449b),
until he provides an adequate answer. In Book 6 Glaucon registers mild
tentativeness about philosophic rule (484b), but Adeimantus is strident:
he denounces philosophers as useless or vicious (487c-d). Later on in the
same book Adeimantus impudently presumes that Thrasymachus would
oppose a view Socrates has expressed (498c). And in Book 8 Socrates has to
correct Adeimantus's overhasty and exaggerated charge that Glaucon fits
the profile of the timocratic man.

Glaucon is more genteel. His early objection to the "city of sows" surely
has more to do with that city's crudeness and rusticity, with its unfitness
for gentlemen, for "men who aren't going to be wretched" (2.372d), than
with the absence in it of a multitude of vulgar sensual pleasures. It is his
aesthetic sensibility that is offended; he is no coarse hedonist. Moreover,
Glaucon seems proud to have had a hand in censoring, purging, and puri-
fying his more gentrified version of the city of sows, the one Socrates labels

---

8. Because Adeimantus does not object—and Glaucon does—to the first, luxury-free, city, the
one Glaucon calls a "city of sows," Bloom concludes (1968, 346) that Adeimantus is the more moderate of the two, that he "has the capacity for self-restraint, a certain austerity not shared by Glaucon" (369). So, too, Strauss (1964, 90–91): "Glaucon is characterized by manliness and impetuosity
rather than by moderation and quietness and the opposite is true of Adeimantus." But Glaucon
is no enemy of moderation, and Adeimantus is not its friend. Indeed, Bloom later calls Adeimantus "a secret lover of wealth" (371). Once Adeimantus realizes that the guardians will be deprived
of lands, fine big houses, accessories, and gold and silver, he is incensed and demands an explanation (419a). Perhaps he didn't object to the first city simply because he did not immediately grasp
its full implications.

9. In this way Adeimantus resembles Callicles, whom Socrates credits with saying what others are thinking but are insufficiently outspoken to say (*Gorg.* 487d).

"luxurious" (*truphōsan*) or "feverish" (*phlegmainousan*) (372e): "That's a sign of our moderation," he says in Book 3 (399e). And he is pleased with Socrates' definition of justice in *Rep.* 4 as health in the soul; he quite likes the idea that, no matter what a man acquires, life would not be worth living for him if his soul were confused and corrupted (445a-b). He comes to embrace the stern measures of the city Socrates fashions (5.471c-e); he protests only when he suspects that Socrates may be treating the philosophers unjustly (7.519d). But even here he takes comfort in knowing that philosophers are being asked to do only what is their duty.

Glaucon is thus admirable in many respects. As David Roochnik puts it (2003, 56), "Glaucon is responsible for the forward momentum of the *Republic*. His energy, his passion for the conversation, his forcefulness, and his crucial insights are necessary goads for an otherwise reluctant Socrates. Glaucon is courageous (357a), ready to laugh (398c7), musical (398e1), and spirited (548d8). Most important, he is erotic (474d); he has both a lover (368a) and a beloved (402e)."

Glaucon may well be eager to participate in philosophic conversation ("For intelligent men the proper measure of listening to such arguments is a whole life," he says at 450b), but still he is no philosopher—nor will he ever become one.[10] (Neither, surely, will Adeimantus.) He is too much the Athenian gentleman—too traditional (he likes things "as is conventional," *haper nomizetai*—372d), too prosaic, too worldly; moreover, smart as he is, he is not smart enough.[11] Indeed, Socrates fairly frequently—though often by way of banter and always good-naturedly (see, for example, 5.474c; 6.507a, 509a, 509c; 7.523b, 527c)—disparages Glaucon's intelligence and philosophic ability. At 7.533a Socrates bluntly informs him of his limitations: "You will no longer be able to follow, my dear Glaucon." And at 10.595e-596a, in a particularly charming exchange, Glaucon freely concedes to Socrates that his vision, as compared with Socrates', is the duller one.[12]

---

10. Bloom (1968, 411) thinks Glaucon "may well be" one of the young men in whom a philosopher's soul delights, "for they have souls akin to his own and are potential philosophers."

11. Commentators on the *Republic* are generally awed by Glaucon's intelligence. See, for example, Dobbs (1994, 263), who raves: "The radiance of his [Glaucon's] intellect renders Thrasymachus . . . virtually invisible". But how impressed is Socrates?

12. Cf. 7.517c, where Glaucon clearly recognizes his own limitations. With respect to the need for a man to see the Good if he is to act prudently in private or in public, Glaucon says: "I, too, join you in supposing that, *at least in the way I can*."

II. Engaging Glaucon and Adeimantus

Socrates undertakes two formidable tasks in the *Republic*. The first is imposed on him by Glaucon and Adeimantus: they ask him to establish for them the worth of justice. The second originates with Socrates: it is he who wants the brothers to value the philosopher as a vital element in a well-governed city. Lest they think that a city can be optimal without philosophers, that it can excel even if no one in it aspires to transcend opinion and custom, Socrates deliberately, though hardly gracefully,[13] injects philosophers and philosophic rule into his beautiful and otherwise complete city, one originally managed quite successfully by guardians noted for their courage and moderation—not for their wisdom.

Glaucon and Adeimantus require an account of the worth of justice because, like many others, they esteem what is profitable—to oneself; both believe that the saving grace of any activity is the benefit or advantage it yields for the agent.[14] In Book 1 Glaucon immediately turns Socrates' question about the superiority of justice into one concerning its greater profitability. Socrates asks: "Which do you choose, Glaucon, and which speech is truer in your opinion?" (347e)—that is, is Thrasymachus right to believe that the life of the unjust man is superior (*kreittō*) as compared with that of the just man, or is Socrates right to oppose him? And Glaucon answers: "I for my part choose the life of the just man as more profitable (*lusitelesteron*)" (347e).[15] To be sure, the profit in justice of which Glaucon and Adeimantus seek to be assured needn't be material:[16] they are well

---

13. Socrates introduces philosophers on the pretext that they alone can turn his imaginary city in speech (one in which women do the same jobs as men, and in which women and children are held in common) into an actually existing one. But surely what is needed to effect a change of such magnitude is political power—not a philosopher's grasp of "what is."

14. See Cicero, *Amic.* 79: "But the vast majority of mankind recognize nothing as good in the human sphere unless it be something profitable." For translated passages of Cicero I use the Loeb Classical Library editions cited in the bibliography.

15. Dobbs (1994, 263) rightly notes that although Glaucon is inclined, as a result of his "native breeding," to prefer justice, he nevertheless lacks what one might call "mature human excellence."

16. Glaucon is not by any means averse to hearing that the just receive material rewards. At 10.612b-614a Socrates restores to the just man his reputation for justice and with it all the "prizes, wages, and gifts coming to the just man while alive from gods and human beings" (613e-614a). And as he is about to add to these good things all the others that "await each when dead," Glaucon says: "Do tell, since there aren't many other things that would be more pleasant to hear" (614b).

aware that material benefit attaches not to the reality of justice but to its appearance—after all, gods and men reward what they see (2.366b)—yet they remain open to the possibility that justice itself, even if unobserved, might be profitable. What they cannot conceive is how a thing might be desirable without affording profit of any kind to its possessor.[17] If justice benefits not oneself but another, Socrates will be hard-pressed to convince the brothers that it is a good of the noblest kind, one that deserves to be liked both on its own account and for its consequences (358).

Socrates' second task is no less daunting. As he anticipates, Glaucon finds the prospect of philosophic rule preposterous (5.473e–474a). Like other men of action and ambition,[18] of courage and dignity, and of purpose, Glaucon doubts the practical value of philosophy, and regards its practitioners as sorely lacking in the requisite sophistication and virility. As someone who is himself "most manly" (*andreiotatos*—357a), Glaucon is apparently less exercised by manly women (female warriors and rulers) than he is by womanly men.

Justice and philosophy as they really are have, then, unfortunately, little hope of winning Glaucon's and Adeimantus's admiration. What is called for, therefore, are slightly distorted versions of each. If the only way Socrates can render justice attractive to Glaucon is by casting it as the soul's healthy condition—Glaucon regards health, whether of body (2.357c) or soul (4.444d), as desirable in itself and advantageous *for the person who has it*[19]—so be it; if the only way he can make the philosopher appealing is by merging him with the warrior (7.525b, 8.543a), that is what he will do. Although the healthy state of the soul is not justice but moderation, and although the true philosopher is no warrior, Socrates knows he cannot be

---

17. For Glaucon, things that are painful but beneficial count as good things (357c); these are the very things that Socrates in the *Gorgias* calls bad (467c-e). And pleasures that are harmless are considered good things as well. The things that Glaucon thinks aren't good, then, are (1) harmful pleasures and (2) unpleasant things that provide no benefit.

18. Strauss (1964, 65), relying to some extent on Xenophon's portrayal of Glaucon at *Mem.* 3.6.16, attributes to him "extreme political ambition," which he thinks Socrates seeks in the *Republic* to cure. Ferrari ([2003] 2005, 13–15) is of the opinion that the brothers have become quietists and need to be coaxed back to an engaged political life.

19. Note that Glaucon is not repelled by Socrates' characterization in Book 1 of good and decent men as those who would never consider something other than their "own advantage," who would never "take the trouble to benefit another" when they might be the ones to be benefited (347d).

effective without compromise. Yet, as I argue in Chapter 5, when Socrates in *Rep.* 4 blurs—and finally effaces—the line between justice and moderation, the sleight of hand is transparent; it is there for any attentive reader to see. And as I show in Chapter 1, the pronounced shift at 6.502c-d from one philosophic paradigm to another[20] enables the reader—if not Glaucon and Adeimantus—to distinguish fairly easily between the pure first philosopher and the composite second one. Although it is philosophers of the second kind whom Glaucon praises as wholly noble (*pankalous*—540b), the reader is in a position to know better because he has already seen better.

III. Two Cities and Two Kinds of Philosopher-Ruler

In Books 2–5 Socrates constructs for Glaucon (and, to a lesser extent, for Adeimantus) a city that he will later call "the beautiful city" (*kallipolis*—7.527c). Callipolis is not Plato's or Socrates' ideal city but is intended to be Glaucon's. Though not the city that Glaucon would have created on his own, it nevertheless reflects his preferences even as it modifies them. Callipolis is a city marked by repression, social stratification, and discipline—in accordance with Glaucon's ideals; but Socrates at 6.503b places philosophers at its helm. These philosophers, designed specifically for Callipolis, come to philosophy by coercion and are made to rule against their will. Chapters 2 and 3 are devoted to them—Chapter 2 to their nature and education, Chapter 3 to their rule. They are shown to be not philosophic but appetitive by nature, intellectually gifted—and so able to scale the heights of wisdom if forced to—and "not unwilling" (519d, 520d-e) to rule when persuaded that ruling is their best option. Rather than pursue as their first concern the improvement of the moral condition of their subjects, however, they seek to secure the city's efficiency or "happiness" by exiling from it all those older than ten. These philosophers represent, on the one hand,

---

20. As I argue in Chapter 1, section IV, the switch between paradigms would have been more evident had Book 7 begun in Book 6 at 502c, where there is, in fact, a clear break. At that juncture Socrates notes that one discussion "has after considerable effort reached an end" (cf. the remarkably similar opening words of Book 6), so that a fresh start is now in order: "But what concerns the rulers must be pursued as it were *from the beginning* (*ex archēs*)" (502e). It is unlikely that the *Republic*'s division into books was Plato's doing.

Socrates' attempt to find for philosophy a place in Glaucon's city and, on the other, his concession to the reality that philosophy as it truly is has no place in Callipolis.

But there is another city, a better city, which, although it appears only briefly (500d-502c), nevertheless offers a distinct alternative to Callipolis. It arises by chance rather than by coercion, and by chance, too, it is governed by philosophers—real philosophers. In Chapter 1, I identify, from among the four philosophic types found in *Rep.* 6 (only two of which are actually called philosophers), the genuine philosopher, the philosopher by nature. This philosopher, first introduced in Book 5's "third wave" (473c-d), is distinguished by possessing, in addition to his intellectual prowess and his passionate love of wisdom, a full complement of moral and personal qualities. Should this philosopher come by chance to rule, his principal aim would be to perfect the city's laws and the soul of each and every citizen (501a-c). It is surely this philosopher whom Plato hopes his readers will admire, one whose love for the transcendent motivates him to promote the moral excellence of other human beings. He provides a welcome contrast to the philosopher who would spend his time contemplating the intelligible realm of being, but would be so profoundly indifferent to other people that he would expend no effort on improving their character (519c-d).

IV. A Third Paradigm?

The one philosopher the *Republic* is virtually silent about is Socrates. Although he is briefly associated with Book 6's philosophers by nature (496c)—for the sake of simplicity, I call the philosophers whose description begins at 5.473c and runs until 6.502c "Book 6's philosophers"—he cannot simply be one of them. Whereas these philosophers "stand aside under a little wall" (496d)—that is, withdraw from the city to keep their souls pure (496d-e)—when they are surrounded by political corruption and have no "ally" with whom to come to the aid of justice (496d), Socrates, as we know from the *Apology* (23b, 31a-c, 36b, 38a), under the very same conditions, makes a point of frequenting public spaces and talking to anyone he encounters. If the philosophers of Book 6 are better than those of Book 7—I call the philosophers whose description begins at 6.502c and runs through Book 7 "Book 7's philosophers"—but Socrates is better still, would he not constitute a third paradigm that is superior to both?[21] In Chapter 4 I argue that Socrates not only surpasses the appetitive men coerced into philosophy in Callipolis but rises, too, above the natural philosophers of the city of chance. His justice reaches the very highest level, that of piety, a virtue as conspicuously absent from *Rep.* 4's list of four cardinal virtues as Socrates is from the four philosophic types specified in Rep. 6. The kind of justice Socrates embodies goes beyond not harming others (the level of justice Book 7's philosophers reach); it even goes beyond helping others when conditions are right (the level attained by the philosophers of Book 6). Socrates fosters justice in others even at his own peril, and so is indeed in a class by himself. He thus represents a third paradigm—but one that lies outside the confines of the *Republic*: none of the philosophers described *in* the *Republic* can meet his standard.

V. Justice

In Chapter 5 I show how Socrates skillfully reduces justice to moderation, the healthy psychic state that Glaucon finds so attractive. It is left to Plato's readers, to those who watch this subterfuge unfold, to raise the question, If the healthy and harmonious condition of the soul is moderation, what is justice? Since Socrates repeatedly insists that justice is a fourth virtue distinct from the other three, one that even "rivals" them (433d), it is up to us, Plato's readers, to recognize that it is justice's unselfishness, the fact that it is concerned for others, that makes it the primary virtue, the "power" that anchors all the others, both producing and preserving them (4.433b-c). It may be salutary for Glaucon and Adeimantus to confuse justice with moderation, but it is not good for us. We must see that there is beauty— nobility—in being concerned for others. It is indeed when one strives to protect the interests of others, and in the best case even to further everyone's most important interest, personal virtue, that one lives well and fares well: *eu prattōmen* (10.621d).[22]

---

21. In the *Apology* Socrates declares that the god has made of him a paradigm: "And he appears . . . to have made use of my name in order to make a pattern (*paradeigma*) of me, as if he would say: 'That one of you, O human beings, is wisest, who, *like Socrates*, has become cognizant that in truth he is worth nothing with respect to wisdom'" (*Ap.* 23a-b).

22. It is with these words that the *Republic* ends.

1

PHILOSOPHERS BY NATURE

A joy to the righteous is the doing of justice, an agony to evil doers.
—Proverbs 21:25

Readers of the *Republic* reasonably expect all its philosophers to be the same. But, just as the dialogue identifies more than one best ruler—first a brave and moderate military man, next a practically wise man, and finally a philosopher—so, too, does it present more than one kind of philosopher: the philosopher by nature and the philosopher by design. These two are the first and last of four philosophic types limned in *Rep.* 6: (1) the philosophic nature that remains true to philosophy to the end; (2) the philosophic nature that becomes corrupted and turns to villainy; (3) the imitation philosopher—the man who wishes to be a philosopher but whose inferior nature prevents him from realizing his goal; and (4) a new breed of philosopher fashioned so as to combine within himself both philosopher and warrior. Although accounts of all four types are found in *Rep.* 6, the first type—the philosopher by nature—makes his initial appearance near the end of Book 5 in Socrates' "third wave" (at 473c), and the fourth type—the philosopher by design—is the subject of Book 7. (There is perhaps a fifth philosophic type found in the *Republic*, the "philosophic" dogs of Book 2 and the guardians who resemble them; they are discussed in the addendum to the current chapter.) Of these four (or five), only the first, the one who is inclined by his nature to strive to grasp the highest realities, the one who is driven to "what is" by an innate desire for truth and love of wisdom and who remains faithful to his calling throughout his life, is fully authentic. In this chapter the genuine philosopher will be distinguished from his three (or four) defective approximations.

I. The Natural Philosopher

Not until Book 5 is there any suggestion in the *Republic* that the rulers of Socrates' city are to be philosophers. In Book 4 the rulers of the new city are the "more moderate few" (434c-d). They are those who are born with the "best natures":[1] their "simple and measured desires, pleasures, and pains [are] led by reasoning accompanied by intelligence (*nou*) and right opinion" (431c). The wisdom they have is practical: it is "knowledge (*epistēmē*) concerning how the city as a whole would best deal with itself and with other cities" (428d).[2]

Socrates recommends the rule of the wise with full assurance, not fearing any resistance to it from his companions. And indeed so long as Socrates positions men of sound judgment—but not philosophers—at the city's helm, his proposal strikes neither Glaucon nor the others assembled in the home of Polemarchus as ridiculous or as lacking in "measure" (cf. 6.484b). It is only Socrates' bold pronouncement near the end of Book 5 that "there is no rest from ills for the cities . . . nor for humankind"[3] "unless the

---

1. "Best natures" will later apply not only to philosophic natures but also to the nature of the philosopher-warrior introduced in Book 6 (from 502c on) and further developed in Book 7. See 491d, 491e, 495b, 497c, 501d, 519c, 526c. In Book 4 it entails no more than moderation and the rule of reason. So, too, in Book 9 (591b). See Chapter 2, section III; and Chapter 2, note 39.

2. Analogously, the wisdom with which reason rules the soul is "knowledge (*epistēmē*) of that which is beneficial for each part and for the whole composed of the community of these three parts" (442c); reason "is wise and has forethought (*promētheian*) for all of the soul" (441e).

3. In earlier books, other remedies are prescribed to save the city. In Book 3 Socrates advises that the overseers in the city be properly harmonized, and hence moderate and courageous, "if the regime is going to be saved" (412a); he also seems to think that the city's salvation turns on the guardians' avoiding contact with gold and silver (417a). In Book 4 he suggests that the city is doomed if the classes fail to do their own jobs (434b-c). In Book 5 "the community of pain and

philosophers rule as kings or those now called kings and chiefs genuinely and adequately philosophize" (473c-d) that arouses skepticism and scorn (473e-474a). Socrates is fully aware of how outrageous his proposition is: because of its unorthodoxy (*para doxan*) he is hesitant to speak (473e); he expects to be "drowned in laughter and ill repute" (473c; cf. 499b-c). And in truth, although the first two "waves"—that women ought to be assigned the same jobs as men, and that women and children should be held in common—are incontestably bizarre,[4] it is the third, philosophic rule, that seems to defy all common sense:[5] could there be any course less reasonable than entrusting the management of a city's internal and external affairs to men who do nothing but daydream and chatter?[6]

Socrates sees only one way to render his proposal more palatable to the present company. He must set the record straight on the nature of the philosopher (474b; cf. 490d, 499e-500a), not only bringing him "plainly to light," but distinguishing (*diorisasthai*) him from the non-philosopher (474b), showing his nature to be extraordinary, superior. Only then, he thinks, will it be possible to show that "it is by nature fitting for philosophers both to engage in philosophy and to lead a city, and for the rest not to engage in philosophy and to follow the leader" (474b-c).[7] Socrates instructs Glaucon to "follow"; Glaucon asks Socrates to "lead."[8]

---

pleasure," and hence "the community of children and women among the auxiliaries," is said to be "the greatest good for a city" (464b). Once the notion of philosophic rule is introduced, however, at 473c, it is only on this that the city's salvation is said to depend: 473d, 473e, 487e, 499b, 500e, 501e, 502d, and 536b.

4. In Bloom's words (1968, 280), the first two waves are "preposterous"; they show "contempt for convention and nature." Aristophanes depicts the first two waves in his *Ecclesiazusae,* probably alluded to in the *Republic* at 5.451c. Ferrari has judiciously argued (in a plenary paper he delivered at the International Plato Society conference in Tokyo in 2010), however, that the first wave is not in fact unnatural, but that Socrates actually appeals to nature in making his case for it. Even if this is so, however, Socrates would be allowing a provision that *is* in accord with nature, viz. that men and women engage in the same occupations, to degenerate into a practice that arguably is not: that women, both young and old, exercise naked with men in the palaestrae (452a-b).

5. Socrates twice characterizes the proposal that philosophers rule as "paradoxical" (472a, 473e).

6. See note 29 below.

7. Socrates here hews to his "priority of definition" principle: one is first to say what something is, and only thereafter to consider its features. See Vlastos 1985.

8. Glaucon is being gently mocked in this brief exchange: not being a real philosopher, he is fit only to follow Socrates. Compare 432c, where Socrates says to Glaucon: "Follow, and pray with me," to which Glaucon replies: "I'll do that; just lead." For other similar passages, see section I of the introduction.

Socrates is quite sure at the start of Book 6 that he has adequately cap-
tured, within the confines of Book 5, the distinctive nature of the philosopher. Indeed, he declares without reservation at the inception of Book 6
(484a): "And so, Glaucon, through a somewhat lengthy argument, who
the philosophers are and who the non-philosophers has, with considerable
effort, somehow been brought to light." The paradigm of the philosopher
advanced in Book 5 is thus intended to be definitive and to set the philosopher decisively apart from those who resemble him merely superficially:
only someone who conforms to Book 5's model will count for Socrates as a
genuine or authentic philosopher.

The distinguishing mark of the philosopher in Book 5, the thing that
makes him genuine or authentic, is what he loves (*philein*—475e, 479e),
or what he "delights in" (*aspazesthai*—475c, 476b5, 476b7, 479e, 480a),
namely, truth and knowledge concerning "what is." Even in his youth, the
true philosopher is not finicky about what he studies; rather, he is willing
to taste every kind of learning; he approaches learning with joy (*hasmenōs*)
and with gusto (*eucherōs*), and is insatiable (475b-c).[9] The philosopher's delight is reminiscent of the delight that reason evokes in properly raised
young men (402a), that the sight of unblemished souls sparks in those who
are musical (402d), and that all sorts of boys (474d) and wines (475a) arouse
respectively in lovers of boys (*erōtikoi*) and wine-lovers.[10] Indeed, by comparing the philosopher to the *erōtikos*, Socrates indicates that the love the
philosopher experiences is intense.[11] Philosophers love, then, as ardently as

---

9. Craig (1994, 53) captures perfectly Socrates' rhetorical hyperbole: "Apparently we are to
understand that with respect to wisdom the philosopher is more like an indiscriminate philan-
derer than a faithful monogamist, more like a wino than a connoisseur (475a), more like a gour-
mand than a gourmet (475c; cf. 354b)." Or as Benardete puts it (1989, 131), "Socrates seems to be
talking about what we call '____-crazy': 'He's girl-crazy,' or 'She's boy-crazy.'" Of course, however, the philosopher restricts his philandering to the realm of being. See, too, 6.485b.

10. Although it is reasonable to think of a lover as a connoisseur (as, for example, Lampert
[2010, 322] does), Socrates' point is that the two are radically different, for whereas the connoisseur
is most discriminating in his taste, the lover loves what he loves almost indiscriminately.

11. There can be no doubt that the philosopher's love for wisdom is passionate; Socrates uses
the term *philein* instead of one that is more emotively charged because of its obvious connection
with *philosophos* (philosopher). In Book 6, however, Socrates replaces *philein* with the more rap-
turous *erān* (485b, 490b, 499c, 501d). In the case of the love of wine and honor, Socrates signals intensity by using the verb of desire, *epithumein*—*erōs* would be odd, which is then applied as well

other lovers do; they differ from those others only in the object of their delight: whereas non-philosophers revel in sights, sounds, arts, opinions, the
many beautiful sounds, colors, and shapes, and all that the crafts fashion
from such things (476a-b, 479e, 480a)—things subject to flux and change,
to coming into existence and perishing, and to variation in accordance with
subjective perspective—philosophers prefer truth and knowledge and the
beautiful itself, things that are real and stable and the same always. The
philosopher loves the things that are "each itself one," the things that only
"look like many" as they "show themselves everywhere in community
with actions, bodies, and one another" (5.476a). Moreover, philosophers
love *all* these "ones" and love each of them in its entirety.

There is no suggestion in Book 5 that among the things the philosopher
loves are war, hunting, and physical labor—things that clearly belong to
the world of flux and change and not to the realm of the immutable and
fixed. Indeed, it is not said in Book 5, as it was in Book 3, that it is gentle
warriors, men of courage and moderation, who are to lead the city, but
rather that the leaders are to be men who fervently love wisdom, truth, and
what is. The philosopher of Book 5 "believes that there *is* something beautiful itself," and he "is able to catch sight both of it and of what participates
in it, and does not believe that what participates is it itself, nor that it itself
is what participates" (476c-d). Insofar as he "looks at each thing itself—at
the things that are always the same in all respects"—he knows rather than
opines (479e), and is awake and not in a dream (476c3, 476c4, 476d).[12] He
is able to follow a leader to the knowledge of beauty itself,[13] and would
therefore not take a mere likeness for the thing itself (476d).

Although Socrates is satisfied that he has extracted in Book 5 the essential core of the genuine philosopher as a lover of truth concerning "what
is," one who indeed not only recognizes the existence of the single Itselfs

---

to wisdom at 475b. Only the tyrant is referred to as erotic as frequently as the philosopher is (572e,
573e, 574d-575a, 578a, 579b, 587b ff.), though the tyrant's pleasures, unlike the philosopher's, are
both crass and "lawless."

12. Another instance in which the dream state signifies an inferior or unreliable form of cog-
nition may be found at 534c-d; see, too, *Meno* 85c, *Symp.* 175e, and *Phdr.* 277d. Cf. *Phaedo* 79c,
where Socrates says that the soul that employs the body and the senses in inquiry is dragged by
them to the ever-changing things and "strays and is confused and dizzy, as if it were drunk."

13. This is something Glaucon cannot do. See note 8 above.

that are manifest in their corresponding manys in the visible realm but is able to see them (476c-d, 479e, 484b), he nevertheless undertakes anew in Book 6 a thorough investigation of the philosophic nature. That Book 6's philosophic natures are the same as Book 5's philosophers is certain: "About philosophic natures, let us agree that . . . just like the lovers of honor and the erotic men we described before [that is, in Book 5, at 474e-475c], they love all of it" (485a-b). And both the philosophers of Book 5 and the philosophic natures of Book 6 are described as loving "that which discloses to them something of the being that is always" (485b; cf. 479e). The full description of the philosophic nature that begins in Book 6 at 485a and ends at 502c thus applies equally to the philosophers of Book 5's third wave. Indeed, both the brief depiction of philosophers in Book 5 and the more expansive elaboration of the philosophic nature in Book 6 culminate in the same way: we have reached our goal "with [or, after] considerable effort" (*mogis*—6.484a; 502c).

What is strikingly new in Book 6, however, is the extensive catalogue it contains of the philosopher's moral, intellectual, and personal virtues. If the extravagant praise it lavishes on the philosophic nature seems exaggerated at first, a second look at the beginning of *Rep.* 6 reveals that it is Glaucon's skepticism that is the cause of the apparent excess. For when Socrates at 484b poses a patently rhetorical question, "Since philosophers are those who are able to grasp what is always the same in all respects, while those who are not able to do so but wander among what is many and varies in all ways are not philosophers, which should be the leaders of the city?" Glaucon's reply is not the expected compliant one "Why, the philosophers, of course, Socrates," but is instead "How should we put it so as to speak in a measured way (*metriōs*)?" Socrates, as we have seen, had assumed (or trusted) that once "who the philosophers are" came plainly to light, it would be immediately evident that they should rule in the city (5.474b-c). Yet apparently, far from being persuaded that philosophers should rule, Glaucon is doubtful: he is not prepared to admit, certainly not without reservation or qualification, that "those who are able to grasp what is always the same in all respects" should lead the city. Indeed, Glaucon is no more sympathetic to the notion of philosophic rule now than he was when Socrates first proposed it at 5.473d. At 473e-474a Glaucon, projecting his own dismay and alarm onto his companions, predicted that they would attack Socrates, both with weapons and with ridicule, should he fail to offer a plausible defense of this view. Thus, when at the beginning of Book 6 Socrates is still promoting the single-minded devotee of "what is" as the best ruler, Glaucon calls for measure: surely a more nuanced figure is in order. Socrates must revisit his depiction of the philosopher if he is to have any hope of persuading Glaucon that philosophers, and only philosophers, should rule.

In an attempt to put the matter "in a measured way,"[14] Socrates takes the sharp-sightedness that is "able to grasp what is always the same in all respects" (484b), that discerns "what each thing is" or "what is truest" and "contemplates it as precisely as possible" (484d),[15] and recasts it as something that is needed and is most useful for guarding (*phulaxai*) or watching over (*tērein*) the laws and practices of cities." (Punning does the work here: how can one watch and guard unless one "sees" well?) In addition, he requires that the men who are to be set up as guardians "not lack experience or fall short of the others in any other part of virtue" (484e). He thus endows the philosopher not only with extraordinary intellect but also with the same qualities that any good leader—whether philosopher or not—would need, qualities that are indeed relevant both to making new law when needed and to preserving existing law (484d).[16] Glaucon is mollified: he is prepared to endorse the rule of those who see well, so long as "these men do not lack the rest"—that is, are not deficient in moral virtue.[17]

---

14. Socrates returns to the notion of "measure" at 490a, saying to Adeimantus: "So, then, won't we make a measured defense in saying . . . ?" to which Adeimantus responds: "Nothing could be more measured" (490b). See, too, 497a, where Socrates again judges that what has been said was "measured."

15. Sharp-sightedness is a recurring theme in the *Republic*: 368c-d, 375a, 484c, 503c, 516c, 519a, 519b, 595c. Socrates asserts in our current passage that there is almost no difference at all between those who lack knowledge of what each thing is, and blind men. See Chapter 2, note 28, where this passage is compared with 484c-d and with 518b-519b.

16. At 501a philosophers are no longer guardians of established law. They wipe the city's tablet clean and draw new laws on it.

17. The need for experience, mentioned at 484c, appears to drop out. It surfaces again only in Socrates' explanation of the fifteen years the philosophers are made to spend in the Cave before their final ascent to the vision of the Good: "so that they won't be behind the others in experience" (7.539e).

As Socrates proceeds, he considers whether it is possible that the same men "will be able to possess these two distinct sets of qualities" (*kakcina kai tauta*—485a)—that is, both the intellectual and the moral virtues. What he argues, however, is not only that intellectual and moral virtues are fully compatible with one another, but that they both attach necessarily to the genuine philosophic nature. Note that this is the second of four occasions on which Socrates raises the question of the compatibility of distinct or opposing qualities or natures: the first time, he asks about savagery and gentleness (2.375c); the second (here), about intellectual qualities and moral ones (485a); the third, about desire for pleasures of both soul and body (485d); and the fourth, about quickness and steadiness (503b-d).[18]

Since it is in the philosophic nature that Socrates expects to find both intellectual and moral qualities, he reaffirms the importance, first noted in Book 5 at 474b, of grasping that nature thoroughly. And, as he had earlier expressed confidence that once the philosophic nature is seen for what it is it would be evident to all that philosophers should rule, he now voices his conviction that all would also agree that philosophers possess both sets of qualities (485b).[19] Although Socrates had offered a definition of the philosopher in Book 5, he did not ask at that time which virtues accompany the philosophic nature. Now, however, he both recalls the traits that he identified in the earlier discussion as distinguishing philosophers from others—namely, that they are always in love with the kind of learning that is related to being and, in loving indiscriminately all of what they love, are like honor-lovers and *erōtikoi*—and ties the philosophers' possession of the moral virtues to these defining features. The moral virtues—justice, moderation, and courage—are found in such men, Socrates explains, *because* they love truth or true being, *because* they have "a soul that is always going to reach out for the whole and for everything divine and human,"[20] *because*

---

18. How are mixed natures to be reconciled with the principle of justice outlined in Book 4 at 434c, according to which natures are distinct and determine the roles people are to play in the city? See Chapter 2, section I.

19. Socrates clearly thinks, both here and in earlier books, that people other than philosophers have moral virtue. In Book 8 we have another case in point, the "aristocratic" father of the timocratic man (see 8.549c): there is no indication that this man is a philosopher.

20. As we shall see, the philosophers of Book 7 (those whose description begins at 6.502c and spans all of Book 7) have utter disdain for human affairs. In this way they are unlike the philosophers of Book 6, who "reach out ... for everything divine *and human*" (486a). See Dobbs 1985, 820.

they have "an understanding endowed with magnificence" (486a). Such a nature is also musical and graceful, measured and charming (485e-486d), one that naturally "grows by itself in such a way as to make it easily led to the Idea of each thing that is" (486d). Indeed, Socrates maintains, *since* when desires incline strongly toward one sort of thing they are weaker with respect to others, anyone whose desires flow toward learning will be so completely enamored of the pleasures of the soul that he will lose interest in the pleasures of the body (485d). (The image Socrates employs here, which Melissa Lane usefully calls the "hydraulic model,"[21] is of a stream that is diverted in one direction, such that the flow in the other direction is cut off.[22]) This phenomenon was instantiated in Book 1 in the person of Cephalus, who reported that as his bodily desires waned his desire for speeches grew (328d); he was finally rid of what Sophocles calls "very many mad masters" (329d), and was now, in his own estimation, "balanced and good-tempered" (*kosmioi kai eukoloi*—329d).[23] Since most vices stem from desires for bodily pleasure, a person without such attachments would be free, too, of the corresponding vices: he would not love money, would not be illiberal, would not be cowardly—since he doesn't place an inordinately high value on life, he would not believe death to be terrible[24]—would not be a boaster, a hard bargainer, or unjust, nor a difficult partner and savage (486b).[25] If, then, a person does desire the pleasures of the body, he can only be a counterfeit philosopher (485d).

In a soul that is genuinely philosophic, the moral virtues (courage, moderation, and justice) are natural consequences of the philosopher's immersion in what truly "is."[26] The intellectual virtues (the ability to learn

---

21. See Lane 2007, 45.

22. The hydraulic effect is most strikingly in evidence in the *Phaedo* (at 64c-e), where the philosopher's orientation to the Forms blunts his interest in and attention to even the most basic material and bodily needs.

23. As Bloom points out (1968, 442 n. 15), this is how Aristophanes characterizes Sophocles in the *Frogs* (82).

24. Contrast Socrates, who does not "even care about death in any way at all" (*Ap.* 32d), with the young guardians in Book 3, who can be kept from being cowardly only by being assured that Hades is not so bad (386a-b). Also see 6.486a-b, where the philosophic nature is described as not regarding human life as something great and as therefore not seeing death as something terrible.

25. The true philosopher is "not harsh" (*mē chalepōi*) and "not jealous" (*mē phthoneroi*) (500a).

26. As Bloom (1968, 395) remarks, the philosophers "do not have to make an effort to become virtuous or concentrate on the virtues; the virtues follow of themselves from the greatest love and

quickly and to retain what was learned) and the personal ones (charm and grace), by contrast, are prerequisites for philosophic engagement: unless a person learns easily, he won't care for learning; unless he is able to preserve what he learns, he will not pursue knowledge, since he would be toiling in vain; and one who is unmusical and lacks grace would not be drawn to the measured nature of truth (486d). Intellectual ability, however, is not the same as *love* of wisdom, and it is the latter alone that necessarily yields moral rectitude. There is little reason to suppose that those who are intellectually gifted but who nevertheless crave pleasures of the body will also possess the moral virtues.

By contending that all types of virtue—moral, intellectual, and personal—come together in the philosophic (wisdom-loving) nature, Socrates hopes to put to rest Glaucon's concerns about philosophic rule. Since one who practices philosophy is not only "a rememberer, a good learner, magnificent, and charming," but also "a friend and kinsman of truth, justice, courage, and moderation" (487a), Glaucon needn't fear his having access to the reins of power. Moreover, by the time the city is turned over to men of this sort, they will have been perfected by education and age (487a). Since we are about to encounter philosophic natures whose education leads them astray and who, as they age, mature not into philosophers but into bad men, Socrates must stipulate that only those philosophic natures that are also properly educated and pursue philosophy into adulthood are suited to rule. Nature alone is not sufficient.

I.A. The Ship Image

Socrates' portrayal of the philosophic nature is sufficiently satisfying to Glaucon that he is willing to grant that "no one could blame" a practice like philosophy (487a). Is he, however, persuaded as well of the appropriateness of having philosophers rule? We never do find out; Adeimantus interrupts the conversation before Glaucon can answer.[27] As in Book 2

---

pleasure of the philosophers. . . . Without sacrifice the philosopher, in addition to possessing the intellectual virtues, will be moderate, courageous, and just."

27. Adeimantus berates Socrates for incrementally misleading by his questions those less skilled at question and answer, causing them to assent to a conclusion far removed from their

where Adeimantus, finding his brother's argument for the inferiority of justice to injustice not quite adequate to the task, bolsters it with an argument of his own, so, too, here, Adeimantus augments Glaucon's doubts about philosophic rule with his own conviction that, however praiseworthy philosophers may be theoretically, the real flesh-and-blood ones are alarmingly flawed. "Someone might say,"[28] Adeimantus ventures, that of those who "linger" in philosophy beyond their youth,[29] "most become quite queer, not to say completely vicious;[30] while the ones who seem most decent,[31] do nevertheless suffer at least one consequence of

---

initial position. Thrasymachus also complains about Socrates' methods—right after Socrates deploys his technique against Polemarchus (1.336b). Socrates' tactics in argument also vex Polus and Callicles in the *Gorgias*, at 461b-c and 482c-483a, respectively; see, too, *Prot.* 334d-e, 360c; *Lach.* 194a; *Meno* 79c-80b; *HMi.* 369b. Unlike the complaints of Socrates' other interlocutors, however, Adeimantus's accusation comes after quite a long stretch during which Socrates has been doing all the talking and has not actually been challenging anyone else's views.

28. Adeimantus hides behind a "someone" when criticizing philosophers, and he continues to hide—behind "those who hear what you now say"—when he berates Socrates (487b, 487d). At first Socrates plays along—"Do you suppose that the men who say this are lying?" (487d)—but by 490c-d no longer pretends that Adeimantus's objection is someone else's; he says simply: "You objected." Glaucon, too, hides behind others when he questions the superiority of justice to injustice. Thrasymachus alone is brazen enough to speak out against justice in his own name. Bloom (1968, 340) thinks Glaucon, unlike Thrasymachus, is worried about how he is perceived. Adeimantus, we may assume, is worried, too.

29. Like Adeimantus, Callicles in the *Gorgias* finds repugnant those who indulge in philosophy beyond their youth (484c, 485a-b), even (or especially) if they "have an altogether good nature" (485a, 485d). He, too, decries their uselessness: they become ridiculous "whenever they enter into some private or political action" (484d-e); they "flee the central area of the city and the agoras," and live the rest of their lives "whispering with three or four lads in a corner, never to give voice to anything free or great or sufficient" (485d-e).

30. Unlike Adeimantus, Callicles sees older philosophers as being useless but not vicious. (See note 30 above.)

31. Cephalus is the first to speak of decent men. He says they would not bear old age well if poor, but adds that even wealth wouldn't help those who lack decency (1.330a). Decency resurfaces in Book 3, as Socrates considers the sorts of men that poets should be imitating (397d, 398b). In Book 4 moderation is said to be a matter of the desires of the common many being mastered by those of the more decent few (431c-d). Decency is most prominent in Book 6, where at 486d Adeimantus first charges the most decent (*epieikestatous*) among the philosophers with being useless. At 488a it is Socrates who then speaks of "the most decent men" and continues to call them "decent" as well as "most decent of those in philosophy" as he compares them to true pilots at 489b. He uses both "most decent" and "decent" again at 489d. Although the "good and decent" men of Book 1 are described not only as "decent" (347c) but as "most decent" (347b), they have little in common with the "most decent" pilots and philosophers of Book 6. Book 1's good and decent men are the subject of the addendum to Chapter 3.

the practice you are praising—they become useless to the cities" (487d). He thus dashes Socrates' hopes that "if we can reach agreement about that [the philosopher's nature] . . . we will also agree that the same men will be able to possess both [sets of qualities] and that there should be no other leaders of cities than these" (485a). Yet Socrates—no doubt to everyone's surprise—accepts the unflattering characterization of the philosopher as vicious or useless (487d), and even commits himself more fully to its aptness than Adeimantus himself does. When Adeimantus is asked, "Do you suppose that the men who say this are lying?" he isn't quite sure: "I don't know," he says to Socrates, "but I should gladly hear your opinion" (487d). But Socrates for his part registers no comparable doubt. The way it seems to him, he says, is that these men are indeed "speaking the truth" (487d).

Turning first to the charge that the decent philosophers are "useless," Socrates affirms their uselessness but blames it on the circumstances in which they find themselves. He defends the philosophers in two separate discussions, the first at 488a-489c (in the ship allegory) and the second at 496a-e, where, after having considered the two vicious types, he returns at last to the decent ones. In the first discussion, Socrates holds the politicians of his day responsible for the uselessness of the decent philosophers: these politicians fail to honor the philosophers as they should, and they imprudently discount their potential contribution. Those who are least qualified want desperately to rule. They are just like inept sailors who vie with each other for command of their ship and who are capable in their frenzy even of killing one another. These sailors attempt to persuade the shipowner to put them in charge or, if need be, they coerce him ("enchaining the noble shipowner with mandrake, drink, or something else, they rule the ship"— 488c), as they "drink and feast" and "sail as such men would be thought likely to sail" (488c).[32] They have utter disdain not only for the man who is an expert at the art of piloting and whose attention is therefore focused

---

32. Keyt (2006, 196) thinks the "political analogue" of the sailors' eating and feasting is the politicians' "entertaining the people and feasting them with what they have an appetite for" in the *Gorgias*. It would be more accurate, however, to see as analogous to the *Gorgias* scenario the sailors' plying the shipowner with mandrake or strong drink. The sailors' own feasting is a separate issue. They squander the city's resources on themselves.

on astronomical, atmospheric, and meteorological matters,[33] calling him "a stargazer" and "a babbler" (*adoleschēn*—6.489a),[34] but also for anyone who so much as suggests that there is a nautical art.[35] They respect only those who are clever at acquiring power,[36] and they think it impossible both to acquire power "whether the others wish it or not" *and* to master the piloting craft (488e).[37]

The sailors in the allegory represent the politicians (489c); the ship, the city; the shipowner, the people; the skilled pilots, the philosophers; the art of piloting, the art of ruling; and the astronomical, atmospheric, and meteorological matters, the true and unchanging nature of justice, moderation, and goodness.[38] "It is necessary," Socrates insists, "for every man

---

33. Benardete (1989, 147) thinks Socrates is at his wittiest in the ship allegory insofar as the pilot he portrays is a landlubber who is not on a ship: he may know many things, but he knows nothing about the sea. Perhaps Socrates' intent, however, is to portray not a pilot ignorant of the sea but one who is relegated to land by those who despise his scientific understanding. That the pilot is not on the ship suggests both his pariah status and his being above the fray.

34. On "babbling" (*adoleschein*), see *Phaedo* 70b-c; *Pol.* 299b; Aristophanes, *Clouds* 1480; Xenophanes, *Oec.* 11.3. Babbling is apparently among the stock charges leveled regularly, and indiscriminately, against "all who philosophize" (*Ap.* 23d).

35. Several commentators note a disanalogy between the pilot and the ruler of a city: whereas the pilot steers the ship but does not determine its destination, the effective ruler needs to determine the city's ends. (See Keyt 2006, 201; Bambrough 1956, 105; Walzer 1983, 285–89.) One way to strengthen the analogy is to take the pilot's task to be to keep the ship on course, and the ruler's to do the same for the city—though in the one case doing so does not include setting the end, and in the other it does. The pilot consults the sky; the philosopher the Forms, including the Form of the Good. Another way to look at it is to say the pilot, like the physician (489b) and the ruler, uses his expertise to supply what is needed: the ship's passengers need to get to their destination; sick people need to be healed; citizens need to be improved.

36. The sailors do not represent orators, as Keyt (2006, 196) thinks they do. They are would-be rulers who are prepared to kill any of their rivals who is more persuasive than they, but who will solicit the help of orators if they cannot prevail on their own. While denying that there is a piloting skill, they flatter and praise as genuine pilots those who are skilled at persuading or compelling the shipowner. The mandrake and strong drink with which the sailors ply the shipowner are to be taken literally; to seize power the sailors use not only words but whatever means are at their disposal.

37. On this last point the sailors are surely right. It is why it proves so difficult to bring into being a city ruled by philosophers.

38. Hitz (2011, 126–27 n. 20), crediting Alexander Nehamas, maintains that the shipowner represents the city itself; the sailors, the demos; and those who succeed in persuading the shipowner to let them rule, politicians or demagogues. But note: a ship has already represented the city at 3.389d ("and destructive of a city as of a ship"), and the sailors are explicitly identified as politicians (*politikous*) at 489c; see also Aristotle, *Rhet.* 1406b25. Following Benardete (1989, 147),

[politicians included] who needs to be ruled to go to the doors of the man who is able to rule, not for the ruler who is truly of any use to beg the ruled to be ruled" (489b-c).[39] It is "not natural" for a true craftsman to beg to be permitted to exercise his craft—especially when his craft is one that stands to benefit the very people he would be begging. The reason the "most decent" among the philosophers (489b) don't rule is that they are unwelcome; they can hardly be blamed if they won't beg to rule. They are useless only because no one cares to make use of their abilities.[40]

By maintaining that the philosophers who are suited to rule, like the pilots who alone are qualified to steer a ship, are useless only because their talents are unwelcome and even spurned, Socrates implies that these men, under more hospitable conditions, would be not only able but also willing to serve. Their love for truth and for the genuine and real, their lack of interest in material goods and pleasures, the magnificence of their nature and their utter fearlessness, their embrace of the whole, of everything divine and human, remove from them all pettiness, all competitiveness, all narrow self-centeredness, all narcissism. All that is required for them to confer their special benefit on those who need it is a knock on their door.

Hitz notes a tension between the portrayal of the shipowner in the ship allegory as somewhat deaf, shortsighted, and ignorant with respect to seamanship, on the one hand, and the characterization of the demos immediately following (at 493a-c) as the greatest sophist—an immensely powerful beast. Dorter (2006, 174–75) similarly observes that the shipowner is called "noble" (*gennaion*), but that the demos is compared at 493b-c to a beast that has only size and power and no nobility. Dorter seeks to resolve the apparent conflict without denying that the shipowner represents the people. He contends that when Socrates addresses the matter of the philosophers' uselessness, he calls the people noble because it is not they but the politicians who are to blame, but when he addresses the philosophers' viciousness, he refrains from calling the people noble because in that case they are to blame. It is likely, however, that there is no real inconsistency (or even tension) here: if the shipowner in the allegory "surpasses everyone on board in height and strength" (488a-b), why is "beast" not an apt label? On this point, see Keyt 2006, 193–94. Furthermore, *gennaion* may connote nothing more than being of good lineage: Socrates applies it to the puppy in Book 2 (*gennaiou skulakos*) to which he compares the well-born (*eugenous*) young man (375a).

39. The very fact that the sailors "beg" the shipowner to grant them the rule (488b-c) thus shows them to be not "of any use." Those who beg to rule can want to rule only for all the wrong reasons. See 494c where the kinsmen and fellow citizens of the young man possessed of a philosophic nature "lie at his feet begging and honoring him."

40. Socrates does not say that the craftsman ought to withhold services until and unless he is begged; his point is rather that the craftsman should not be the one doing the begging.

I.B. The Small Band of Worthy Philosophers

Having digressed to consider the two larger, vicious philosophic types (489d-496a), Socrates returns at 496a-e to take up again—this time directly—the rare decent but useless philosophers whom he had previously, in the ship allegory, considered only by analogy.[41] This very small group, which "remains to keep company with philosophy in a way that is worthy" (496a-b), contains, Socrates tells us, those philosophers who fail, for one reason or another, to become politicians. Some have a "genteel and well-reared disposition" but are in exile and therefore do not attract corrupters. Others have a "great soul"[42] but hail from a small city and despise its politics. Still others start out as lowly craftsmen (and hence, one would suppose, lack the good birth or wealth that makes politics a viable option).[43] Some are sickly, like poor Theages, whose frailty, "shutting him out of politics, restrains him" (496c). And Socrates, perhaps unique among philosophers, remains faithful to philosophy when his "daimonic sign" places politics off-limits to him.[44] It is noteworthy that on this occasion Socrates cites not the oracle, which ostensibly spurred his philosophic activity, but his *daimonion,* which prevented it, suggesting that with respect to all the members of this select group we are learning not why they were drawn to philosophy in the first place but why they did not in the end pursue the life of politics.

---

41. The vicious constitute the great majority of philosophic types, both for Adeimantus at 487d and for Socrates at 489d (*tōn pollōn*). More rare are people with philosophic natures (476b, 491b, 495b). Decent but useless philosophers are rarer still. Extremely rare is the fourth philosophic type consisting of philosophers who are also warriors (503b). Not only are there few fine minds—even in Book 4, the class of the wise was designated the smallest in the city (428e)—but the combination of fine minds and the qualities of a warrior is quite exceptional.

42. Compare the "great soul" (*megalē psuchē*) of Book 6's philosophers (496b) with the "puny soul" (*psucharion*) of the future philosopher-ruler in Book 7 (519a). On *psucharion* see Chapter 2, note 34.

43. Craftsmen were apparently not held in high esteem. Socrates observes in the *Gorgias* that Callicles wouldn't let his daughter marry an engineer's son or an engineer's daughter marry his son (512c). And in the *Apology*, Socrates refers to craftsmen as "those with more paltry reputations" (*Ap.* 22a).

44. The nature of the *daimonion* is a matter of some dispute (see Vlastos 1991, 283–87; Brickhouse and Smith 1994, 190–95; McPherran 1991, 368–73; Reeve 1989, 70–73). In my view, it needn't be thought literally to emanate from a god. It appears to be triggered either by a conflict between what Socrates is about to do and his own reasoned belief or better judgment, or by an

Interestingly, there is no hint of grandeur in any of these men—Socrates included: none of them is said to be tall, handsome, strong, charming, clever, or magnificent; and none is said to have powerful political connections. Perhaps it is because they lack a certain splendor, because they are on the surface rather ordinary, that they succeed in avoiding the corruption that, as we shall soon see, frequently besets those endowed with a philosophic nature. Like the useless philosophers in the ship allegory who would rule if only they were asked, these philosophers, too, would "come to the aid of justice" if only they had an "ally" (a "fellow fighter," *summachos*) with whom to do so. And just as in the first discussion the unwanted philosophers go on with their seemingly useless stargazing, not putting it to the good use it might have served, so, too, in the second discussion, the philosophers, despite their ability to do considerable good, to "save the common things along with the private" (497a), if only the regimes in which they found themselves were suitable, end up shunning public life. As Socrates says, each of them elects to "keep quiet and mind his own business,"[45] and, "seeing others filled full of lawlessness," "stands aside under

---

imminent prospect of his being deprived of an experience of the sort he himself values. That it began coming to him in childhood (*Ap.* 31d) suggests that, even as a child, he had a highly developed sense of right and wrong and an intuitiveness about what is and what is not of worth. Socrates need not be taken to imply at 496c that the *daimonion* is unique (or nearly unique) to him; he may be indicating instead that no one else has ever been kept from politics in this way. (For a fuller discussion of the *daimonion*, see the section entitled "Gods and 'The God'" in Weiss 1998, chap. 2. See, too, Weiss 2005.)

45. "Minding one's own business" is here less than ideal. So, too, at 2.369e-370a, where Socrates gives the name "minding one's own business"—literally, "himself by himself doing what is for himself" (*auton di' hauton ta hautou prattein*—370a)—to a plan according to which each member of a four-man city would take care of himself, devoting one-fourth of his time to producing for himself alone (*heautōi monon*) each of his four basic needs: food, housing, clothing, and shoes. Socrates makes clear that this sort of "minding one's own business" entails "neglecting" (*amelēsanta*) the other three men and "not taking the trouble (*pragmata echein*) to share in common with them." The *Charmides* contains another such instance: "Do you think a city would be well governed," Socrates asks, "by a law commanding each man to weave and wash his own cloak, make his own shoes and oil flask and scraper, and perform everything else by this same principle of keeping his hands off other people's things and making and *doing his own*?" (161e-162a). As Socrates concludes (163a), craftsmen "make or do" not just their own business but that of others. Similarly, Socrates in the *Apology* always minds "your" business (*to . . . humeteron prattein aei*), *neglecting* (*ēmelēkenai*) his own affairs (*Ap.* 31b); indeed, in his case, minding your business is the way in which he does his own (*ta emautou prattontos*) (33a); he is nothing less than a "busybody" in private (31c)—for others' sake. In yet another use—one that Socrates clearly regards favorably— minding one's own business entails escaping "the honors, the ruling offices, the lawsuits,

a little wall," "as a man in a storm, when dust and rain are blown about by the wind."[46] Such a man is content to live a life "pure of injustice and unholy deeds" and to "take his leave from it graciously and cheerfully with fair hope" (496d-e).[47]

The "decent but useless" philosophers of Book 6, then, would rule, if they could, for the sake of justice—that is, for the sake of improving people's souls with respect to justice. Their wisdom is such that it makes them able "pilots," but it is their *love* of wisdom that makes them willing ones. They show no signs of reluctance or aversion to ruling;[48] it is only as a last resort that they "mind [only] their own business." There is, Socrates assures Adeimantus, but one reason that they are useless, and that is that others are too foolish, arrogant, greedy, or ambitious to appreciate and to use them.

We have now seen the first—and best—of the four types discussed in Book 6: those who have a genuine philosophic nature and stay true to philosophy.[49] Because these people are decent, they are useless in the prevailing political climate—and in every other one that has existed thus far.[50] Indeed, Socrates contends, no current regime is deserving of the philosophic nature (497b)—that is, of the nature that "remains to keep company with philosophy in a way that is worthy." It is a sorry situation all

---

and everything of the sort that is to the busybody's taste" (*Rep.* 8.549c; cf. *Ap.* 36b, *Gorg.* 526c). The timocratic youth soon learns that men like his good father who "mind their own business" in this way are called simpletons (*ēlithious*) "and are held in small account" (*Rep.* 8.550a). In Book 4 (443c-d) Socrates sharply distinguishes minding one's external business from minding one's business internally, and commends the latter as personal justice. See Chapter 5, addendum II. "Minding one's own business" cannot without qualification define justice because it is not uniformly good.

46. The *Gorgias* (510d-e) teaches that the only way to avoid suffering wrong is to master the art of doing wrong with impunity. The decent and worthy philosophers, seeking to avoid both suffering wrong and committing it, live not as public but as private men.

47. These philosophers, like Socrates and unlike the philosophers depicted in the *Phaedo*, do not prefer death to life. So long as they are alive, they wish to continue living.

48. They thus contrast sharply, as we shall see in Chapter 3, with the philosophers of Book 7.

49. Of the four types discussed in Book 6 this type is best. In Chapter 4 we will entertain the possibility that there is an even better philosopher or philosophic type, Socrates or the Socratic type, who, though not described in the *Republic* directly, is nevertheless on display on its every page.

50. In the final analysis, all Socrates really concedes is that these philosophers are *called* useless (499b). See, too, 488a, where the sailors (who represent the politicians) *call* the true pilot (the philosopher) "a stargazer, a prater, and useless," as well as 489a, 489c, and 490e. Socrates hints that in fact the ruler is "truly of use" (*tēi alētheiāi . . . ophelos*) (489c).

around: philosophers fall short of their potential ("in a suitable one he him-self will grow more"—497a), and regimes are not "saved" (497a).

I.C. The Natural Philosopher's Rule

Although Socrates has determined that no regime past or present has been worthy of the genuine philosophic nature, he proceeds to imagine what a good regime and the philosophers in charge of it would be like. Indeed, once it has been agreed that the only way the philosophic nature, the best nature,[51] can avoid ending up "twisted and changed" is for it to be sown in the soil of the best regime (497b-c), the logical next step is to inquire into the nature of that regime (497c).

The best regime is one that is ruled by true philosophers, by individu-als blessed with the entire spectrum of admirable qualities—intellectual, moral, and personal. Unfortunately, however, people are generally unac-quainted with anyone who is "perfectly balanced with virtue, in deed and speech," and who also "holds power in a city fit for him" (498e-499a). Nor have they been privileged to hear speeches that "strain with every nerve" in pursuit of truth for the sake of gaining knowledge (499a). It is no wonder, then, that they perceive philosophy as a frivolous pursuit hardly appro-priate for respectable grown men, a child's sport in which it is unseemly for gentlemen to engage. They cannot but think that the only adults who practice it are uncouth quibblers.

For that reason, Socrates explains, "we" have been reluctant to speak of the need for philosophic rule—even though, ultimately, "compelled by the truth" (499b), we did so anyway. We declared that "neither city nor regime will ever become perfect, nor yet will a man become perfect in the same way either, before some necessity by chance imposes on those few philosophers who are not vicious, those now called useless, to take care of a city, whether they want to or not, and the city to become obedient" (499b).[52] The reader already knows the circumstances under which those

---

51. See note 1 above.

52. Although some scholars have been led to emend the text (Stallbaum 1881, for example, has *kat.ēkoois*) and to translate "and makes them [the philosophers] pay heed to the city" (see, e.g., J. Sachs 2007), I follow Schleiermacher (1855–62), who emends the *katēkooi* found in MSS A, F, and M (Slings [2003] attributes it to A, D, and F and follows the MSS to *katēkoōi*. Burnet (1902)

who are decent but useless *would* wish to rule: if their rule were welcomed by those in need of it, if they had an ally with whom to come to the aid of justice, or if politics were not a den of corruption.[53] And he knows, too, the circumstances under which they would not wish to rule: if they had to beg to rule or if the corruption in the city were such that they were left isolated and unsupported and in fear for their very lives. Unless, then, something were to happen that would make the city obedient, philosophers couldn't rule and couldn't wish to.

Since the reason cities balk at philosophic rule is that people mistake fake philosophers for real ones, the only remedy is for them to see the philosopher as he truly is. And so once again Socrates finds it necessary to describe the true philosopher.[54] He tells Adeimantus (500b-d) that the genuine philosopher is drawn to the things that *are,* and that he therefore has no leisure to be envious or to bear ill will toward human beings because he regards them as rivals. He is immersed in things that are regular and unchanging, things that neither commit nor suffer injustice; and it is out of his admiration for them that he imitates and consorts with them[55]— indeed he cannot be kept from doing so. His association with the "divine and orderly" makes him, in turn, as orderly and divine as "is possible for a human being." Should the necessity arise for him to form not only himself but others in accordance with what he sees, he would be, both privately and publicly, a good craftsman of moderation, justice, and demotic virtue generally.

It may seem that the same philosopher who cannot be kept from shaping his own soul in accordance with the beautifully ordered Forms (500c)

---

and Adam (1969) adopt this emendation as well. Schleiermacher's view is supported by the text at 502b: "if he has an obedient city."

53. In light of the notorious unwillingness of the philosopher of Book 7 to rule, it is actually the "want to" in "whether they want to or not" that is surprising.

54. This is in fact the sixth of Socrates' descriptions of the true philosopher. The first appears in Book 5 at 475d-480a; all the others are in Book 6: 485a-487a, 490a-c, 491c, and 494b.

55. It is not the heavens but the Forms that the philosopher imitates (see Miller 1986, 187 n. 30). (1) The passage states that the philosopher's understanding is "toward the things that *are*" (*pros tois ousi*—500b-c); (2) if the philosophers mold human dispositions, looking to "the just, fair, and moderate in nature and everything of the sort" (501b)—that is, to the virtue-Forms— these must be what the philosopher sees at 500c; and (3) the expression used at 500c, "keep company with" (*homilei*), is used as well at 496b for the philosopher's association (*homilountōn*) with philosophy.

is perhaps less eager ("if some necessity arises"—500d) to mold the dispositions of others. But Socrates has already argued that decent philosophers
would indeed go to justice's aid were it not for their fear of corruption or
death, that they are useless only because their services are rebuffed (488a-
489c, 496c-d). What he has not yet stated explicitly, however, and therefore
still needs to affirm, is that their uselessness is not due to incompetence.
His current contention, then, is that philosophers who out of love for
the Forms enthusiastically introduce the Forms' perfect orderliness into
their own souls are also skilled at improving the character of a city and its
inhabitants.

The way the true philosopher would form the city—though to do so
is "hardly easy" (*ou panu rhadion*—501a)[56]—is by first wiping it clean as
if it were a tablet, and then outlining the shape of the regime and drawing laws (501a).[57] With respect to the individual human beings in it, he
would scour their dispositions and, looking back and forth from the just,
noble, and moderate by nature to the people he is to mold, would mix and
blend practices as ingredients and produce an image of man (*andreikelon*)
that approximates the image that Homer called "godlike" (*theoeides*) and
the "image of god" (*theoeikelon*) (501b). He would "rub out one thing and
draw in another again, until [he] made human dispositions as dear to
the gods as they admit of being" (501c).[58] To be sure, the notion of wiping the slate clean and producing new human dispositions is not fully

---

56. The matter of ease or difficulty arises several times in the *Republic*: 370a, 358a, 363e-364a,
473c, 497d, 519d, 520d, 540e-541a. For further discussion of this last instance, see Chapter 3, section IV.

57. As noted above (note 16), the philosophers who were initially to preserve, as guardians,
the already established law, are now primarily (if not exclusively) makers of new law. (That is
not to say, however, that none of the new laws can be the same as the old. See Chapter 3, note 71.)
Both the philosophers-guardians at 6.484c and the philosopher-rulers at 6.500e-501a are likened
to painters who "look off" to the unchanging realities.

58. Benardete (1989, 145) contends that the *Republic*'s philosophers rule the city but not human
beings. Although, as we shall see in Chapter 3, section IV, this is true of the philosophers of Book 7,
it is clearly false with respect to the philosophers of Book 6. Relying on the ship analogy, Benardete
writes: "The city is not the people, and since the art of rule has nothing to do with human beings,
the philosopher can rule the city without ruling them" (145). Even in the ship allegory, however,
it is not the ship that Socrates says should knock on the pilot's door, but "every man who needs to
be ruled" (*panta ton archesthai deomenon*) (489c).

perspicuous—after all, one cannot literally scour a soul[59]—but Socrates may have in mind something resembling the proper political practice he describes in the *Gorgias,* one whose concern is "to take care of (*therapeuein*) the city and the citizens, making the citizens as good as possible" (513e), and which attempts to "lead desires in a different direction and, not yielding, to persuade and force them toward the condition in which the citizens would be better" (517b-c).[60] Indeed, the first step in the process may be something like Socrates' own elenchus, whose intent is to disabuse people of their false beliefs: could this practice not legitimately be called "scouring the soul"? Since, however, in the current case, those effecting the change neither are nor profess to be ignorant of the most important things (*ta megista*), the process's second step may be less tentative. Even so, the practice Socrates describes is complex and involves continual adjustments. The philosophers do not simply impose their vision of the just, noble, and moderate on human souls, but rather, in an iterative procedure, they "look away frequently (*pukna*) in both directions" (501b) and "rub one thing out and draw in another again (*palin*)" (501c).[61]

The philosophers by nature of Book 6, then, keep company with the divine, are themselves "orderly and divine," and try to paint a close-to-divine image on the clean slates of cities and men. They "see," they grasp, the models whose essences they are to imprint on the materials they mold. They strive to perfect their own souls and are willing and able to transform the city and souls that are amenable to their project. They are lovers of truth—and indeed Socrates neither imagines that they need to be lied to nor asks them to lie. They are thus unlike the guardians or rulers described earlier, who are both lied to and lie. "Useful lies," Socrates says, are to be told to future guardians "because we don't know where the truth about ancient things lies" (see 2.377d-e and 2.382c-d); the notorious "genteel lie" is to be propagated in the hope that it might persuade, "in the best case," not only "the rest of the city" but "even the rulers" (3.414b-c); the privileged

---

59. By contrast, there is no need to construe figuratively the practice of sending out to the country "all those in the city who happen to be older than ten" (540e-541a)—which is the way the philosopher-rulers of Book 7 will secure the city's obedience. See Chapter 3, section V.

60. See Aristotle, *EN* 1102a9: the genuine *politikos* aims at making the citizens good.

61. Cf. the *au* at 501b3.

rulers of Book 3 are, in turn, permitted or encouraged to lie while everyone else is forbidden to do so (389b; compare 5.459d: "It's likely our rulers will have to use a throng of lies and deceptions for the benefit of the ruled"). Now that both the nature of the philosophers and their way of ruling have been made clear, Socrates is hopeful that those who fiercely objected to philosophic rule will finally be able to see its value. Since it is undeniable that philosophers are lovers of that which is and of truth, and that their nature is akin to the best, the skeptics can be expected to accept that only with men such as these in charge of the city will the city and its citizens enjoy respite from ills (501d-e). The opponents of philosophy should have by now become gentle and, from shame—presumably shame at having so egregiously misjudged the philosopher—if from nothing else, should agree that philosophers alone are suited to rule (502a). Indeed, since the philosophers of Book 6 are not warriors, they will rule if and only if the people willingly obey them.

Perhaps the most striking feature of the new philosophic regime discussed at 499a-502c is the prominence in it of chance. (It is remarkable, too, that nothing is left to chance in the regime discussed after 502c; on the contrary, chance is something to be guarded against [539d].) When the need for philosophic rule is first introduced at 5.473d, Socrates speaks of the "falling together" or the coincidence (*sumpesēi*) "in the same place" of political power and philosophy.[62] And in the ten Stephanus pages spanning 6.492a-502a, chance appears seven times: the philosophic nature "chances" on a suitable course of learning (492a); "one of the gods chances to assist it" (492a); "from these men [with the best nature] . . . come those who do the greatest harm . . . as well as those who do the good, if they chance to be drawn in this direction" (495b); "if he [the philosopher] didn't chance upon a suitable regime" (497a); "before some necessity by chance imposes upon those few philosophers who aren't vicious . . . to take charge of a city . . . and the city to become obedient" (499b); "such a nature, when it chances upon suitable practices" (501d); and "will anyone argue that there

---

62. By adding "while the many natures now making their way to either [i.e., political power or philosophy] apart from the other are *by necessity* (*ex anankēs*) excluded" (473d), Socrates intends not that force is needed to keep distinct natures from going their separate ways (pace Benardete 1989, 128), but that it is an ineluctable consequence of the coincidence of political power and philosophy that natures that currently diverge will no longer do so.

couldn't chance to be children of kings, or of men who hold power, who are born philosophers by their natures?" (502a). The nature of the natural philosopher "grows by itself" (*autophues*—486d, 520b), and the philosophers who have this nature "grow up spontaneously" (*automatoi*)—even *against* the will of the regime (520b). It is only by chance, then, that philosophic natures receive proper education, engage in suitable practices, or are graced with needed divine assistance. If men possessed of these natures are drawn to good rather than ill, find themselves in an appropriate regime, or come to rule and to be obeyed by citizens who are gentle and who welcome them, they are just lucky. It is, in the final analysis, largely in the hands of fortune whether philosophic men are born to politically powerful fathers,[63] manage somehow to escape corruption, or find themselves in a position to mold the people's souls in justice, moderation, and the rest of demotic virtue. A good regime is neither guaranteed nor ruled out. It is possible—if only barely so (499c, 499d, 501d, 502a-b, 502c).

II. The First Deficient Philosophic Type: A Philosophic Nature Gone Bad

Socrates' account of the first philosophic type—the decent but useless philosopher—is found, as we have seen, in two distinct passages: 488a-489c and 496a-502c. What occupies the space in between these two passages is a full consideration of the "vicious" (*ponēroi*) philosophic types to whom Adeimantus had alluded at 487d. There are two such types identified at 490e-491a: (1) "the corruptions of *this* nature" (that is, of "the nature of the true philosophers" [as depicted at 490d]); and (2) "the natures of souls that imitate the philosophic nature and set themselves up in its practice, and . . . who approach a practice that is of no value for

---

63. By no longer entertaining at 502a (as he had at 473c-d and 499b) the possibility that philosophers might become kings but only that children of kings or of men who hold power might be born philosophers by their natures and somehow avoid corruption and be saved, Socrates may be suggesting that the only hope for the philosophic city's coming into existence is if the philosopher already has access to the reins of power. As we observed in connection with the ship allegory, the "sailors" are probably right to think that a person cannot at the same time acquire skill at "getting hold of the helm whether the others wish it or not" and at "piloting" (488e).

them, and who often strike false notes." It is, Socrates says, only when the first of these, the true philosophic natures who become corrupted, neglect philosophy, and leave her "an orphan bereft of relatives" (495c), that the second, the sham philosophers, can move in, "thereby attaching to philosophy everywhere and among all men a reputation such as you say" (491a; cf. 495c).

Socrates has by now defined the philosophic nature twice: first in Book 5, after proclaiming the need for philosophic rule at 473d; and then, as we have seen, in the early part of Book 6, in response to Glaucon's skepticism with respect to philosophic rule (485a-487a). It was this second Socratic encomium to the philosophic nature that prompted Adeimantus's complaint that philosophers are useless or vicious (487d). Socrates now, in taking up Adeimantus's charge that many philosophers are vicious (490e), reviews yet again—that is, for a third time—the essential elements of the philosophic nature, elements that those who become corrupt nevertheless share with those who remain worthy. Socrates reminds Adeimantus that one who has this nature[64] is guided by truth and is not a boaster; he is a real lover of learning who strives for what "is," leaving behind matters of opinion, but holding fast to his passionate love, a love that does not abate until he grasps the nature of each of the things that are (490a b).[65] It is the love of "what is," a love that precedes the philosophic nature's actual grasp of the highest truths, that drives the ascent. Once the journey is completed, once the lover of learning draws near and grasps that which truly is, only then, "having begotten intelligence and truth," does

---

64. Socrates now calls the man who has a philosophic nature a "gentleman" (*kalon te kagathon*—489e), as he had earlier and will subsequently call him "decent" and "most decent." He is indeed a gentleman—until he is corrupted.

65. Socrates' point is not that the philosopher's passionate love ceases once he attains knowledge (though the "labor pains" do subside), but rather that it persists through the entire arduous learning process. In the famous passage in the *Symposium* (200a-e), whose argument is generally taken to imply that love ceases once its object is secured, Socrates in fact tells Agathon (at 200d-e) that it is possible for a person to wish to *continue* to possess a good that he already has—to wish even to hold onto it forever—so that one may indeed still love what one has already attained. (But see *Lysis* 218a: "Those who are already wise no longer love wisdom [*philosophein*], whether they are gods or men." This inference, however, relies on the dubious premise that like cannot be friend to like.) Certainly the verb *aspazesthai*, "to take delight in," applies to things one has—not only to those one aspires to. And at the end of Book 5 the lovers of wisdom not only delight in but love (*philein*) that on which knowledge depends (479e-480a), even though they are already able to "look at each thing itself" and do actually "know" rather than "opine" (479e).

he "know and live truly, is nourished, and so ceases from his labor pains, but not before" (490b).[66] These are men who hate falsehood, and, in addition, possess the whole range of virtues—moral, personal, and intellectual—associated with the love of wisdom: a healthy and just disposition, accompanied by moderation, courage, magnificence, facility at learning, and memory (490b-c).

Yet even natures such as these can sour—indeed, they are far more likely to go bad than not. Those who have these natures have philosophic potential—that is, they are men "for whom philosophy is most suitable" (495b)—yet most become corrupted by bad rearing and never follow through on their early and natural attraction to philosophy. Instead, they "go into exile and leave her [philosophy] abandoned and unconsummated" (495b). They turn vicious, and are distinguishable from other villains, if at all, only by the enormity of the evil they are capable of perpetrating (491e, 495b; cf. 7.519a).[67] Everything seems to conspire against the pursuit of philosophy by these rather spectacular men who are "first among all in everything" (494b). Their magnificence attracts corrupters (492a-e). If one of them should have, besides his philosophic nature, external assets as well—"beauty, wealth, strength of body, relatives who are powerful in a city, and everything akin to these" (491c), "if his body naturally matches his soul" (494b), "if he chances to be from a big city, is rich and noble in it, and is, further, good-looking and tall" (494c)—all these advantages will ensure his downfall (491c) as evil men exploit him for their own ends. (As we saw, these external goods, these things that are merely "said to be goods" [491c] or that are "so-called goods" [495a], seemed to elude the small group of men who are described at 496 as not only having philosophic natures but also remaining faithful to philosophy.) "Most surprising of all" (491b), however, is that even the moral virtues—courage and moderation—of these men blessed with a philosophic nature destroy their souls and tear them

---

66. The ascent to truth is admittedly painful even for those who fervently wish to embark on it. But, the pains of learning are like labor pains (*ōdinos*—490b); they are pains that anticipate great joy, pains that one undergoes happily for the sake of the end (in this case, the "begetting" of intelligence and truth [*noun kai alētheian*]—490b). And they end, as do labor pains, when the glorious goal is reached.

67. See *Crito* 44d for the similar point that the many can do nothing great—whether good or bad; only a big nature can do much good or much harm.

away from philosophy (491b).[68] Moral virtues, no less than intellectual and external goods, are empowering.[69] Moral strength when corrupted is still strength, and so is dangerous and corrosive in a way that moral weakness could never be. And because good natures that are improperly educated turn out worse than inferior natures ("bad is more opposed to good than to not-good"—491d), the damage suffered by superior young men when exposed to corruptive influences is far greater than that suffered by average men.[70] These young men are flattered and honored, and they begin

---

68. The list of moral virtues associated with the philosophic nature grows progressively shorter, as they drop out one by one. At 487a and 490c, justice still appears among them. At 491b, where Socrates begins to consider the corrupted philosophic nature, moderation remains, but justice is gone. By 494b, only courage is left (here Socrates enumerates specifically those assets that attract would-be corrupters); it alone remains to the end along with the intellectual virtues and with magnificence. Bloom (1968, 396) suspects that justice is omitted because the philosopher is not really just; it is only "that there are certain kinds of things he is likely to abstain from"; he does not have "a disposition to render unto others what is due to them" (396) and forms no attachment to the city. Perhaps, however, the reason justice drops out is that, as difficult as it is to see how having the moral virtues of courage and moderation could be the cause of villainy, it is far harder to see how justice could; after all, justice is the virtue that keeps people from harming one another. A similar development is found in the *Meno* (88a–b) and in the *Euthydemus* (279b–281c), both of which contain lists of good things—external as well as intellectual and moral—that make possible greater evil as well as greater good. Found initially on both lists are the moral virtues moderation, justice, and courage. Yet in the *Meno* (88b), Socrates uses only moderation and courage as examples; and in the *Euthydemus* justice drops out at 281c, where Socrates asks: "Would a courageous and moderate man do less, or a coward?"

69. The *Meno* does not offer much in the way of an account of why good things are more harmful than inferior ones when used wrongly or under the influence of ignorance, but the *Euthydemus* does say at 281d: "In all those things which we said at first were good, ... if ignorance leads them they are greater evils than their opposites, inasmuch as they are more able to serve the leader which is evil." See, too, the *Hippias Minor*, esp. 373c–376c, and *Rep.* 1.332d–334b. In Book 7 (519a), those who see most sharply are the ones who do the most evil when they are wrongly "turned." One reason Socrates may be insisting that the moral virtues play a role in the corruption of the philosophic nature is in order to emphasize that they are part of that nature; they aren't simply cultivated by habit. Those who lack the philosophic nature, the guardians of Book 3, for example, can acquire moderation, courage, liberality, and magnificence only through training (402c). In Book 7, where, as I shall argue, the philosophers lack a philosophic nature, the moral virtues are said to come through habituation and practice (518d).

70. When speaking of plants Socrates maintains that the more vigorous ones do especially poorly when they fail to get suitable nourishment (491d), implying thereby that philosophic natures need more than protection from harmful instruction; they need good education. Although when he turns directly to the philosophic nature his concern is lest they receive "*in*appropriate rearing" (*allotriōterāi trophē*—491d), "*bad* instruction" (*kakēs paidagōgias*—491e), and "*bad* rearing" (*kakēi trophē*—495a) (see also 497b, where even in using the plant imagery, Socrates attributes

to believe that they can manage the affairs of both Greeks and barbarians. If someone gently tries to tell one of them otherwise, tries to tell him he needs to expend effort in order to acquire intelligence, the young man won't even be able to hear this remonstrance through the wall of "pretension and empty conceit" (494d) that the corrupters have erected. Moreover, should this young man, because of his good nature, nevertheless be turned and drawn to philosophy, both he and his gentle persuader will be maligned and will be targets of "private plots and public trials" (494b-c);[71] the corrupters will stop at nothing to win him back. Once the philosophic nature's natural love of philosophy is suppressed, the moral qualities that are normally consequent on it are perverted and made to serve immoral ends.

Who are the corrupters who impede the philosophic nature's natural progression toward philosophy? As Socrates sees it, it is too easy to blame professional sophists for spoiling the philosophic nature; indeed, the very people who blame the sophists are the biggest sophists of all (492b): professional sophists, after all, merely regurgitate the beliefs of the multitude and praise what pleases it—and call that wisdom (493a).[72] The masses, whether

---

the failure of the philosophic nature to its being "a foreign seed *sown in alien ground*"), it is clear that in his view good instruction is also required. The only way the philosophic nature can hope to remain true to philosophy is if it "chances on a suitable course of learning," in which case it will "grow and come to every kind of virtue" (492a; cf. 497a: in a good regime it will "grow more"); but "if it [the philosophic nature] isn't nourished in what's suitable, it will come to all the opposite [i.e., to vice], unless one of the gods chances to assist it" (492a; cf. 499b). The reason it is not sufficient simply to leave the philosophic nature alone is that the surrounding moral climate is not neutral but egregiously detrimental. Indeed, Socrates says, good instruction cannot even be heard over "a wall of so many evils" (494d). Maybe there is, then, some validity to the idea, entertained briefly in the *Meno* (89b), that if men are good by nature, it would be prudent to sequester good children in the acropolis until they grow up. Book 6's philosophers may be protected, as was argued, by their superficial blandness.

71. It is a young man's own good nature that inclines him to philosophy; the man who gently encourages him along that path helps him to resist the forces that oppose his natural bent.

72. Socrates says of the professional sophists that they "call the necessary just and noble" (493c). McCoy (2008, 126), relying on the later discussion of necessary and unnecessary desires and also on the earlier "city of utmost necessity" (396d), understands by "the necessary," bodily needs. Reeve (2004, 187), however, translates: "but calls everything he is compelled to do just and fine." In support of Reeve it may be noted that Socrates characterizes the sophists as sharing the many's understanding of the noble and shameful, good and bad, just and unjust, and the many, as Glaucon observes in Book 2, regard the just as something hard (358a) that people are compelled to do, though they would prefer not to ("no one is willingly just but only when compelled to be so"—360c).

in assemblies, courts, theaters, or army camps, determine by their shouting and clapping what is good and what is bad—and brook no dissent.[73] And they cannot be philosophic: they are not capable of the belief that there is a beautiful itself in addition to the many beautiful things. As a result, both they and the sophists who wish only to gratify them (494a) condemn those who philosophize (though, as we shall see in a moment, some sophists secretly admire and want to be philosophers) and quash the tendency to philosophy found in the best young men. No attempt to educate the young that runs counter to the conventional bad instruction is tolerated (491e); none is permitted to succeed (494d).

We have now seen the second of Book 6's four philosophic types: men who possess a genuine philosophic nature but who nevertheless never become philosophers. For the most part, those who have the genuine philosophic nature, replete with all the virtues that attach to it, will fail to realize their potential (494a).[74] The prospects are even grimmer for those whose inner qualities are enhanced by the external adornments of wealth, good looks, and political connections (494c): they are corrupted before they can even begin to develop their natural penchant for philosophy. Neither the uselessness of the philosophic nature nor its viciousness can be blamed, however, on the nature itself. It owes its uselessness to those who fail to appreciate it, and its viciousness to those who value it too highly, seeking to enlist it for their own ignoble ends.

III. The Second Deficient Type: The Pseudo-Philosopher

Members of the third philosophic type that Socrates discusses in Book 6, the second of the vicious types, lack a philosophic nature, and thus can only be "counterfeit" (*peplasmenōs*) philosophers (485d). Initially contrasted with true (*alēthōs*) philosophers (at 485d-e), they are subsequently

---

73. We may compare with Socrates' denunciation of the multitude Meletus's assertion in the *Apology* that not only the judges but also all the others present in court—the councilmen, the members of the Assembly, and indeed all Athenians but Socrates—are improvers of the youth; Socrates alone, he says, is a corrupter (*Ap.* 24e-25a).

74. These men never actually become philosophers, and so cannot be held responsible for philosophy's bad repute. It is the pseudo-philosophers, those whose nature is not philosophic, who bring shame upon philosophy (490e-491a, 495c, 500b, 535c).

described (at 491a) as men who "imitate the philosophic nature and set themselves up in its practice": they merely pretend to philosophy but are unworthy of her (495c). Insofar as these sham philosophers don't have a philosophic nature, they are distinct not only from the "decent but useless" philosophers Socrates considered first but also from the "vicious" philosophers he considered next—those who have an authentic philosophic nature that fails to thrive. The current vicious group is most likely composed of sophists of some kind, who practiced a vulgar craft before leaping into philosophy (495d-e). Socrates indeed says of professional sophists that they "organize" their mastery of the anger and pleasures of the many "into a craft" that they then teach (493b). So, whereas Socrates absolves the sophists, as we have seen, of primary responsibility for corrupting budding philosophers, he nevertheless charges them with sullying philosophy's reputation by pretending to be what they are by nature unworthy to be.

These are the men who are responsible for philosophy's bad name: "By far the greatest and most powerful slander comes to philosophy on account of those who claim to practice such things" (489d); they "approach a practice that is of no value for them and is beyond them; they often strike false notes, thereby attaching to philosophy everywhere and among all men a reputation such as you [Adeimantus] say" (491a); they "come to her [philosophy] and disgrace her" (495c).[75] Since these pseudo-philosophers are men who "keep company" with philosophy "in an unworthy way" (*homilōsi mē kat' axian*—496a), they are the polar opposites of the decent men who "keep company with philosophy in a way that is worthy" (*tōn kat' axian homilountōn*—496a-b). The reason they are attracted to philosophy is that it surpasses the crafts in magnificence (495d). Socrates colorfully compares them to "a little, bald-headed worker in bronze who has gotten some silver, and, newly released from bonds, just washed in a bathhouse, wearing a newly-made cloak and got up like a bridegroom, is about to marry his master's daughter because she is poor and destitute" (495e).[76] In other words, these unworthy men can disguise their nature and sidle up

---

75. Cf. 7.535c, where Socrates speaks harshly of the "bastard" men who take up philosophy and bring dishonor to her.

76. The reference to bronze and silver calls to mind the metals in the city (Bloom 1968, 462 n. 15). These unfit philosophic aspirants are bronze; they *get hold of* some silver; but they wish—in

to philosophy because she has been left "poor and destitute" by the worthy natures that became corrupted and abandoned her. They produce "sophisms" (*sophismata*), connected with nothing genuine (496a); they deliver highly stylized ("balanced"—*hōmoiōmena*) speeches (498d-e) and indulge in "subtleties and contentious quibbles that strain toward nothing but opinion and contention in trials as well as in private groups" (499a); they are philosophic frauds, "drunken revelers, who abuse one another and indulge a taste for quarreling, and . . . always make their arguments about persons" (500b). In their quibbling and quarreling and resorting to ad hominem arguments, they are the cause of philosophy's bad reputation.

Let us pause for a moment to review our inventory of the philosophic types in *Rep.* 6 encountered thus far. Two of these possess genuine philosophic natures; one does not. Of the two that do, men of the first type remain true to philosophy and become philosophers—they are decent but useless; men of the second type become corrupted, abandon philosophy, and turn vicious: although they start out as gifted youngsters who might have become philosophers under other circumstances, they are led astray and deflected from their natural course. The one type that does not possess a philosophic nature is the sham would-be philosopher, the charlatan who never actually becomes a philosopher but only imitates philosophers and gives philosophy a bad name. Philosophy itself is not to blame for the defects of any of the three types thus far considered: not for the uselessness of the decent ones—they would prove quite useful if only given a chance; not for the viciousness of the philosophic natures that are corrupted—these abandon philosophy; and not for the villainy of the philosophic imitators— these are not genuinely philosophic. To these three types Socrates will now add a fourth, thereby making his list both complete and symmetrical. The full list will thus contain, in addition to (1) philosophic natures that become philosophers, (2) philosophic natures that do not become philosophers, and (3) nonphilosophic natures that do not become philosophers, also (4) nonphilosophic natures that *do* become philosophers.

---

vain—to *be* gold. They could not marry the "master's daughter" unless she had become impoverished—that is, unless those in possession of the true philosophic nature had turned their backs on philosophy.

IV. The Third Deficient Type: The Philosopher-Warrior

At 502c, Socrates declares the discussion of the philosophic ruler complete. He has determined that the city ruled by philosophers is both best and not impossible. The remaining topic, Socrates says, is the matter of how the "saviors" are to be educated when they "come to be present within the regime for us" (502c-d): which studies and practices are they to take up, and at what ages? He calls for a fresh start: "What concerns the rulers," he says, "must be pursued as it were from the beginning (*ex archēs*)" (502e).

If, as is likely, Plato is not responsible for the *Republic*'s division into books (as was observed in note 20 of the introduction), it is legitimate to ask whether 6.502c is not a more fitting starting point for Book 7 than the actual one: 514a. We find at 502c a precise parallel to 484a, which marks the beginning of Book 6. At 502c9 Socrates says: "Now that this discussion has after considerable effort (*mogis*) reached an end"; this perfectly matches 484a1-3: "And so, Glaucon, through a somewhat lengthy argument, who the philosophers are and who the non-philosophers has, with considerable effort (*mogis*), somehow been brought to light." Furthermore, the task taken up in Book 7, namely, determining the course of the rulers' education, is the one that Socrates sets for himself and Glaucon at 502c: "which studies are to be taken up, and at what ages." Indeed, the break at 514a seems awkward: Socrates' elucidation of the nature of the highest study is by then already well under way. It is still in Book 6 that Socrates instructs Glaucon to "take these four affections arising in the soul in relation to the four segments [of the divided line]" and to "arrange them in a proportion, and believe that as the segments to which they correspond participate in truth, so they participate in clarity" (6.511d-e). Yet, when Socrates proceeds to the next stage—"Next (*Meta tauta*), then, liken our nature in its education. . . ." (514a)—we are suddenly in Book 7.[77]

Whether or not Book 7 would more appropriately have begun at 502c, it is clear that Socrates takes himself to be starting over at this point, to be beginning "from the beginning," *ex archēs*. The fresh start ushers in his

---

77. The image-making (*apeikason*) with which Book 7 begins (514a) and the *eikona* Socrates there produces (515a) are also connected with the image (*eikona*—509a) he fashions of the sun at the end of Book 6.

fourth and final philosophic type. Admitting that it was not very wise of
him to have initially omitted from his discussion of the "wholly and completely true institution" the "unpleasantness" of the three waves, namely,
(1) women taking up the same tasks as men, (2) the communism of women
and children (450b: "I saw it and then passed by so as not to cause a lot of
trouble"), and (3) philosophic rule, he will now remedy his lapse in judgment with respect to the rulers, as he has already done with respect to
women and children.

Philosophic rule, however, initially formed no part of the plan for the
new city and so was not simply an underdeveloped idea in the way the other
aspects of Callipolis were. When Adeimantus at the start of Book 5, giving
voice to Polemarchus's concerns, challenges Socrates to flesh out what he
had no more than mentioned at 423a, namely, the matters of women and
children, philosophic rule is not even on the horizon; the third wave when
it appears (at 473c-d) thus comes as an almost complete surprise. (The wise
rulers of Book 4, as we have seen, are not ever called philosophers.) Indeed,
the outline of Callipolis is already complete at 471c-d, where Glaucon asks
to be assured only that the city as described is possible. The philosopher-
rulers are brought in at that moment, ostensibly as the "one change—not,
however, a small or an easy one, but possible" (473c)   that could transform
the city in speech into a real one.[78]

Even though philosophic rule was not part of Socrates' original plan,
nevertheless, once he introduces it as his third wave, that is, from 473c
on, he takes up, along with his companions, not only the matter of the nature of philosophers but also that of how they would rule, reaching an end
(*telos*), as he says, "after considerable effort" (*mogis*—502c). But if Socrates
has indeed already discussed the nature of philosophic rule, describing
how ruling philosophers would go about revamping the city's laws and
refurbishing its citizens' imperfect souls (501a-c), why would he say at 502e
that "what concerns the rulers" has yet to be addressed?

It seems that the philosophic rule Socrates has considered at 501a-c is
appropriate not to Callipolis but to Book 6's city of chance. He has apparently ridden the third and biggest wave (473c) far too far out to sea, dock-
ing in a city that bears virtually no resemblance to Callipolis as outlined in

78. See the introduction, note 13.

Books 2–5. At 502c-e Socrates realizes how far he has strayed and heads back to shore, taking up, as he says, the question of how philosophers who "come to be present within the regime for us" (*hēmin . . . enesontai tēs politeias*)—that is, within Callipolis[79]—are to be educated, and the way in which they are to rule there. We have seen that for philosophers of the first paradigm, those who have a true philosophic nature, Socrates creates no scripted (or coercive) educational program; instead, it is hoped that (by chance—492a, 501d) they will be "perfected by age and education" (487a). It is only for Callipolis's philosopher-rulers that an educational curriculum must be planned to the last detail. We have seen, too, how philosophers rule in the city of chance; what remains to be explored is how philosophers would rule in Socrates' beautiful, carefully orchestrated, and rigidly structured city.

Revisiting, then, the city he envisioned in Books 2–5, a city that had utterly vanished from view in Book 6, Socrates revives the guardians of Book 3 to serve as its rulers. Yet, even the best of those guardians, the ones Socrates had singled out to rule, were not distinguished by any sort of wisdom; they were not said to be capable either of making laws or of determining which opinions the laws should reflect. They were to be prudent in the matter of guarding the city; they were to be powerful; and they were to care for the city (412c). In particular, they were to be "skillful guardians of the conviction" that one must do what is best for the city (412e). In the wake of Book 4's division of the city into three classes—ruling, military (auxiliary), and producer—and its insistence that those in the ruling class be wise, Book 3's guardians would no longer qualify for rule. And so, even though nothing explicit is said about it, they had to have been demoted in Book 4 to the military class, to the class that is characterized as having a "kind of power and preservation, through everything, of the right and lawful opinion about what is terrible and what not" (430b), having received "from us" the opinions favored by the law "in the noblest way possible like a dye" (430a). If such men are to regain their former status as rulers, wisdom must augment their courage and moderation.

---

79. The city that philosophers perfect at 501a is not itself "the regime" (*politeia*) that the founders have been constructing. There the philosophers take a city and outline the shape of its regime or constitution (*tēs politeias*) (501a). At 502c-d, however, *politeia* denotes the founders' regime; it is *hēmin . . . tēs politeias*, that is, "for us . . . the regime"—or simply "our regime"—in which the saviors will take their place (*enesontai*).

Building with Adeimantus on what "we were saying" earlier (502e)—
though it was actually Glaucon with whom Socrates had been conversing
for the better part of Book 3[80]—Socrates now fashions from the sturdy
warrior stock of Book 3's guardians the hybrid philosopher-warrior, who
is to rule the beautiful city.[81] It is no doubt in part for Glaucon's sake that
Socrates produces a more virile philosopher than the one he described at
the end of Book 5 and for most of Book 6, a new type that embodies the
spiritedness and physical strength that would otherwise be associated exclusively with the auxiliaries. The pure unmixed philosopher who, like
the true pilot, has his head in the clouds, is surely not to Glaucon's liking:
we recall that Glaucon found the initial suggestion of philosophic rule at
473d worthy of contempt if not of violence (473e), and that he regarded
Socrates' exuberant endorsement of such rule as lacking in measure (484b).
Moreover, it is unlikely that Glaucon would think the artless intellectu-
als of Book 6 capable of radically restructuring a city and effecting a new
social order.

Socrates' new philosophers (as he calls them, on account of their at-
tainment of wisdom if not of their love for it: 6.503b; 7.520a, 525b2, 525b6,
540d; 8.543a) depart markedly from the other types identified in this
chapter—from the decent but useless men of whom he speaks admir-
ingly as well as from the two vicious sorts of whom he clearly disapproves.
Individuals of the fourth type, as we shall see in Chapters 2 and 3, are,
once they are turned to philosophy, neither useless nor vicious (7.518e).
So long as they agree to rule, they will rule ably. Yet, insofar as they lack
the genuine philosophic nature, they can only be, in Socrates' eyes, poor
substitutes for the naturally wisdom-loving, decent, and morally upright
philosophers who, as Socrates has argued—and as he hopes all will agree
(485a)—are alone truly suited to rule.

---

80. Perhaps Socrates is hoping to goad Glaucon into more active engagement in the current
argument by misidentifying his partner in the earlier conversation as Adeimantus. Glaucon soon
does take his brother's place—at 506d. A similar misidentification was made just before at 501c;
and at 465e Socrates pretends not to remember whose argument it was (it was Adeimantus's) that
"reproached us for not making the guardians happy."

81. See Dawson 1992, 80: "The rule of the guards must be united to the rule of the wise" if the
defect in Plato's first, "low," utopia is to be corrected and Plato's second, "high," utopia is to take
its place. See Chapter 2, note 26.

V. Conclusion

We have identified four philosophic types in *Rep.* 6: (1) those who possess the genuine philosophic nature and become philosophers, (2) those who possess the genuine philosophic nature but fail to become philosophers because they are corrupted, (3) those who lack the philosophic nature and for that reason do not become philosophers, and (4) those who lack the philosophic nature yet do become philosophers. Of these, (1) and (3) are examples of natures left alone—good natures that turn out good and bad ones that go bad; (2) and (4) are natures that are manipulated—good natures that are not permitted to stay good and bad ones that, as we shall see in Chapter 2, are prevented from remaining bad. We are left, however, with the nagging suspicion that those who lack the philosophic nature can never—no matter how they are sculpted—become true philosophers. After all, according to Socrates in Book 6, philosophy is "a practice that a man could never adequately pursue if he were not by nature a rememberer, a good learner, magnificent, charming, *and* a friend and kinsman (*philos te kai sungenēs*) of truth, justice, and moderation" (487a). The philosopher-rulers who are introduced in Book 6 (after 502c) and developed in Book 7 may have superior minds but they are not, by their natures, as we shall see, friends and kin of truth, justice, and moderation.

Addendum: Philosophic Dogs and Their Human Counterparts

Well before philosophers and philosophic types are discussed in Books 5–7, the label "philosophic" is attached in *Rep.* 2 to dogs. The comparison of people to animals and particularly to dogs runs through much of the *Republic*.[82] On several occasions young boys are likened to puppies. In Book 2, for example, Socrates suggests that "for guarding" there is no "difference between the nature of a genteel puppy and that of a well-born young man" (375a). At 7.537a and 539b, two puppy images follow one another in quick succession: in the first passage Socrates recommends that children be taken

---

82. On animal imagery in the *Republic*, see Saxonhouse 1978.

to war as spectators and, like puppies, taste blood; in the second he urges that precautions be taken lest young men abuse arguments once they get a taste of them, because young men tend to play like puppies at contradiction and refutation and enjoy "pulling and tearing with argument at those who happen to be near."[83]

Socrates' purpose in describing dogs as philosophic is to shed light on the nature of the city's future guardians who are likened to them. Although dogs are essentially spirited creatures, Socrates insists that their nature contains a philosophic element that enables them to be gentle toward people they know even as they are ferocious toward strangers.[84] But, of course, even if Socrates calls this aspect of a dog's nature philosophic, indeed even if he calls dogs philosophers (375e), he cannot mean literally what he says. They are, after all, dogs.[85] If dogs are vicious toward people they don't know and amiable toward those with whom they are acquainted, that surely has nothing to do with anything that can reasonably be called "love of learning" (376b)—no matter what Socrates asserts. For if, as Socrates makes a point of saying, dogs dislike strangers even when they have had no bad experience of them, and like the people they know even when they have had with them no good experience (376a), then they are anything but philosophic. Responding to others on the basis of familiarity alone is hardly a sign of love of learning; on the contrary, the dogs' attitude reveals a distinct lack of interest in knowing or discovering the nature of those with whom they associate, or in tailoring their responses accordingly. They are in this respect reminiscent of Polemarchus in Book 1 (334c ff.), who defines justice as helping friends and harming enemies—without having given any sustained thought to what kinds of people should count as one's friends and enemies. Those who love learning, truth, and wisdom do not

---

83. It is hard to miss the juxtaposition of tasting blood and tasting argument. In Book 5 the true lover of learning, "especially when he is young," "is willing to *taste* every kind of learning with gusto" (5.475c). This youngster is drawn, however, not to the sport of philosophy but to the "sight of truth" (475e). Taste also appears at 496c, where Socrates speaks of the few who "have tasted how sweet and blessed a possession" philosophy is.

84. Insofar as it is not toward the same people that the dogs are both vicious and gentle they avoid violating Book 4's law of noncontradiction.

85. See Ranasinghe 2000, 13: "Unless the reader recognizes that this passage reeks of irony, he or she will miss the point."

simply trust what is familiar; on the contrary, they challenge the familiar and endorse the true—whether familiar or foreign.

What *is* true of dogs is that they are fiercely loyal. But knee-jerk loyalty is neither the same as, nor even reliably compatible with, philosophy— that is, with the love and pursuit of wisdom with respect to "what is."[86] Perhaps, then, the aspect of the philosophic nature that Socrates wishes to emphasize is its gentleness. Since his aim in speaking of philosophic dogs in Book 2 is to teach us something about the guardians—and, in particular, to prepare the ground for his more extensive discussion of them in Book 3—we may assume that he wishes to assure us that, like dogs, the guardians, if they are "philosophic" at all, can be so only in the sense that they are able to be not only fierce but gentle.

The guardians of Book 3, like their canine counterparts, are, then, essentially spirited creatures[87] who also have a softer side. In dogs, that softer side manifests itself in friendliness to people they know; in the guardians, in the use of persuasion rather than force and in a certain gracefulness (411d-e). When the future guardians are young, they are trained in music and gymnastic in order to calm their excessively savage spirited aspect and to toughen their too tame "philosophic" side.[88] The resultant psychic harmony is expected to yield men of courage and moderation. It is not, however, expected to produce wise men. Indeed, the guardians' philosophic nature is never associated with mental acuity—with such things as facility at learning and having a good memory (as the philosophic nature of philosophers is in Book 6 at 486c-d, 487a, and 490c).[89] Since Socrates ascribes a

---

86. In Book 4 the auxiliaries are compared to dogs inasmuch as they are obedient to rulers who are likened to the shepherds of a city (440d). Indeed the spirited part of the soul is compared to a dog that can be tamed by a herdsman. The herdsman is reason (440d).

87. As in Book 4, the virtue associated in Book 2 with spiritedness is courage: "Will horse or dog—or any animal whatsoever—be willing to be courageous if it is not spirited?" (375a).

88. The reasoning part of the soul in Book 4's rulers, like the gentle aspect of Book 3's guardians, is supposed to be "in tune" with the spirited part. In Book 3, training in music and gymnastic tunes the guardians' "philosophic" (gentle) and spirited natures to each other; in Book 4, the same training brings about accord between the *reasoning* and spirited parts of the rulers' souls, "tightening the one and training it in fair speeches and learning, while relaxing the other with soothing tales, taming it by harmony and rhythm" (441e; cf. 411e-412a).

89. The guardian does need to have a good memory (and be hard to deceive); the only thing he has to remember (or not be deceived out of), however, is the conviction (*dogmatos*) that he must on every occasion do what seems best for the city (413c-d).

philosophic nature not only to people who are like animals but even to the animals themselves, the reader is duly forewarned: not everyone Socrates calls a philosopher is one. Indeed, the philosophic dogs and their human counterparts—the guardians of Book 3—do not love wisdom, have wisdom, or even wish to be thought wise. The guardians who become the philosopher-rulers of Book 7, then, are a rare—and comic—breed indeed: insofar as they have the abilities and qualities of warriors but are also intellectually gifted, they are as improbable as dogs who can read.[90]

---

90. Steinberger (1989) forcefully argues that the guardians of Book 3, with respect to their education, character, and regard for truth, are not philosophic, so that the *Republic* would make better sense if the guardians could be kept separate from the philosophers: guardians would rule Callipolis; philosophers would reform already existing cities (1223). As Steinberger concedes (1223), however, the passage at 502d-503b precludes keeping the two apart. (Steinberger does note [1224] that Aristotle's critique of Callipolis in Book 2 of the *Politics* treats Plato's city as if it contained no philosopher-kings.)

2

PHILOSOPHERS BY DESIGN I

The Making of a Philosopher

> Nothing can . . . be called good, without qualification, except a good will.
> Intelligence, wit, judgement, and the other talents of the mind, however they
> may be named . . . may also become extremely bad and mischievous if the
> will which is to make use of them, and which, therefore, constitutes what is
> called character, is not good.
>
> —Immanuel Kant, *Groundwork of the Metaphysics of Morals*, chapter 1

Socrates expects of his philosophers nothing less than the salvation of cities. Only philosophers, he tells us repeatedly, can save regimes from all ills, public and private (5.473d; 6.487e, 499b-c, 500e, 501e, 506a-b; 7.536b); they "perfect everything" (*pant' epitelesai*—6.502b); they are "saviors" (*hoi sōtēres*—502d).[1] We have seen that the philosophers of Book 6,[2] who possess the philosophic nature and also somehow remain loyal to philosophy, would satisfy Socrates' high expectations should they happen on a city willing to obey them. Their love of wisdom, truth, and being endows them with every quality, moral and personal; they are blessed with superior intellects; and, given reasonably favorable conditions, they would fight for justice in service to their cities. The question at the core of this chapter is,

---

1. See Chapter 1, note 3.
2. As already noted, I refer to the philosophers whose description begins at 5.473c and runs through 6.502c as "the philosophers of Book 6."

Are the philosophers designed by the founders of Callipolis from 6.502c through the end of *Rep.* 7[3] equally up to the task?

Chapter 1 sought to dispel the illusion that all philosophers in the *Republic* are the same. Not only does Socrates playfully permit even dogs to be philosophers (and even to have a philosophic nature),[4] but he also recognizes philosophic natures that do not mature into philosophers, as well as pseudo-philosophers who lack a philosophic nature. Chapter 1 showed, too, that Socrates introduces in *Rep.* 6 at 502e a new type of philosopher, one who is to rule not in a city that happens, by chance, to welcome him, but in the planned city made for him. This chapter will show that this new philosopher, a man (or woman) not only intellectually gifted but also fit for battle, is nevertheless not by nature philosophic, so that in making him (her), Socrates must defy nature and deny chance.[5] Chapter 3 will then explore how a philosopher of this kind, formed out of a nature not in its essence philosophic, rules the city designed for him (her).

There can be little doubt that this new type of ruler—a blend of sharp wits and mulish constancy—appeals to Glaucon in a way the earlier one never could. Glaucon congratulates Socrates on producing, "like a sculptor (*andriantopoios*), ruling men who are wholly noble (*pankalous*)" (540c).[6] The modified philosopher Socrates creates at the end of Book 6 and through all of Book 7 is one Glaucon can respect. By supplementing intellectual qualities with those typical of a soldier, Socrates keeps Glaucon from dismissing the value of philosophy and encourages him to admire the smart and manly philosopher-warrior.[7] Glaucon had offered no resistance to the

---

3. I call these "Book 7's philosophers," as noted earlier.

4. As we saw in the addendum to Chapter 1, philosophic dogs are gentle and are even amusingly said to "love learning," because they love the people they *know*. Socrates never says of them, however, not even in jest, that they love "what is"—same for the guardians, who are compared to these dogs.

5. It is probable that what Socrates attempts cannot be done. As Benardete notes (1989, 119), "The city may ultimately make its citizens, but it will never make the philosopher. Nature in the form of chance frustrates the true city."

6. Glaucon is clearly repaying Socrates' compliment. At 2.361d, Socrates had said: "My, my, my dear Glaucon, how vigorously you polish up each of the two men—just like a statue (*andrianta*)—for their judgment."

7. As Ferrari ([2003] 2005, 29) puts it, Socrates makes the ruler in Book 7 "a real man." See Craig, 1994, 79: "As for someone with a genuinely timocratic nature [i.e., someone like Glaucon], of which the finest embodiment is he who wishes to be honoured for his virtue, he can be made

notion of rule by the spirited guardians of Book 3 or even by the practically wise rulers of Book 4. As we have seen, only the suggestion that philosophers make the best rulers arouses his spirited indignation.[8]

I. Philosophic Hybrids

The philosopher-warriors that Socrates fashions represent a flagrant violation of his one-man, one-job principle: each citizen "must be brought to that which naturally suits him—one man, one job—so that each man, practicing his own, which is one, will not become many but one" (4.423d). The principle was first established in Book 2 as the foundation for the "city of utmost necessity" (369d) (later called the true and healthy city [372e]), and was decisively reaffirmed specifically when Glaucon questioned the need for special military men to fight the city's battles (374a). It was then that Socrates insisted that "it is impossible for one man to do a fine job in many arts" (374a). Moreover, as Socrates warned at 4.434a-b, the incursion of citizens into the wrong classes poses a particularly great danger when "one who is a craftsman or some other kind of money-maker . . . tries to get into the class of the warrior, or one of the warriors who is unworthy into that of the adviser and guardian . . . or when the same man tries to do all these things at once." (See, too, the disparaged "tendency" of the rulers in an oligarchy to be "busybodies"; they "engaged in farming, money-making, and war-making at the same time" [551e-552a].) It is astonishing that Socrates' mongrel philosopher-warriors fail to provoke an outraged outcry from either the dialogue's participants or its readers.[9]

---

into a true gentleman by his coming to respect philosophy, and to honour wisdom as the highest virtue. He needs only be assured that philosophy is manly—that it is not corrupting if pursued in the right way by those who are naturally suited for it."

8. Unless Socrates were fashioning a figure agreeable to Glaucon (and Adeimantus), it is hard to see why the rulers could not be philosophers pure and simple; any battles, internal or external, could be waged by their allies, the auxiliaries. Indeed, if the rulers are warriors, is the auxiliary class needed?

9. Bloom (1968, 407) and others see the philosopher-ruler as a violation of the one-man, one-job principle. But philosopher is not a job—ruler is. And warrior is. So, the problematic combination is actually ruler-warrior. The philosopher of Book 7 is in violation of the principle because he is to be both ruler and warrior.

Indeed, a closer look at these new rulers reveals not only that they are dual-natured but that their two natures are diametrically opposed to each other. Unlike those men with philosophic natures described earlier in Book 6, who combine easily within their souls the fully compatible, if distinct, intellectual and moral qualities (485a-487a), the men of 503b-d are to contain in their natures two components that "are rarely willing to grow together in the same place" (503b; also 503d).[10] On the one hand, these men are to be intellectually gifted—that is, they are to be good at learning, have good memories, and be mentally agile, sharp,[11] brimming with youthful exuberance (*neanikoi*; cf. 491e), and magnificent, the sort whose sharpness carries them away "wherever chance leads" (503c). On the other hand, they are to be steady, trustworthy, and implacable in the face of fears; they "must show themselves to be lovers of the city (*philopolidas*), tested in pleasures and pains, and . . . that they don't cast out this conviction (*dogma*) in labors or fears or any other adversity" (503a).[12] Generally speaking, however, as Socrates observes, people whose minds are mercurial tend not to be reliable and orderly. And people who are immovable in war are likely to be plodding in their studies. Yet this new and exotic (503b) breed of men is expected to excel at both war and studies. Socrates will withhold "a share in the most precise education, in honor, or in rule" (503d) from anyone who fails to participate in both natures, from anyone who fails the tests either in "the labors, fears, and pleasures[13] we mentioned then" (503e; a reference

---

10. In Book 4 Socrates makes a point of keeping the spirited nature and the reasoning one decisively apart (439e-441e). To combine them now in one nature is surely to violate Socrates' hard-won principle.

11. See Chapter 1, note 15; and note 28 below.

12. In this way the philosophers of Book 7 replicate the guardians of Book 3, whose love of city essentially consists in holding on tight to the conviction (*dogma*) that the city's interests come first (cf. 412e, 413c). Socrates cannot (and does not) long keep up the pretence, however, that these philosophers are lovers of the city or in any way identify their own interests with the city's. The rulers of Book 7 are apparently not subjected to the "genteel (*gennaion*) lie" of 414b-c, nor are they likely to be taken in by it. They are not bound to their fellow citizens "as brothers and born of the earth" (414e); indeed, they pity them (516c). There is no mention of love of city even at 535–536. See section IV in this chapter.

13. Cf. *Theaet.* 144a-b, where Theodorus remarks that Theaetetus seems to blend within his character qualities that are normally at odds with one another: he is sharp and quick, yet extraordinarily gentle rather than rash; he is steady, without having a sluggish mind and poor memory. Theodorus had previously thought these qualities—of keenness and retentiveness, on the one hand, and gentleness and steadiness, on the other—never come together: "I never thought such a combination could exist" (144b).

to 3.413d[14]) or in "the greatest studies." By mastering both endeavors, these "most precise (*akribestatous*) guardians" (503b),[15] however few (503d),[16] surpass Book 3's "most complete (*panteleis*) guardians" (414a): superior intellect now complements natural spiritedness. *Love* of wisdom, however, forms no part of the nature of the philosopher-warrior.

Socrates leaves no doubt as to the need for a warrior component in the nature of his new rulers. Not only are they "champions of war when young" (521b), but they are to be "warlike men" (521b). "Our guardian," Socrates says, "is both warrior and philosopher" (525b), one who is to be "steadfast in studies and steadfast in war" (527d); only "those . . . who have proved best in philosophy and with respect to war" are to be kings (543a). Indeed, because "our guardian is both warrior and philosopher" (525b), his education, even though its aim is to direct him away from the sensible realm and toward the intelligible, "mustn't be useless to warlike men" (521d); his studies must be "necessary for a warrior to learn . . . and for a philosopher" (525b). Socrates and Glaucon agree that gymnastic is not the sort of study that will begin to effect the ascent to philosophy: it is "wholly engaged with coming into being and passing away" (521e). And Glaucon recognizes that even music is not "a study directed toward something of the sort you are now seeking," insofar as it inculcates instead a certain harmoniousness—not knowledge—through habit and rhythm (522a). The curriculum Socrates designs, therefore, to set the soul on an upward trajectory begins with calculation (arithmetic). As he explains, however, calculation is appropriate not only because it properly orients the soul but also because it is something a warrior needs (522e): the guardians are "to stay with it [calculation] until they come to the contemplation of the nature of numbers with intellection itself, not for the sake of buying and selling like merchants or tradesmen, but *for war* and for ease of turning the soul itself around from becoming to truth and being" (525c). To be sure, the relevance of the philosophers' studies to war steadily diminishes. By the

14. These new guardians are connected with those of Book 3 also by undergoing tests in the way gold is tested in fire (503a, 413d-e). Socrates never says of the philosophers of Book 6 that they need to be tested.

15. Socrates' use of "most precise" recalls the "ruler in the precise sense" of 1.341b. For Thrasymachus, this was the "strong" man who never mistakes his own advantage; but for Socrates, it was the one who cares for "the weaker."

16. See Chapter 1, note 41.

time the third and fourth subjects are considered there is no longer any
mention of war at all, and even in the case of the second, geometry, it is
Glaucon who emphasizes its value for war: as much of geometry must be
studied, he says, "as applies to the business of war" (526d). Socrates for his
part in fact minimizes not only geometry's but even calculation's usefulness for war, "For such things only a small portion of geometry—as of
calculation—would suffice," now directing Glaucon's attention to the
greater part of these studies, which "compels one to look at being" (526e).
Socrates continues to maintain, however, that geometry's "by-products"—
the "nobler reception of all studies" that it fosters as well as the efficacy in
war that Glaucon had mentioned—"aren't slight" (527c).

In all of Book 6 there was not a single mention of war—until 502e,
of course, where the dual-natured philosopher-warrior enters the scene.
Indeed, what possible need would there be for the natural philosopher of
Books 5–6 to be warlike, to study subjects that are useful in battle, or to
engage in fighting? Yet in Book 7, war is mentioned frequently: 521d5,
521d11, 522c10, 522e1, 525b3, 525b8, 525c4, 526d1, 527c5, 537a4, 537d2,
539e4. Indeed, the philosophers are compelled near the end of their training to descend to the Cave and rule in affairs of war (539e) in order to gain
sufficient experience. And, as the short summary at the start of Book 8
plainly stipulates, the city that is "going to be governed on a high level"
must have kings "who have proved best in philosophy and with respect to
war" (543a). The only war Book 6's philosophers are prepared to engage in
is the fight for justice (496c-d).[17]

The future rulers' "steady, not easily changeable dispositions, which...are
trustworthy and which in war are hard to move in the face of fears" (503c-d),
recall those of the guardians described in Book 3: "moderate and courageous men who are champions of war" (416d-e; also 404a). In Book 3 the
guardians' dual nature, spirited and philosophic, was trained in music and

17. Craig suggests (1994, 79) that "perhaps the ones best suited for philosophy are not those
who are gentle by nature . . . but rather those whose great spiritedness makes them passionate lovers of victory." Yet the philosophic nature in Book 6 is gentle: the soul that has such a nature is both
just and tame (*hēmeros*), not hard to be a partner with nor savage (486b). There is no reason to assume, however, that the philosophic nature, even if generally gentle, is passive in the face of evil,
in deed or in speech. For one thing, the philosophic nature hates falsehood (485c). And for another,
Socrates, and philosophers generally, fight for truth and justice, and are prepared to battle their
opponents (*Ap.* 32a; *Meno* 86b-c; *Phaedo* 89a, 89c; *Gorg.* 503a, 505e, 521a; *Rep.* 335e, 496c-d, 499d).

gymnastic in order to moderate the tendency to savagery while preventing excessive softness. At the end of Book 6 it is once again spirited men who rule, though now with intellectual vibrancy improbably complementing their dull doggedness.[18]

II. The Cave

The allegory of the Cave is indispensable to achieving an understanding of the nature of these new philosophers. It is our guide to the question of who these philosophers are, what sort of life they prefer to lead, how they come to be philosophers, and the sense in which they are philosophers. It tells of three realms: the Cave, the visible realm, and the intelligible realm, and of two analogous ascents: the ascent out of the Cave into the visible realm and eventually up to the sun, and the ascent out of the visible realm into the intelligible realm and eventually up to the Good. Each step of each ascent represents progress toward Being, toward what is most real.

The ascent out of the Cave begins with the perception of (1) shadows of various artifacts and statues of animals and men, continues on to (2) artifacts and statues of animals and men in the Cave, next to (3) reflections (in water) of artifacts, actual men (and other things), heavenly bodies, and heaven itself outside the Cave, then to (4) artifacts, actual men and other things such as animals and plants (532b), and heavenly bodies and heaven itself not re-flected in water or other media but viewed directly, and finally to (5) the sun. In the Cave, then, the prisoners perceive only reflections of artificial originals: "Such men would hold that the truth is nothing other than the shadows of artificial things" (515c).[19]

The ascent out of the visible world begins with step (3) of the ascent out of the Cave, that is, with the perception of reflections of artifacts, actual

---

18. See Chapter 1, section IV, where the oddness of transforming the former guardians of Book 3 into philosophers suited to rule in Callipolis is noted and discussed. See, too, Chapter 1's addendum. I use the term "doggedness" advisedly.

19. The Cave does in fact contain natural things. The prisoners are themselves natural, as are the "puppeteers"—those who parade the artifacts and statues along the wall behind the prisoners—and the sounds they make are natural. Moreover, if the prisoners converse with each other, they might even hear some natural sounds directly. Socrates would no doubt have us bracket these non-artificial things in the Cave for the sake of his analogy's efficacy.

human beings and other things, and heavenly bodies and heaven itself. It proceeds to steps (4) and (5) and goes on from there to (6) intelligibles ac cessed by way of hypotheses and images, then to (7) Forms, and finally to (8) the Good. (Steps 3 through 7—with 5 included in 4—are represented in the four divisions of the divided line at 6.509d-511e.) The prisoners in the Cave mistakenly believe that the shadows they see are the only reality there is; the people in the visible realm take the actual visible things they see to be the ultimate reality.

Each of the three realms has its own source of light: the Cave, fire; the visible realm, the sun; the intelligible realm, the Good. Just as fire makes it possible for the prisoners to see the shadows on the Cave wall, so the sun enables people to see visible things, and the Good makes it possible for philosophers to "see" intelligibles. Actually viewing the sun and the Good apparently also opens the eyes of the viewer to the other roles these two sources of illumination play in their respective realms. The sun is the source of seasons, and is steward as well as cause of all things in the visible realm (516b-c), providing generation, growth, and nourishment (509b); the Good is the cause of "all that is right and noble in everything" (517c): it gave birth to light and to the sun (517c); it is sovereign in the intelligible realm, pro-viding truth and intelligence (*noun*); and it is responsible for the being or existence of the intelligibles in the intelligible realm (509b).

The prisoners in the allegory who find themselves in the Cave from childhood, "with their legs and necks in bonds so that they are fixed, see-ing only in front of them, unable because of the bond to turn their heads all the way around" (514a), are, Socrates tells us, "like us" (515a). And in truth, we are similarly bound. We are tied to the visible world as surely as the prisoners are tied to the Cave. Our bonds, "like leaden weights" (519b), are our appetites, the desires we have for pleasures of the body and all other things that delight the senses. We are lovers of sights and sounds, lovers of opinion rather than of wisdom (5.475d-480a).

In yet another way the prisoners are "like us." The condition in which they find themselves is quite to their liking. They do not chafe against their bonds. They do not wish to be released. They savor the comfort of the fa-miliar. Indeed, being bound is their natural state, the one in which they are most at home. The matter-of-factness with which Socrates describes the prisoners' situation suggests that they were not thrust into it against their will. Whereas Glaucon speaks of the prisoners' having been "compelled" to keep their heads motionless throughout life (515a-b)—implying that being immobile is not their preferred position—from Socrates' perspective it is not their severely restricted movement but their release that is compelled (515c). Socrates envisions a releaser who compels (515d, 515e), forces (515e), and drags (515e-516a) his hapless victim out of the Cave.[20]

The fact is that in Socrates' telling of the tale, the prisoners make no effort to identify and punish those responsible for their imprisonment; it is rather the one who would seek to liberate them, "the man who attempts to release and lead up" (517a), whom they would slay. They mock the returning released prisoner, who, having been in the light, now sees less clearly in the dark (518a). We, too, relish our passivity, our weakness, our impotence in the face of temptation. We are ignorant conformists, too lazy, too lax, to buck convention and custom. We are content to remain as we are, and we laugh at those who swim against the tide.

There are, to be sure, ways in which the prisoners are not like us. First, the prisoners have never seen anything but shadows, have never heard anything but echoes; they lack the very concepts of original and copy. When we, however, look at reflections of things in water, for example, we are well aware (on most occasions) that there are originals of which these are mere reflections. In a sense, then, we are more blameworthy than the prisoners when we doubt or deny or ridicule the possibility of a transcendent realm of which our own world might be only a copy.[21] Second, our bonds are merely metaphorical. We can turn our heads, we can resist what is ignoble, we can oppose what is merely traditional or popular. Yet, we act as if we have no choice, as if our hands are literally tied.

---

20. It is clear that there is "someone" (*tis*—515d2, 515e5; implicit at 515d9 and at 517a4–5) who does the releasing and compelling. Socrates' expression "if something of this sort were by nature (*phusei*) to happen to him" (515c) is therefore odd. It may well signify that in the unlikely event that such a thing were to happen it would not be the result of "some divine inspiration" (*theias epipnoias*), as, for example, the flowing of *erōs* into the sons of those in power or into the powerful fathers themselves (499b-c; see, too, 492a, 492e-493a), but it would come about in a quite natural way: the prisoner would simply be compelled by a human compeller. Howland's view (2004, 139), "that a soul without philosophical *erōs* could never be compelled to philosophize," does not seem right: only such a soul would require compulsion.

21. In principle, of course, the prisoners in the Cave might conceivably be tipped off to the unreality of the shadows when they find something contradictory or puzzling in them. The intellect, we know, is awakened by puzzling features of large and small, hard and soft (523a-524d).

Are we all this way? Does no one in the Cave set his sights on something better, something more stable and more real? Although the human
condition is such that we all have bodily needs and an inborn desire to
satisfy them, and we all from the outset imbibe our city's customs and the
ways it thinks, it is not the case that all of us are in chains. The philosopher by nature, discussed in the previous chapter, is explicitly not "like
us"—as we have seen, Socrates takes it as his task not only to set forth the
nature of the philosopher but to distinguish him from the non-philosopher
(474d, 499e-500a). The philosopher of Book 6 knows he is in a Cave, is
sure there is something more real than his everyday experiences, a "what
really is," a "what always is," even before he sees it (476c-d). It is indeed the
philosopher's conviction that there is a reality beyond what meets the eye
that distinguishes him from the non-philosopher, from the lover of sights
and sounds and of opinion, who denies that there is anything in existence
beyond what he can see and hear (476b, 476c, 480a). The natural philosopher thirsts for truth and wisdom, for a transcendent reality purer and
more ennobling than the one he is born into. He is "a man whose intellect
(*dianoian*) is toward the things that are" (500b-c), a "real lover of learning"
whose *nature* it is "to strive for what is," not "to tarry by the many things
opined to be" but to "go forward without losing the keenness of his passionate love (*erōtos*) or ceasing from it before he grasps the nature itself of
each thing that is" (490a-b). The philosopher by nature is not trapped by
his bonds in the way other prisoners are. He will "forsake those pleasures
that come through the body," since "he isn't a counterfeit but a true philosopher" (485d-e). Propelled by the force of his love for what is, he persists
through the difficult ascent until he reaches his goal (490a-b); his nature
"grows by itself (*autophues*) in such a way as to make it easily led to the
Idea of each thing that is" (486d); it "grows by itself (*autophues*) and does
not owe its rearing to anyone" (520b).[22]

---

22. It is instructive to compare the natural philosopher of Book 6 with his closest counterpart,
described in the *Phaedo* at 82e-83e. There, the philosopher's soul, like all others, is said to start out
imprisoned in the body, to be indeed a willing captive. But, in the case of the soul of the lover of
learning, philosophy need only "gently encourage" it to sever its ties to the sensible and visible.
This soul, that "of the true philosopher," does not resist or oppose deliverance but, on the contrary,
aids it by keeping away from the violent pleasures, pains, and passions that would weld it to the
body, preventing it from keeping company with the divine, the pure, and the constant.

The philosopher by nature is thus not like the prisoner who is released from the Cave; indeed, he is not "like us." No one is needed to remove his shackles. No one must compel him to stand up, to turn his neck around, to walk and look up toward the light (515c). Whereas the released prisoner who is told that he now sees "more correctly" cannot divest himself of the belief that "what was seen before is truer than what is now shown" (515d), the natural philosopher is fully confident that with every step he takes away from the visible realm he is nearing reality and truth. The light that is a source of joy for the philosopher by nature only blinds and confuses the prisoner who is compelled to see it: when the latter is made to look at the light, his eyes hurt, and he turns away and flees (515e). Indeed, unlike the philosopher who is "easily led" (486d), the prisoner will ascend only if someone drags him (*helkoi*)[23] by force (*biāi*). And throughout his ordeal, as he is dragged "along the rough, steep, upward way" and not let go until he is out in the light of the sun, he is "distressed and annoyed" (*odunasthai te an kai aganaktein*) (515e-516a).[24]

Once the prisoner is in the light, his eyes take time to adjust to the brightness (516a). He proceeds gradually from the darkest things (shadows), to reflections in water, to the things reflected, to the dimmer heavenly bodies, which are visible at night, and finally to the brightest heavenly body, the one visible by day: the sun. He no longer wishes to dwell in the Cave; he is happy now and feels only pity for those who remain there. He is not the least envious of those in the Cave who are powerful and honored. Rather, he would prefer, to quote Homer, "to be on the soil, a serf to another man, to a portionless man" (*Od.* 11.489–91) than to live among them. A condition so repugnant that only death, as Achilles thinks, could be

---

23. *Helkein* is found at 515e5, 515e6, and 516a1. It is the term used as well in Book 4 for the way in which the reasoning part of the soul pulls or is pulled by the others (439b, 439d, 440a), and in Book 7 to describe how study "drags" the reasoning part to ever higher levels of understanding (521d, 533d). *Helkein* is found, too, in the *Theaetetus* (at 175b-c), where Socrates describes how when a philosopher drags upward (*anō*) someone who is not philosophical, the latter will no longer ask which particular injustice has been committed or suffered but will ponder instead what justice and injustice are in themselves. Note, however, that in the *Theaetetus* the person dragged is "someone who is willing" (*ethelēsei tis*) to leave the old questions behind; in the *Republic* the man dragged is clearly unwilling to change: he is "distressed and annoyed" as he is dragged (515e-516a).

24. Popper (1945, 1:148) thinks these philosophers are special by their nature, that they "are not like other men. They belong to another world, they communicate with the divine." As we have seen, however, Socrates makes a point of their being "like us." It is the philosophers of Books 5–6, those who have philosophic natures, who are truly distinctive.

deemed worse (see *Rep.* 3.386c) thus holds greater appeal for the released prisoner than the prospect of returning to the Cave. Indeed, he would "undergo anything whatsoever rather than to opine those things and live that way" (516d).

III. The Nature of the New Philosophers

If we are like the prisoners in the Cave, then the philosophers Socrates fashions in Book 7 are like the prisoners who are released from the Cave. Just as the prisoners start out happy in the Cave, the new philosophers are content with their world—the visible realm. They neither recognize anything better or higher nor want to know of any such thing. They don't resent their fetters, their attachments to the things of this world; they don't yearn to be free. They don't leave the visible world of their own accord, fueled by their own longings; someone—the founders—releases them. Like the prisoners who are freed, they ascend only reluctantly ("distressed and annoyed"); they, too, have to be dragged. The dragging continues for both prisoners and philosophers as they travel "along the rough, steep, upward way." In the case of the philosophers, the dragging takes the form of compulsory studies, which themselves compel a turn away from the material and toward the intelligible. And just as the prisoners who see the sun have no desire to go back to the Cave, so, too, the philosophers, once they see the Good, wish to remain in the intelligible realm, having nothing but disdain for human affairs.[25]

Two critical differences, however, distinguish the philosophers' experience from that of the released prisoners: (1) as the released prisoners' eyes become accustomed to the light, they make steady progress toward the sun; the philosophers' progress, by contrast, is interrupted: they are compelled to descend to the visible realm and to remain there for fifteen years

---

25. Bloom (1968, 409) supports his view that the philosopher cannot look directly at the Good by pointing out that a man cannot actually look directly at the sun. (See, too, Lampert 2010, 365). We may wonder then why Socrates in the *Republic* treats both feats as achievable (516b, 540a). In the *Phaedo*, by contrast, Socrates remarks that gazing at the sun even during an eclipse destroys the eyes of some; he therefore decides not to attempt to use his senses to grasp "things" (*pragmata*), but instead to seek the truth about "beings" (*ta onta*) by taking refuge in *logoi* (99d-100a).

before they (or some of them) continue their ascent to the Good; and (2) the released prisoners do not have to be forced to look at the sun once they can; yet the philosophers have to be compelled to look at the Good (540a). These two differences are not unrelated: it is because the released prisoners' ascent to the sun proceeds without interruption that their eyes don't need to undergo a painful readjustment as they approach the sun; but, as we shall see, the philosophers' fifteen-year sojourn in the visible realm complicates their otherwise straight and steady climb toward the Good. (Why the philosophers' ascent is put on hold for so long, and how this delay impedes their progress, will be discussed later on in this section.)

And there is yet a third difference: in the case of the Cave no indication is given as to why a particular prisoner is selected for release; yet we are indeed told with respect to Book 7's potential philosophers which feature distinguishes them from all others, what it is that makes them special. As we turn to our new philosophers, we shall note, however, not only what it is about them that disposes the founders to choose them but also where they are deficient so that the founders must fix them.

At 502c, as we have seen, Socrates snaps out of his happy reverie in which philosophers rule in a city that happens to welcome their rule, and finds himself once again in the city in which women do the same work as men and are shared, along with their children, with the men of their class. Starting from scratch, he proceeds to add to this city those who are to rule it. Unlike the philosophers of Book 6 (before 502c) who come about by chance and rule by chance, the philosophers of Book 7 (beginning at 6.502c) are part of a planned city; they are created by the founders for the express purpose of ruling Callipolis.[26] Since, however, philosophic natures

---

26. Vegetti (2000, 350–53) recognizes differences between those he calls philosopher-kings, who are the rulers described in Books 5–6, and the philosophers he calls dialecticians, the rulers described in Book 7. (The earlier rulers he calls simply *archontes*.) (The change from philosopher-kings to dialecticians occurs for him not at 502c, but between Book 6 and Book 7.) For Vegetti, the regime depicted in Books 5 and 6 is not Callipolis but merely a "historical" regime that is transitional to it. (Books 2–4, he thinks, contain intimations of what Callipolis will be like, but it is not until Book 7 that the beautiful city is fully fleshed out.) Callipolis is the necessary condition for the emergence of the dialecticians and regimes depicted in the *Republic*, see Reeve (1988, 204), for whom "the Third Polis . . . incorporates the Second, which incorporates the First" and "is intended to be Kallipolis for everyone— money-lovers, honour-lovers, and philosophers"; and Dawson (1992, 77–81), for whom the span

cannot be manufactured—they are, after all, *natures*—the founders set about to produce philosophers who mimic the real thing, philosophers who, though their first and natural love is the realm of sights and sounds, the realm of opinion, can nevertheless be trained to prefer the intelligible realm. The founders' goal is surely laudable: they seek to spare their fair city the compromised rule of those who are unsuited to rule.

There is to be sure something perverse about fashioning philosophers out of nonphilosophic natures. It calls to mind the second wave, in which the founders seek to improve on nature (in the way animal breeders do) by strictly regulating the sexual partnering of men and women. It would no doubt be far better to educate genuine philosophic natures to become the rulers of Callipolis, a plan that more closely resembles the first wave, in which the founders permit the innate talents and skills of women to follow their natural course rather than artificially (or conventionally) suppressing them. (See Chapter 1, note 4.) Reforms that support nature seem both more promising and more realistic than reforms that attempt to bend nature to human ends. Philosophic natures, however, are extremely rare, so that we could not rely on finding a sufficient supply of them either to get Callipolis off the ground or to keep it going. But, more than that, Socrates pairs philosophers by nature with a natural—that is, a chance—city, and designed philosophers with a designed—that is, chance-free—city. The components of the two paradigms fit each other; they cannot be mixed and matched.

What, then, is the nature of the philosophers who are to rule Callipolis? If they are distinguished from the general run of men, in what way are they different? They are, we know, "like us," but *they* become philosophers. If the aim of the Cave image is to capture "our nature," the nature we all share, "in its education and lack thereof" (514a), to juxtapose, as it were, our "before" and "after" snapshots, it must attend specifically to those of us who leave. Those of us who remain imprisoned have only a "before." None but the "best natures" among us (519c) have "afters."

---

of text 2.374—5.473 presents a "low utopia," a city with a Spartan constitution that is unworkable because its communism cannot be implemented unless philosophers rule, and that from 5.473 to 8.544 an ideal but unattainable philosophically governed city, the "high utopia." Burnet (1914, 339) distinguishes an "earthly city" favored by the (historical) Socrates from the "heavenly city" inserted by Plato. And Thesleff (1997) conjectures that the *Republic* was composed in two different periods, the first circa 390, and the second after 367, following Plato's second trip to Sicily.

What sets these "best" natures apart? What makes them best? Why are they particularly suited to a philosophic education? They certainly aren't best in that they start out from a better place, for we all—that is, all of us who lack a philosophic nature—start "from the dark" (518c). We share the same material attachments; we love the things of this world more than truth, wisdom, and what is. Furthermore, as Socrates assures his companions when he explains what education is, those who are to become philosophers do not come equipped with faculties the rest of us lack. Despite what some would have us believe, education is not putting knowledge (*epistēmē*)[27] into souls that don't have it, as though putting sight into blind eyes; rather, "this power (*dunamin*) is in the soul of each," as is "the instrument (*organon*) with which each learns" (518c); the intellect is "a certain instrument of everyone's soul" (527d-e). In other words, all of us have in our souls an instrument with which we learn—the analogue of the eye, which is the instrument of vision—as well as the power to know, which is the analogue of sight. Unless we are blind, unless we lack the power of sight, we can see—so long as not only our eye but our whole body is turned to the light. (If one is to recognize shadows as shadows, it is insufficient that one turn just the eye to the light; a person's entire orientation must change.) Similarly, unless we lack the power to learn, we can be educated—so long as not only the knowing part of the soul but the whole soul is turned to face the Good ("the brightest part of that which is"—518d).

Yet, we are not equal. Just as some see more sharply than others because their eyes are keener, so do some understand more clearly because their intellects are superior.[28] Even if all people can be turned, not all can see or

---

27. Since knowledge is being compared to sight, *epistēmē* in this passage has to be the power—not the content—of knowing. Indeed in the divided line (6.509d-511e) it is through *epistēmē* that we access the intelligible realm about which we also have *epistēmē*, and in *Rep. 7*, *epistēmē* replaces *noēsis* as the name for the highest faculty in the divided line: *dianoia* is said to be brighter than opinion but dimmer than *epistēmē* (533d). All four—*noēsis*, *dianoia*, *pistis*, and *eikasia*—are called *pathēmata* at 511d. In our passage Socrates in fact refers to *epistēmē* as a power—*dunamin* (518c, 518d). Yet if, as it appears, *epistēmē* is a power, then Socrates is refuting a straw man: there probably isn't anyone who thinks education is endowing someone with the power to know.

28. The distinction between merely having sight and seeing well was already introduced in Book 1, where at 353b-c Socrates makes the point that the virtue of the eyes, as of all things, is that by which they do their work *well*—not, then, sight simpliciter (as Thrasymachus wrongly thinks—353c), but sharpness of vision. In Book 6 at 484c-d, the sharp-sighted are those who attain knowledge of "what is," and the blind those who come back empty-handed even when they try to

understand equally well when turned. (Indeed, even in the darkness of the Cave, some discerned the various shadows more sharply than others [516c].) As Socrates repeatedly tells Glaucon, not all who are led can follow (476c, 479e, 533a [here Socrates is not sure that Glaucon can follow], 534b [here Glaucon himself is uncertain]). Some cannot follow because they won't acknowledge the existence of the "Itselfs" (476c, 493e-494a); but some are simply not sufficiently smart. As Socrates points out to Glaucon, of the two of them, Socrates is the more sharp-sighted and Glaucon the duller (10.595c-596a). Although Socrates acknowledges that everyone subjected to the "gymnastic" of calculation becomes "quicker" (526b), it is nevertheless only those who are "naturally quick in all studies" (526b), the "best natures" (526c), who are to be educated in calculation (526c) (and presumably, too, in the more intellectually taxing subjects).[29] Furthermore, Socrates identifies "a nature that is dialectical and one that is not" (537c). Indeed, when the time comes for the philosophers to see the Good, it is the "brilliant beams of their souls" (*tēn tēs psuchēs augēn*) that they lift up (540a). And when they finally train others to take their place, they "educate other *like* men" (540b). Sharp intellects, like sharp eyes, are natural endowments.

And indeed Socrates selects for the ascent those who are most intellectually fit for it. He distinguishes the exercise of the mind, *phronēsai*,[30] from the other virtues: the others, though called virtues "of the soul," are

---

see. In Book 7 (518b-519b), sharp-sightedness is the ability to see *well* no matter which way one is turned; blindness is the inability to see at all. Book 7 assumes that unless one is blind, unless one lacks the power to see, one will be able to see something of the higher reality if one is turned in that direction—which is not to deny that some will see more sharply than others. In Book 6, Socrates' point is that one might just as well be blind if one looks off to the intelligible realm but derives nothing from it. In both passages, however, it is clear that anyone who is not blind can look.

29. In mathematical studies it quickly becomes evident that we are not all equal. Even though Socrates pronounces in the *Meno* (85c-d) that the slave will in the end come to know "these things"—that is, the truths of geometry—"as accurately as anyone," it is clear that mathematics, like most crafts, is a discipline in which some people will be more proficient or expert than others.

30. *Phronēsai* normally signifies practical wisdom and is frequently translated "prudence." Here at 518e, however, it is clearly a matter of intellect. So, too, at 530b-c, where, in a clear reference back to 518e, the "*phronimon* by nature" will be converted from uselessness to usefulness through the proper study of astronomy. Also in Glaucon's and Adeimantus's lists of things delightful and good in themselves—at 357c and 367c-d, respectively—*phronein* appears alongside seeing, hearing, and being healthy. Other instances are 505b-c, where Socrates says that some think the good is pleasure, while the more refined think it is *phronēsis*, though when asked to say what sort of *phronēsis*, they say "about the good"; and 572a, where, once the spirited and appetitive

actually "close to the body" and are acquired through habits and practice.[31] *Phronēsai*, by contrast, is a virtue one either has or doesn't have; it cannot be cultivated. As Socrates puts it, it is in one's soul—if one has it at all— "beforehand."[32] *Phronēsai* is the only real virtue; it is "more divine" than the others; moreover, it never loses its power (518d-e).

One implication of Book 7's emphatic division of *phronēsai* from the moral virtues is that those who are blessed with the keenest intellects are not necessarily also courageous, moderate, and just. The intellectual aptitude of the philosophers of Book 7 is indeed seen to be fully compatible with vice no less than with virtue—it all depends on the direction in which their soul is turned (518e-519a). In this way, being smart is significantly different from loving wisdom: as we learn in Book 6, in the wisdom-*loving* nature cognitive abilities and moral virtues, though two distinct sets of qualities (*kakeina kai tauta*—485a), are joined together. The soul's passionate desire for the higher things ensures the presence in it of all the moral virtues. In philosophic natures the virtues are "natural"—not cultivated; they do in fact come "beforehand"—if not by birth then as a by-product of the love of wisdom; they do not require "habits and exercises"—and can only be subsequently eroded through exposure to improper nurture or corruptive influences. As the philosophers of *Rep.* 7 unseat their counterparts in Book 6, however, the orderliness and love of wisdom (*philosophia*) on account of which the latter were called divine ("But if it [the philosophic nature] ever takes hold in the best region, just as it is best, then it will make plain that it really is divine as we agreed, and that the rest are human" [497b-c]; "it is the philosopher, keeping company with the divine and orderly, who also becomes orderly and divine, to the extent possible

---

parts of the soul are silenced, the *phronein* in the reasoning part of the soul is activated and "lays hold of the truth." See, too, 582a, 582d, 583b (where "the pleasures of the *phronimos*" are clearly pleasures of the intellect, as is confirmed at 585b-c), 586a, 586d, and 603b. In the *Republic*, the various wisdom terms—*sophia, epistēmē, phronēsis*, and others—span the spectrum from practical to theoretical.

31. Cf. Aristotle, *EN* 2.1, for the need for habituation to produce moral virtue.

32. Aristotle notes that the virtues, like crafts, do not come to be present in people until they are practiced, but powers or capacities (*dunameis*) and the senses (*aisthēseis*) exist in them "beforehand" (*proteron*) (*EN* 2.1.1103a). Aristotle thus says about the virtues precisely what Socrates says about them at 518d-e; but what Aristotle says about powers and senses Socrates says about *phronēsai*.

for a human being" [500d][33]) are replaced by the divine *phronēsai* of the former (518e). The philosophers of Book 6, though no less sharp-sighted than those in Book 7 (6.484c), are endowed with a nature that is accounted divine not for its brilliance alone, but insofar as it comprises a whole spectrum of virtues—intellectual, moral, and personal.

It is noteworthy that the "puny soul" (*psucharion*—519a)[34] of *Rep. 7*'s sharp seers can take them in either of two directions: it can make them useful and beneficial (*chrēsimon te kai ōphelimon*) or useless and harmful (*achrēston au kai blaberon*—518e-519a). Conspicuous in its absence from Book 7 is the term "decent" (*epieikēs*), which was regularly paired with "useless" in Book 6.[35] The concern in Book 6, raised by Adeimantus and seconded by Socrates (487d), was that the decent philosophers might be useless; it was thought only of the *in*decent ones that they might actually be harmful. Indeed, Socrates makes a point of characterizing Book 6's philosophers as "those whom they call *not vicious*, but useless" (490e), "those few philosophers who are *not vicious*, those now called useless" (499b). Moreover, the only reason Book 6's philosophers are useless is that others do not care to use them; they would turn useful the moment others would put them to use. Book 7's philosophers, however, are not decent; they are intelligent. They are thus either very good—useful and beneficial—or very bad: not just useless, but actually harmful, even vicious (*ponerōn*). If they are not somehow made useful, are not in some way compelled to be of

---

33. There are other references in the *Republic* to a divine nature. At 2.366c-d, Adeimantus expresses his expectation that a man who knows adequately that justice is best will also know that the only person who is willingly just is one who "from a divine nature" either finds doing injustice repugnant or keeps away from it because he has gained knowledge. This idea is picked up by Socrates at 492e where he maintains that none but a "divine" character can become "differently disposed toward virtue," as a result of receiving an education that is contrary to the prevalent one, but notes that even for such a nature the ability to resist the pressure to conform requires "a god's dispensation." See, too, 492a.

34. As we saw in Chapter 1, section I.B, one member of the small band of "worthy" philosophers in Book 6 (496b) has a "great soul" (*megalē psuchē*); none of them has a "little soul." *Psucharion* is used pejoratively at *Theaet.* 195a; and at *Theaet.* 173a and 175d, respectively, Socrates speaks of nonphilosophical men whose souls are caused to be "small and not straight" (*smikroi de kai ouk orthoi*), and of men who have "a small (*smikron*), sharp (*drimun*), and legal (*dikanikon*) soul" and see "sharply" (*oxeōs*—175e), but are nevertheless unable to get past the question of particular acts of injustice to the consideration of justice and injustice themselves. *Drimu* is paired with *oxeōs* at *Rep.* 519a.

35. See Chapter 1, note 31. The only person who is called "decent" in Book 7 is the adopted child who upon learning that he is adopted nevertheless continues to honor his "parents" (538c).

service, they will apply their intelligence to evildoing. We have here, then, a new category: "vicious but wise" (*poneron men, sophon de*—519a).[36] The souls of these men are compelled "to serve vice" (519a).[37] The more sharply their souls see, the more evil they accomplish. They are in this way like the corrupted philosophic natures of Book 6, who, because of their superior abilities, become "exceptionally bad" and a "source of great injustices and unmixed villainy" when under the sway of pernicious influences (491e).[38] But whereas Book 6's corrupted philosophic natures start out good and are made bad, Book 7's philosophers start out bad and have to be made good.

Clearly, then, the sense of "best nature" has changed. Socrates had first spoken of the "best" among the guardians who were to be prudent in the matters of guarding and caring for the city, trained in music and gymnastic to be properly spirited—not too savage, not too soft—and older (3.412). At 4.431c the "best natures" were those rare men whose simple and measured desires and pleasures and pains are accompanied by intelligence (*nou*) and right opinion. In Book 6, "best natures" were philosophic natures: 495b, 491d, 491e, 497c, 501d. But once the new philosophers arrive on the scene it is they who are the "best natures"—they have the sharpest intellects (519c and 526c).[39] Although these best natures are called philosophers (503b, 520a, 525b5, 525b8, 527b, 536c, 540d), they are never said to have a philosophic nature. In this way they are decidedly unlike the philosophers of Book 6, whose philosophic nature is frequently noted: 4585b, 486a, 490c, 490d5–6 ("the nature of the true philosopher"),[40] 490e1 ("this nature"), 491a1 ("this one," *tauten*), 491a8-b1 ("such a nature, possessing everything we prescribed just now for the man who is going to become a

36. In the *Theaetetus* (at 177a) those who have the small soul also pride themselves on being "clever and villainous" (*deinoi kai panourgoi*). See note 34 above.

37. The compellers are likely the men themselves. At 4.443d the just man compels the parts of his soul to mind their own business. At 8.554c-d the oligarchic man, who merely seems just, forcibly holds down his soul's bad desires with some decent part of himself.

38. See Chapter 1, note 70, and corresponding text.

39. In Book 9 the "best nature" is no longer philosophic or even smart but morally virtuous: a soul is "brought to its best nature" when it "acquires moderation and justice accompanied by prudence" and "gains a habit worthy of honor" (591b). The "form of the best" is "by nature weak" when a man isn't capable of ruling—but only of serving—the beasts in himself (590c); the "best man" at 590c-d is one who is ruled by "what is divine and prudent."

40. The philosophers of Book 7 are called "true philosophers" (*hoi hos alethos philosophoi*—540d), but they are not said to have the true philosopher's nature.

perfect philosopher"), 491b8 ("that nature"), 492a ("the nature we set down for the philosopher"), 494a, 495a, 497b, 501d, 502a.

Despite the absence of a philosophic nature in *Rep. 7*'s wise men—the nature they do have, "such a nature" (519a), is sharp-sighted but vicious— they are nevertheless designated to make the ascent to the Good. Since they are neither virtuous nor enamored of "what is," the only thing that qualifies them to commune with the Forms is their intellect. Yet their intellect, "their vision," starts out facing the wrong way; their souls are tied to the wrong things. Intellects, however, can be turned and trained; ties can be cut. Even this nature, therefore, can be salvaged. "This part of such a nature (*touto . . . to tēs toiautēs phuseōs*)," Socrates says, will be "hammered" into shape (*koptomenon*) straight from childhood, and the soul's ties of kinship with Becoming lopped off, as if they were "leaden weights." These bonds, analogous to those that prevent the Cave's prisoners from looking at anything but the Cave's wall, are "naturally" affixed to the souls of these future rulers by such earthly pleasures as food (or eating—*edōdais*) and delicacies (or gluttony—*lichneiais*), and these pleasures in turn have the effect of directing the intellect's vision "downward" (519b).[41] But once these ties are cut, the whole soul is free to turn along with the intellect. And once the intellect, "this same part of the same human being," is turned, it will continue to see sharply (we recall that *phronēsai* "never loses its power"), but this time the things it will see are "the true things" (519b).[42]

Rep. 7's philosophers, Socrates thus plainly informs us, are appetitive by nature[43]—their appetitiveness, that which makes them vicious when wrongly turned, is the second component, after sharp-sightedness, of "such a nature" (519a). Their souls are naturally yoked to the realm of Becoming by the vulgar pleasures it affords. These pleasures—and not the delights of beholding the "true things"—are what entice them. If a man's "whole

---

41. Cf. *Phaedo* 83d: "Every pleasure and pain provides, as it were, another nail to rivet the soul to the body and to weld them together."

42. Cf. 10.611e–612a, where the soul that naturally loves wisdom becomes encrusted in rocks and shells because of its indulgence on earth in feasts. To release the soul these encumbrances must be "hammered off" (*perikroustheisa*). How much more encrusted, then, is the soul that does not naturally love wisdom but only sees sharply.

43. As we have seen, Book 7's philosophers are also warriors and so must be spirited. Their natures are thus an odd mix of intellectual aptitude, appetitiveness, and spiritedness. What they lack is love of wisdom.

soul" must turn if his intellect is to ascend to the Good, its appetitive ties must first be severed; it must be liberated from bodily lusts. Only then can "what is best in the soul" (the part that sees or understands—intellection, *noēsis*—532b) be led up to the contemplation of "what is best in the things that are" (the Good)—just as "what is clearest in the body" (the eyes) is led to the contemplation of "what is brightest" in the region of the bodily and the visible (the sun) (532c).

Appetitive natures are not, however, philosophic: even if dogs could learn to read, they would rather eat. This, as we have seen, is the lesson of the earlier "hydraulic model" (485d): "When someone's desires incline strongly to some one thing, they are therefore weaker with respect to the rest, like a stream that has been channeled off in that other direction." This model cuts both ways: not only will someone who loves the soul and the pleasures of learning (specifically, learning directed to the highest truths) not yearn for the pleasures of the body, but someone enamored of pleasures of the body will not love the pleasures of the "soul itself with respect to itself" (485d). Whereas the natural philosopher of Book 6 cares for his body so as to secure it "as a helper to philosophy" (it will not then oppose him when he takes up the "more intense gymnastic" of the soul—498b), one who loves the pleasures of the body is, as we have seen, a "counterfeit philosopher" and not a "true" one (485d-e).

And, indeed, there is no mention of intellectual *erōs* in Book 7[44]—not at the end once the philosophers have seen the Good, and certainly not

44. Scholars note the absence of *erōs* in the craftsmen and auxiliary classes, yet many think it is present in the *Republic*'s philosopher-ruler. Nussbaum (1986, 182) and Klosko (1986, 98), for example, link the *erōs* of the philosopher-rulers to that which crowns Diotima's ladder of love in the *Symposium*; Reeve (1988, 229) and Voegelin (1966, 5) (along with others to be discussed in Chapter 3, section I) think that the philosophers' love of the Forms generates a desire to change the world in accordance with the order underlying the highest realities. According to Nussbaum, Plato regards *erōs* as compatible either with a tyrannical and antipolitical life (Alcibiades) or with the philosophic and apolitical life represented by Diotima's sublime lover (1986, 201)—not, however, with things of ordinary value (153). For a similar view, see Strauss 1964, 110–12; cf. Bloom, 1968, 425. Strauss thinks the philosopher's *erōs* leads him away from the city, but, at least in 1964, 128, as I read him, he does not think that justice *must* be divorced from *erōs*, and so does not regard it as impossible that a philosopher might wish to care for his city. Other things Strauss has written, however, particularly his correspondence (in German) with Jacob Klein of February 16, 1939 (2001, 566–68), suggest less openness on his part to the possibility that Plato's philosophers might be just or willingly care for the city: "The *Politeia* [*Republic*] is starting to become clear. What I suspected last year, . . . that it is devoted to a radical critique and condemnation of the political

when they are still on the path to it.[45] It is in fact not until these philosophers actually see the Forms that they display a marked preference for the higher realm (and so have to be "compelled" to go back down to the Cave [539e]),[46] and not until they see the very highest Form that they feel as if they "have emigrated to a colony on the Isles of the Blessed while they are still alive" (519c). Unlike the philosophers of Book 6, those of Book 7 are driven to philosophic heights, not by their own *erōs*, but involuntarily, by the coercive measures taken by the founders of Callipolis. Coercion replaces the erotic impulse and is required in its absence. Although once they are in the light they are eager to remain there (517c-d), it is nevertheless the case that until they get there they don't want to go. Moreover, even at the final stage of their ascent, which we shall turn to momentarily, they have no desire to see the Good, but have to be forced to do so (540a). Although they cannot bear to relinquish the life of contemplation once they experience it—as Socrates will tell us in Book 9, pleasures of the intellect are consistently judged best by those who are capable of enjoying them

---

life has been fully confirmed. . . . It is dedicated to a critique of *dikaiosunē* [justice]: the *Republic* is indeed an ironic justification of *adikia* [injustice], for philosophy *is adikia*—this comes out wonderfully in the dialogue with Thrasymachus. *Dikaiosunē loses* its case; in the final analysis, it *wins only* in myth, i.e. through a *kalon psuedos* [noble lie], that is, through a deed that is, strictly speaking, *adikon* [unjust]" (567–568) (emphasis in original; "strictly speaking" appears in English) (my translation, adapted from William Altman's [2009, 90]). See, too, Strauss 1952, 36: "This is not to deny that some great writers might have stated certain important truths quite openly by using as mouthpiece some disreputable character." It is interesting that Strauss mistakenly quotes Socrates as speaking in the *Republic* of a *kalon pseudos*, a noble lie. The expression Socrates actually uses is *gennaion*, which has connotations of patrician origins or breeding rather than of the nobility associated with morality. It is perhaps more telling that it is not a "disreputable character" who advocates lying but Socrates. (On this point, see the introduction, note 6.) See the end of section IV of this chapter, where it is noted that the philosophers of Book 7 are called *gennaioi* but not *kaloi*. See, too, Chapter 1, end of note 38.

45. Even if one were to contend that the language of *erōs* is absent because *erōs* is experienced by one who longs for something not yet possessed, and thus by those who love wisdom and not by those who are wise, the fact is that the philosophers of *Rep.* 7 are not said to experience *erōs* at any stage of their journey. On the *Symposium*, see Chapter 1, note 65. See Nichols (1987, 118–19), who says of the philosophers of the Cave allegory: "Indeed, they are not attracted to philosophy at all. . . . They are not characterized by any erotic striving that urges them out of the cave, any intimation that there is anything dissatisfying about their life there, or any sense of insufficiency. . . . He presents philosophers as nonerotic, moved by external compulsion rather than by their own motion." See also Annas 1981, 259.

46. Socrates emphasizes the philosophers' preference for the higher realm in part, no doubt, in order to call attention to their contempt for the lower, and thus to explain their unwillingness to rule there.

(580d-585e); indeed, how could anyone while in the light not prefer it to darkness?—that is hardly the same as loving the Good. (Do the prisoners released from the Cave love the sun or any of the things they are now able to see, or do they simply enjoy living in the light?) Book 7's philosophers are thus oddly unlike any others: the usual worry is that those who love "what is" may nevertheless fail to attain it; with respect to *Rep.* 7's philosophers, however, the concern is that though they attain it—they actually see the Good—they never quite love it. They are sharp-sighted, to be sure, and they prefer the intelligible realm to the sensible and regard themselves as happy once they are in it, but it is not their love for the Good that propels them upward or keeps them there. Those who see well can indeed be led to the Good; to be more precise, they can be dragged. It is only those who love it, however, only the philosophers of Book 6, who are "easily led" (486d).

Whereas expressions such as "loving" (*philein*) or "taking delight in" (*aspazesthai*)[47] (also *hasmenōs*—"with gladness") are featured prominently in Book 5 in Socrates' description of the philosopher's relationship to the objects of knowledge (474c-475c, 476b, 479e, 480a), we are never told that Book 7's philosophers "love" or "take delight in" the eternal verities they are privileged to see—not even when they have seen the Forms and the Good Itself and wish to remain outside the Cave. We are not told that Book 7's philosophers love the Forms passionately (*erān*), though in Book 6 Socrates underscores the philosopher's passionate love (*tou erōtos*), which is neither dulled (*ouk amblunoito*) nor surrendered (*oud' apolēgoi*) for the duration of the ascent (490b). Socrates speaks there of philosophic natures as being "always in love with" the learning that discloses to them something of true being (485a-b). He hopes in Book 6 that true erotic passion (*alēthinos erōs*) will be infused into those in power (499c), and describes philosophers as "lovers" (*erastas*) of that which is and of truth (501d). And he calls Book 6's philosopher a "real lover of learning" (*ho ontōs philomathēs*—490a). Book 7's philosophers, to whom such terms are never applied, are, then,

---

47. "Taking delight" appears (1) at the beginning of Book 2 in connection with Glaucon's three types of goods, the first two of which are sources of delight (357b); (2) in Book 5 with respect to the *erōtikos*, the lover of boys, to whom all boys in the bloom of youth seem worthy of attention and delighting in (474d); and (3) twice at the end of Book 5 in describing the philosopher's love for the only things that can be known, the things that "are" in themselves (479e-480a). See, too, 3.402a, 402d.

however paradoxically, not real lovers of wisdom. They may finally deem themselves "happy" and pity those who remain in the darkness of the Cave (516c-d), but their happiness is without ardor.[48]

In selecting and training the philosophers of *Rep.* 7, who lack the natural love of wisdom and truth that define their philosophic predecessors in *Rep.* 5 and 6, Socrates is settling for a poor substitute—men who see and know the Good rather than men who love it: "Our regime will be perfectly ordered if such a guardian, one who knows (*epistēmōn*) these things, oversees it" (506a-b). Once the philosophers' eyes adjust to the darkness, they will see "ten thousand times better than the men there"; they will "know (*gnōsesthe*) what each of the phantoms is, and of what it is a phantom" because they "have seen the truth about noble, just, and good things" (520c). Competence takes the place of love.[49]

Lacking genuine love of wisdom, the philosophers of *Rep.* 7 miss out, too, on the full complement of moral virtues that comes with that kind of love.[50] Since they are appetitive by nature they are not really moderate; they only simulate moderation.[51] And since they are not really moderate they are not really just. To be sure, once their ties to this world are cut, and they are turned toward the Good, they no longer crave the material goods whose pursuit easily leads to injustice. But let us note that Socrates sees fit to interrupt the philosophers' ascent at the point at which they have seen all the Forms except the Form of the Good, and to "compel" them to return to the Cave for fifteen years. One reason for the interruption, Socrates says, is "so that they won't be behind the others in experience" (539e). But there is a second reason: "And here, too, they must still be tested

---

48. Book 5's indiscriminate "philanderer-philosopher" (in Craig's perfect phrase [1994, 53]) thus stands in stark contrast to the affectless philosopher of Book 7. See Chapter 1, note 9.

49. Like the craftsmen in the first planned city, the philosophers of *Rep.* 7 are assigned roles in accordance with their natural aptitudes; the question of what they love never arises. (See Chapter 3, section II.) At 486c it is suggested that one is not likely to love something one is not good at. Perhaps that is true for difficult undertakings that require much effort—mathematics, for example. If only it were true of singers! See *Gorg.* 502a, where Meles' singing was not only not aimed at "the best" but apparently not at pleasure either; it is said to have pained the audience.

50. Pace Lane (2007, 65), who says: "And we see that the philosopher-rulers of the *Republic* will retain at their psychic core the hydraulic effect of the love of knowledge and its associated evaluative outlook, even when they have fully completed their education."

51. They thus resemble the oligarchic man who suppresses his desires (though only because they threaten his wealth). (See note 37 above.) Oligarchic men, however, at least do their own repressing (even if by necessity and fear rather than by way of argument [544c-d]).

whether they will stand firm or give way when pulled in all directions"
(539e-540a). Apparently, then, despite the twenty years the philosophers
have already spent in study outside the Cave, despite the fact that they
have by now seen the Forms, including, presumably, the Just Itself and
the Noble (or Beautiful) Itself, Socrates is nevertheless not convinced that
all are fit to see the Good. For how can he be sure that when these trained
philosophers return to the Cave, their old bonds to the realm of Becoming
will not re-form? How can he trust that when they live once again among
people who indulge their cravings for food, drink, and sex, and their thirst
for honor, power, and money, their own dormant desires will not be re-
awakened? Will their natural appetitiveness, forced underground by the
founders, not surface once again? Will they not succumb to the allures
of a world to which they are attracted by nature once they are given the
chance? And will they not, with their capacious native intelligence now
honed to exquisite perfection, be even more dangerous than they were before, if their souls are once again "compelled to serve vice" (519a)? If it was
by being turned toward the intelligible realm that their ties to the realm
of Becoming were weakened, would not their being turned once again
toward the material realm restore and strengthen those ties?

It is all but certain that it would—at least for many of them. Only "those
who have been preserved throughout and are in every way best at everything, both in deed and in knowledge" (540a), will ascend at last to the
vision of the Good. Yet even these exceptional few don't go on their own.
They "must be led (*akteon*) to the end"; they "must be compelled to look
(*anankasteon . . . apoblepsai*) toward that which provides light for everything" (540a).[52] None of them, it seems, escapes completely the effects of
the return to the Cave. Having returned to the visible realm, they have to
be prodded to direct their gaze toward the Good.

Education, then, no matter how rigorous and thorough, does not fully
expurgate natural dispositions; it only suppresses them, forces them into
hiding. Indeed, it is clear at the end of Book 3 that even the guardians' (or
the auxiliaries') extensive training in music and gymnastic is not a wholly

---

52. Whereas the philosophers of Book 7 have to be compelled to look away toward (*apoblepsai*) the vision of the Good (540a), those of Book 6 "look away (*apoblepoien*) frequently in both directions, toward the just, noble, and moderate by nature and everything of the sort, and, again,
toward what is in human beings" (501b) as they seek to improve the souls of the ruled.

reliable guarantor of virtue (416b-c): "Wouldn't they have been provided with the greatest safeguard if they have been really finely educated?" Socrates asks, but then he answers his own question as follows: "It's not fit to be too sure about that." The guardians, despite their education, cannot be permitted to own private property, to keep secret storerooms, or to possess gold and silver; if they did they might turn savage or form factions (see 5.464d-e).[53] Socrates has to hope that a wildly implausible myth will persuade them that they possess these precious metals in their souls (416e; cf. 7.521a, 8.547b) and so won't lament not having them in their pockets. If the guardians' education is no guarantee of virtue, then there is not much reason to think that the philosophers' education will be. Despite their having been turned and trained, they are not likely to have been fully immunized against the attractions of the world of sights and sounds.

Surprisingly few commentators have been struck by how odd it is that the philosophers must be compelled to undertake the final ascent to the Good. Two exceptions are Ellen Wagner and Christopher Shields.[54] Wagner suggests—and Shields concurs—that the reason compulsion is needed is that the philosopher's spirit, his *thumos*, is not yet quite under the control of his reason.[55] (For this insight Wagner credits Taft 1982.) Yet, the culprit is clearly not spirit but appetite.[56] During the fifteen years the philosophers find themselves back in the Cave it is surely their dormant appetites—not

---

53. There is no comparable worry with respect to the philosophers of Book 6: in their case, preoccupation with the things that "are" leaves no time for envy and ill will toward human beings (500b-c).

54. See, too, Barney 2008.

55. As noted above (see note 43), since the philosophers are warriors they are necessarily spirited. Nevertheless, in Socrates' description of the philosophers' ascent it is their appetitiveness, not their spiritedness, that needs to be overcome (519a-b).

56. Socrates clearly identifies "food and such pleasures and delicacies" (519b) as the ties to "becoming" that need to be trimmed. In Book 4's account of the soul, the soul's spirited part, the *thumoeides*, is the swing vote; it is not an independent motivator. In the healthy soul, it rushes to reason's side in its battle with appetite; in the unhealthy soul it is appetite's ally. If appetite does not oppose reason, the *thumoeides* cannot but support reason. Until it becomes a force in its own right (as it most likely does in Book 8's timocracy and timocratic man), it is not, on its own, reason's rival. In Socrates' frequently misunderstood illustration, Leontius's desire to gaze upon the corpses is appetitive—"He desired (*epithumoi*) to look" (439e)—but his initial disgust with himself emanates not from his spirited element but from his reason. At first he averts his eyes, but finally, "overpowered by the desire," he opens them. It is when he runs to get his fill of the sight of the corpses that his spirit, his *thumos*, scolds his eyes, calling them "you damned wretches" (440a). As Socrates goes on to explain, this is a case in which a person's desires (*epithumiai*) force him to act

their spirit—that are revived. The reason the philosophers need to be compelled to turn their gaze on the Good is that they don't want to see it; they want, once again, what the Cave has to offer. Their resistance, as we observed earlier, has no counterpart in the experience of the released prisoner in the Cave allegory, who, once out in the light, "gets accustomed (*sunētheias*)" gradually to the brightness (516a) until he is able on his own to make out the sun itself (516b). The prisoner, not having returned to the Cave, proceeds willingly to the final stage of his journey. The philosophers, by contrast, need to be compelled to the bitter end: in the aftermath of their return to the visible realm, the light of the Good is just too bright.

Yet another oddity that has gone largely unnoticed by Plato scholars is that the philosophers must even be compelled to order their own souls:[57] "Once they see the Good itself, they must be compelled, each in his turn, using it as a pattern, to order city, private men, *and themselves* for the rest of their lives" (540a-b). (The *anankasteon* at 540a7 governs not only *apoblepsai* at 540a8 but also *kosmein* at 540b1.) As we shall see in Chapter 3, ruling is something the philosophers don't want to do, but why should they regard ordering themselves as an unwelcome chore? After all, even the oligarchic man of Book 8 who holds down his bad desires does so by his own volition: he forcibly (*biāi*) suppresses them with "some decent part of himself" (554c-d).

As we have seen, so long as the philosophers are turned away from the realm of the visible, their desires for the vulgar pleasures abate, and their appetites are in remission. To all the world, therefore, they seem moderate (just as the oligarchic man seems just—8.554c-d). But the fact is that they have never had occasion to attend to their souls, and they have never done so. Their moderation comes from without: their ties to pleasures are cut and their souls are made to turn. The first time they have to deal with their desires is during the fifteen-year span between their training in dialectic and their being led to the Form of the Good. This preliminary return to the Cave is, as we saw, a test; only some, only the best, pass it; the rest never resume their ascent. Indeed, even those who are chosen to complete the

---

in opposition to his reason (*logismos*), and his spirit (*thumos*) is aroused against the coercive agent. There are but two parties "at faction," appetite and reason; and Leontius's spirit, in reproaching his eyes, is reason's ally (440b). See, too, 9.589a, where the lion (representing spirit) is the ally of the human being in the healthy soul and of the many-formed beast in the unhealthy one. In this case, too, the lion has only a supporting role.

57. Here Ferrari ([2003] 2005, 31) is the exception.

journey to the highest Form may be assumed to retain some of their earlier fascination with the pleasures of the material world; otherwise it would not be necessary to compel them to undertake the last leg of the ascent. Surely, however, once they actually see the Good and bask in its brilliance they are rid, finally and utterly, of their taste for the delights of the flesh.[58] Why, then, must they be compelled to order themselves "for the rest of their lives"?

What needs to be controlled at this last stage of ascent is likely no longer the vulgar appetites but something else in the philosophers' souls. If they are to devote themselves, despite not wanting to, to the service of others, if they are to perform for the city the task to which they, of all men, are most suited, it is their appetite for philosophy that must be tempered,[59] their desire to continue to dwell only in the light.

How willing are the philosophers to suppress their desire to live practicing only philosophy? G. R. F. Ferrari thinks that although the philosopher regards caring for his soul as something necessary but not as something splendid, as something he must do as the human being he is fated to be ([2003] 2005, 31, 34), nevertheless, the philosopher's desire to understand, to find the "best answer" to the question of how all the parts of the soul can live together well, will determine for him that his reason should mind the soul's other parts—not for its own sake but for the sake of the whole soul (2007, 196–99). On this account, the philosopher thus does, not unwillingly, what he knows to be best.

The language of compulsion, however, now applied to self-governance, surely suggests otherwise: the contrast with Book 6's philosopher in this regard could not be more striking. Not only does the philosopher of Book 6 not have to be compelled, but when he finally sees and contemplates "things that are set in a regular arrangement and are always in the same condition . . . [and] remain all in order according to reason," he "imitates them and, as much as possible, makes himself like them"; indeed, there is no way of "keeping him" from doing so, that is, "from imitating that which he admires and therefore keeps company with" (500c). Even though the philosophers of *Rep.* 6 are by nature just and moderate, they nevertheless

---

58. The philosophers who have seen the Good must be compelled to return to the Cave (540b; also 519c-d, 519e-520a); they clearly have no desire to do so.

59. In Book 9 Socrates recognizes that reason, too, has appetites (*epithumiai*) (580d).

also actively want to model their souls on the pattern they witness in the higher realm. Not so the philosophers of *Rep.* 7, who have to be compelled to order their souls even after seeing the Form of the Good.

IV. Second Thoughts

Rather belatedly, Socrates does attribute to the rulers of *Rep.* 7 many of the qualities that characterized the philosophers of Book 6. In considering how dialectical studies are to be "distributed," that is, who should be permitted to advance to this pinnacle of the curriculum, Socrates revisits the nature of his students. He now advises that they are to have a whole host of attributes not previously assigned to them. Indeed, he counsels vigilance lest unfit men proceed to this most sublime study. Just as the young, as Socrates will soon argue, are not to be trusted with the study of dialectic (539b-d), so, too, those whose characters are deficient are to be kept from it. A "special guard" is needed to bar those not suited for dialectic from its study (536a).

    Those to be allowed to advance to the study of dialectic are to be, like the former rulers—the guardians of Book 3—steadiest and most courageous (and best-looking, if at all possible) (535a-b), genteel (*gennaious*) and tough (*blosuros*) (535b), but also keen at studies, able to learn without difficulty, blessed with a good memory, and willing to endure the labors both of the body and of study (535b-c), men who have, in Glaucon's words "an entirely good nature" (*pantapasi . . . euphuēs*—535c). Socrates cautions against allowing men who are not worthy, "bastards," to take up philosophy (here, specifically, dialectic) (535c). Those who approach this study must not be "lame" (*chōlos*) in their love of labor, loving only gymnastic and the hunt and all bodily labor but not learning, listening, and inquiry—or the reverse (535d).[60] They must hate the willing lie as well as ignorance (the unwilling lie) (535d-e), and must be moderate, courageous, magnificent, and virtuous in all ways (536a). They are to be "straight of limb" (*artimeleis*) and "straight of mind" (*artiphronas*)—that is, not lame in either respect—and

---

60. Book 7's "bastards" who are unworthy of dialectic recall the frauds of Book 6 who produce "bastard" things (*notha*) and were thus "unworthy" (*anaxioi*) of education and philosophy (496a).

genuine (*gnēsion*) rather than bastard (536b). Only thus will justice herself be satisfied, and philosophy escape ridicule, so that "we shall save the city and the regime" (536b).

In this span of barely one and a half Stephanus pages, Socrates turns into paragons of virtue the exceedingly intelligent appetitive men he just finished sketching at 519c, men who were seen to lack the philosophic nature along with its attendant virtues. He also casts them as lovers of both bodily and intellectual pursuits—and this despite the unlikely prospect that the same people will exhibit all these qualities: for the most part, those who love the physical activities of gymnastic and the hunt dislike the learning and inquiry that are the province of the soul.[61]

In addition, Socrates' laudation of this new nature implies that the philosopher of Book 6 is somehow "lame" or "bastard": after all, that philosopher, as we saw in Chapter 1, is not described as a lover of war; nor is he portrayed anywhere as a lover of gymnastic and the hunt. The pure lover of wisdom, whose nature "really is divine" (*tōi onti theion ēn*—497c), the man whose *erōs* is directed upward to the realm of Being, can hardly be expected to love the labors of the body. Indeed, in all the accolades Socrates heaps on the natural philosopher in Books 5 and 6, in all the moral and personal qualities he lavishes on him, he never so much as hints that this philosopher is nevertheless incomplete or deficient in some way because he does not love war, gymnastic, and the hunt.[62]

One can only suppose that this dual-faceted new nature, suddenly assigned to the philosopher-warrior type, is designed to appeal to Glaucon. For Glaucon in fact calls it "an entirely good nature" (535c), and calls those

---

61. If these new philosophers are not to violate the "hydraulic model," they may not love "that learning that discloses to them something of the being that *is* always" (485b), for love of that sort precludes love of material pleasures. Lovers of sights and sounds also qualify as lovers of learning of a sort—this is how Glaucon understood them (5.475d)—and Glaucon is himself a lover of listening and learning (see 450b) without loving "what is." Glaucon may indeed have the two sets of qualities Socrates outlines at 535–536, and may well pass the tests for steadfastness in studies and in war. Socrates commends him twice for having a good memory (543c, 544b), and Glaucon twice says that he wouldn't be worth much if he didn't (504a, 612d). He also learns without difficulty. As for his being an accomplished warrior, both brothers distinguished themselves in the battle at Megara (2.367e-368a).

62. In Book 4 the wise rulers, who are explicitly sundered from the warriors, are called "perfect" (*teleous*—428d) and "true" (*alēthinous*—428e) guardians. And in Book 6 Socrates' ideal is a city ruled by the "perfect philosopher" (*teleōs . . . philosophos*—491a-b).

who have it "ruling men who are wholly noble (*pankalous*)" (540b). But, whereas it may be in the main for Glaucon's sake that Socrates at last endows the philosopher-in-training with so broad an array of virtues, there is undoubtedly a second motivation at work as well. As Socrates makes clear, he fears that unless he supplements the nature of his new philosophers, he will be "pouring even more ridicule over philosophy"; he will be inviting censure by "justice herself" for having brought "men of another sort," vicious men, to philosophy, and for having put no screening mechanism, no "special guard" (536a), in place to test for anything but aptitude. As he gazes on his own creation, he is dismayed.

But Socrates is pained, too, by the embellished natures he has now produced; he is frustrated—with himself. In a momentary fit of self-reproach, Socrates confesses that in his attempt to shield philosophy from ridicule (*gelōta*—536b), he himself has been "somewhat ridiculously (*geloion*) affected" (536b).[63] He berates himself for having "forgotten that we were playing," and for having consequently spoken too intensely. What can he have forgotten other than that his nonphilosophic philosophers are only make-believe; that they cannot be real (indeed he had warned at 487a that those who lack philosophic natures cannot adequately pursue philosophy); and that they therefore don't merit or require so vehement a defense? Yet he evidently could not help himself, could not stop himself. Seeing philosophy defiled by the suggestion—his own suggestion—that even men of poor character who relish the vulgar pleasures of the body can scale philosophy's heights, he had to come to philosophy's rescue: he had to ensure that the wholly unworthy are not permitted to darken her door, that such men are barred at least from the study of dialectic.

There can be no doubt that it is Socrates who is the anonymous party responsible for philosophy's having been "undeservedly spattered with mud." For, even if it was Glaucon's and Adeimantus's resistance to Socrates' rarefied philosopher-ruler of Book 6 that prompted Socrates to craft Book 7's philosopher-warriors in the first place, it is he who is ultimately to blame for bestowing the name "philosopher" on such flawed men. Furthermore,

---

63. Socrates worried in Book 6 about philosophy's being subjected to ridicule on account of unworthy men who pass for philosophers (491a, 495c, 500b).

Glaucon and Adeimantus can hardly be guilty of any recent besmirching: it has been a rather long time since anyone other than Socrates has said much of anything; indeed, not since the beginning of Book 6 has Glaucon or Adeimantus challenged Socrates in any way. If, then, Socrates' *thumos* is "just now" (*en tōi paronti*—536b) aroused "against those who are responsible," it can be aroused only against himself.[64] (As Socrates taught in Book 4, in an uncorrupted soul, *thumos* rushes in to make common cause with reason when it sees the desires getting the upper hand.[65]) Glaucon, to be sure, sees nothing untoward in Socrates' immoderate embellishment of the character of those to be led to dialectic, but Socrates is adamant: it certainly does seem to him—"to me, the speaker" (536c)—that he has spoken "too seriously" (*spoudaioteron*). It was bad enough that in his desire to please his companions he made philosophers of men who do not love wisdom and are essentially appetitive, thereby spattering philosophy with mud—this malefaction is what first arouses his *thumos*; it is surely worse that he has now compounded that transgression by speaking too seriously, that is, by bestowing on the new philosophers virtues they simply don't have: he has overcompensated for his first misstep by taking a second.

Let us note that in Book 6 Socrates is plagued by no comparable self-doubt and unleashes on himself no similar barrage of self-recrimination. There, as we saw, Socrates unabashedly lavishes on the philosophic nature every conceivable commendable trait—intellectual, moral, and personal; yet he experiences neither remorse nor regret. Even the philosophers' uselessness, as Socrates sees it, is not the philosophers' own fault but the fault of those who are too foolish, too greedy, or too ambitious to appreciate the philosophers' true value. It is only in Book 7 that Socrates castigates himself for bedecking the philosophers with many virtues. Yet, strikingly, even in his impulsive thumotic rush to philosophy's defense, he will go only so far in rehabilitating his flawed philosophers. He is willing to say that they hate the lie and ignorance but will not add, as he does in the case of Book 6's philosophic natures, "while cherishing the truth" (*tēn d' alētheian stergein*—485c). He can bring himself to say that they are lovers of learning and of listening but will not use an expression like "a lover of wisdom . . . [who] strives for

----

64. Since Socrates calls himself "the speaker," and Glaucon declares himself "the listener" (536a), it is likely that the spatterer is Socrates.

65. See note 56 above.

every kind of truth" (495d). Nor will he call the new philosophers "real lovers of learning [who] strive for what is" (490a): he will not pretend that they long for the transcendent realm. Moreover, the love Socrates attributes to these philosophers never exceeds *philia*: it lacks the fire of *erōs*. In addition, Socrates holds out no hope that *Rep.* 7's philosophers will be decent (*epieikeis*) or good (*agathoi*); at best they will be courageous, moderate, and magnificent—qualities that suit warriors. They are to be *gennaioi* (genteel) but not *kaloi* (noble).[66] And though, as we shall see in Chapter 3, Glaucon assumes they are just (520e), the term *dikaios* never crosses Socrates' lips. Indeed, although justice is mentioned ten times in Book 7, the only time it is used for the philosophers is when *Glaucon* calls them just men.

With his outburst behind him, Socrates goes on. He considers the age at which the study of dialectic should be undertaken, dealing first with the appropriate ages for the earlier studies—calculation, geometry, and the other studies that pave the way for dialectic (536d), as well as for gymnastic (537b). But he has been chastened: all that remains of the long list of qualities just enumerated is that of being "steadfast in studies and steadfast in war and the rest of the duties established by law" (537d). These are the traits that were attributed to the original philosopher-warriors at 6.503b-504a. Moreover, it is once again their *aptitude* for war and studies that is emphasized—love of these things has dropped out. Gymnastic is "compulsory" (*anankaiōn*—537b); and the young men will be tested: in gymnastic (537b), in studies and war (537d), in dialectic (537d). They will indeed have to have "orderly and stable natures" (539d)—but this is the conservative standard of 503c-d, not the extravagantly overblown one of 535a-536b. Socrates' short-lived spurt of misplaced intensity has ended and is forgotten. He is no longer "too serious" (*spoudaioteron*—536c); he is back at play.

V. Education

Unlike in Book 6, where education was to happen by chance—"if the nature we set down for the philosopher *chances* on a suitable course of learning" (492a); "such a nature, when it *chances* upon suitable practices" (501d)—the program of instruction Socrates sketches in Book 7 is compulsory: "Then our job as founders is to compel the best natures to go to the

---

66. See Chapter 1, end of note 38.

study which we were saying before is the greatest, to see the Good and to go up that ascent" (519c-d).[67] In *Rep.* 7 the formal regimen begins in early childhood, with children being exposed, on the one hand, to calculation and geometry and other preparatory studies by way of play (536d-e)—because "no forced study abides in a soul" (536e)[68]—as well as, on the other, to war, where they will be led as spectators on horseback near enough to the action to "taste blood" (537a). (The philosophers of Book 6, even when young, love truth and wisdom [475b-c, 485d] and need no incentive—neither play nor coercion—to pursue them.) The boy who acquits himself best in all these "labors, studies, and fears"—all tests are tests of aptitude—is selected for further education, which will proceed systematically and rigorously through all the studies outlined: calculation, plane geometry, mathematics of the third dimension, astronomy, harmonics, and, finally, dialectic. Each of these studies both is compelled and compels: after the young men are released from the "compulsory gymnastic" (537b) in which they are also tested, other studies that are "compulsory for us" and that "compel the soul to use the intellect itself on the truth itself" (526a-b) follow.[69] The compulsory educational program to which the philosophers of Book 7 are subjected, along with the coercive nature of the subjects taught, conspire to produce philosophers with sharpened intellects who think abstractly and move farther and farther from the world of Becoming.[70]

In Socrates' fully developed educational program, then, training in music and gymnastic soon gives way to studies that turn the soul to the intelligible

67. Whereas Glaucon had protested against the unhappiness to which the founders would be subjecting the philosophers in compelling them to rule, he registers no complaint concerning compulsory education. The demanding discipline to which the philosophers-in-training are subjected is probably quite to his liking: it is fully consonant with his manly ideal.

68. The fun in learning does not appear to persist beyond its earliest stage. Once the more talented youngsters are identified, they are launched on a course of structured, formalized instruction.

69. In the timocracy, the rulers are stingy, honor money but won't possess it openly, spend other people's money, harvest pleasures stealthily, and run from the law, as boys do from a father—all because "they were not educated by persuasion but by force—the result of neglect of the true Muse accompanied by arguments and philosophy while giving more distinguished honor to gymnastic than to music" (8.548b-c).

70. The *Theaetetus* gives us reason to wonder if mathematics is in fact the best preparation for dialectic or philosophy. Theodorus praises Theaetetus, his gifted math student, for many things but never describes him as philosophical (despite what Socrates says at 155d). Theaetetus indeed seems to be not particularly good at philosophical discussion, and Theodorus, the far more accomplished mathematician, seems even worse. Theodorus confides to Socrates that he left philosophy or, at any rate, Protagorean philosophy, which he calls *tōn psilōn logōn* ("dialectical abstractions"), *for* geometry (165a).

realm. As we have seen, gymnastic, as Socrates points out, "is wholly engaged with coming into being and passing away. For it oversees growth
and decay in the body" (521e). And music, as Glaucon acknowledges,
does nothing to, as Socrates had put it, "draw the soul from becoming to
being" (521d): "As for a study directed toward something of the sort you are
now seeking, there was nothing of the kind in it" (522a-b). Though music
"transmits by harmony a certain harmoniousness . . . and by rhythm a certain rhythmicalness," what it does not yield is knowledge (*epistēmēn*—522a).

By the time the budding philosopher is seventeen or eighteen, then, his
musical studies have ended; by the time he is twenty he is no longer receiving instruction in gymnastic. Is there not, however, some danger in allowing these prospective leaders to abandon training in music and gymnastic
at so young an age? Without the studies that tame and strengthen their
souls, will their moral virtue endure? Unlike the philosophers of Book 6,
whose moral virtues come as by-products of their love of wisdom and who
are less in need of any special training than they are of protection from
corruption, the philosophers of Book 7, like their guardian predecessors,
rely on music and gymnastic to instill in them courage and moderation. If
the only thing that keeps them from vice is being forcibly deprived of the
pleasures that bind them to the material world, it is no wonder that upon
returning to the Cave, many of them, as it seems, fail to "stand firm" as
they are once again "pulled in all directions" (540a). The studies that follow music and gymnastic—even the first and most elementary, calculation
and geometry—"by nature lead to intellection" (523a), "in every way are
apt to draw men toward Being" (523a), "lead the soul powerfully upward"
(525d), "compel the soul to use the intellect itself on the truth itself" (526b),
"make it easier to make out the Idea of the Good" (526e), and "compel one
to look at Being" (526e). Though calculation and geometry are touted as
being suited to war as well, their most important function, as we saw in
section I, is to turn the soul (526d-e). The future philosophers' educational
program is almost wholly abstract and theoretical in nature; its goal, after
all, is to lead them to knowledge of the Good.

VI. Conclusion

The course Socrates charts for the philosopher who is to be the "guardian of a city and of laws" (504c), the curricular path that is to direct him to

"the end of the greatest and most fitting study" (504d), is, as Socrates memorably calls it, a "longer way around" (504c). The first time Socrates had spoken of a longer road (at 435d) it was to disparage the city-soul analogy shortcut, which, he thought, would inevitably fail to yield a precise account of the virtues. He now reminds Adeimantus of that earlier needed but neglected longer road (504b-c, 504d), and contrasts it with the current longer road that is to lead to something "still greater" than "justice and the other things we went through" (504d).[71] The greatest study is designed to take the philosopher to the greatest thing there is: the Form of the Good. It is, after all, good things that every soul yearns for and pursues—indeed the soul does everything for the sake of what is good—so that those who care for a city must not be ignorant of that which makes all good things, including the virtues, good (505d-506a). Even if the "best men in the city" come to know the Good, however, and even if as a result they rule successfully, it is never suggested that their souls yearn for this highest reality or pursue it any more fervently than any other soul does.[72] Education may indeed lead the philosophers to the Good. But what nothing and no one can do for them is endow them with an ardent love for wisdom and truth concerning "what is always" (527b). Only nature can do that.

---

71. Although Socrates identifies two distinct longer roads, each to be preferred to a corresponding distinct shorter road and each having its own distinct goal—the first, the nature of the virtues, and the second, the Form of the Good—scholars have tended to confuse the two, thinking that Socrates recommends taking the longer road of the study of the Form of the Good as a way to understand the virtues or the soul. Scott (2000, 9), for example, sees the longer road to discovery of the Good as a "revisiting" of justice—that is, as the better way to reach a fuller understanding of justice; for Howland (2004, 109) the longer road that is alone adequate for a precise grasp of the soul "is identified with the study of the Good." White (1978, 174) thinks Plato is saying at 504 that if the rulers now traverse the longer road mentioned at 435d, they will "thoroughly know the principles" that determine "with certainty" whether the soul has the tripartite nature that was earlier argued for merely provisionally. Cf. Yu (2000, 136), who thinks the short way, the discussion of virtue and the soul, leads to practical justice and happiness, and the long way, the theory of Forms, to the achievement of intellectual justice and happiness.

72. Shields (2007, 24) thinks that the philosophers are compelled to look at the Good by the goodness of the Good itself. Since we all pursue the Good (505e1–2), he argues, the philosophers, when in its presence, must want to see it (23). Yet the philosophers are not said to have any greater desire than anyone else for the Good. If wanting genuinely good things does not make others strive for a vision of the Good, it needn't make the philosophers do so either.

3

Philosophers by Design II

The Making of a Ruler

If a man looks down on the life of the city as unworthy of him, he should, if
he so wishes, remain in this world above. This does indeed happen to those
who have contemplated much.

—Plotinus, "The Good or the One," *Enneads* 6.9[9].7

The allegory of the Cave not only makes plain that the philosophers
of *Rep*. 7 have no native interest in the pursuit of wisdom and the Good,
but it exposes as well their unabashed disinclination to rule. Just as the
released prisoners, having seen the sun, prefer virtually any fate to a return to the darkness (516c-e), so, too, do the philosophers who have seen
the Good wish only to remain in its presence. All Glaucon need do if he
is not to "mistake my expectation," Socrates says, is to "liken" each facet
of the Cave imagery to "the soul's journey to the intelligible place" (517b).
"Come, then," he continues, "and join me in supposing this, too, and don't
be surprised that the men who get to that point [the vision of the Good]
are not willing to mind the business of human beings, but rather . . . their
souls are always eager to spend their time above" (517c-d). That the philosophers are unwilling to rule is likely, Socrates says, "if indeed ["since" is
implied] this, too, follows the image of which I told before" (517d).

I. Unwillingness to Rule

Scholars struggle mightily to view Book 7's philosophers favorably. Despite Socrates' depiction of them as unwilling to involve themselves in human affairs, it is widely held that they do, that they must, if not at first, then eventually, wish to rule.[1] Some believe that the philosophers' vision of the Good inspires them to return to the city, that as soon as they see this most dazzling of Forms, they want nothing more than to enable others, too, to bask in its glow.[2] Others suppose that *Rep.* 7's philosophers, like the good and decent men of Book 1 (347a-d), rule in order to avoid being ruled by their inferiors.[3] One scholar has proposed that it is the *law* mandating philosophic rule that tips the scale for them in ruling's favor.[4] Another is sure that these philosophers are, qua philosophers, inevitably like Socrates, and so descend to the Cave willingly, as Socrates does.[5] And many commentators expect these wisest of men to recognize that ruling is in their interest: they either will be persuaded by the founders' argument,[6] or will come to appreciate on their own,[7] that ruling is required by justice, and will immediately draw the connection between justice and their own happiness: however unappealing ruling might have seemed to them in any other context, in the context of its justness it becomes instantly desirable and no longer even an act of self-sacrifice.[8]

---

1. For a fuller discussion of the views of these scholars, see Weiss 2012. There are, of course, some scholars who recognize that the philosophers do not wish to rule, do not regard ruling as beneficial to them in any way. These include Bloom (1968, 407–8), Sallis (1975, 379–80), Brann (2004, 95–96), and Scott (2007).

2. Among the scholars who pursue this tack are Kraut (1997, 213–14), Irwin (1977, 241; 1995, 300), Cooper (2000, 20–21), Demos (1964), Gosling (1973), Kahn (1987), Mahoney (1992), and Vernezze (1992). Scholars cite the *Symposium*'s notion of "giving birth in the beautiful" (206e), yet there is no reason to assume that the same desire guides the lover of wisdom in the *Symposium* and *Rep.* 7's philosophers. Scott wonders (2007, 149) why "there is not the faintest whisper about *erōs*" in Socrates' account of the philosophers' agreeing to rule. What is perhaps more surprising, however, is that the philosophers of Book 7, as was argued in Chapter 2, section III, are wholly unerotic; there is no context in which they are moved by *erōs*.

3. Sedley 2007, Cross and Woozley 1964, and Davies 1968.

4. E. Brown 2004; Scott (2007, 148) agrees.

5. Miller 1986.

6. Dorter 2006.

7. Brickhouse 1981.

8. See Irwin (1995, 300), who dismisses as a momentary lapse on Plato's part the text's intimation that the philosophers are reluctant to rule; Plato, he says, "mistakenly" loses sight of his

The fact is that none of these well-intentioned suggestions is borne out by the text. As Socrates portrays *Rep.* 7's philosophers, not only does their vision of the Good fail to make them willing to rule; it is precisely this vision that makes them *un*willing: "Men who get *to that point* are not willing to mind the business of human beings" (517c). Just as it is the vision of the sun (516b) that makes the released prisoner prefer "to undergo anything whatsoever" rather than be drawn back into the Cave no matter how many of its "honors, praises, and prizes" (516c) he might attain there, so, too, in the case of the philosophers, it is once they see the Good that they must be "compelled" to order the city (*anankasteon . . . kosmein*—540a-b) in accordance with their vision. It is unlikely, then, that imitating the Forms, giving birth in the Beautiful, or advancing rational order is these philosophers' own chosen aim. There are simply no textual grounds in Book 7 for concluding that the experience of seeing the Good is profoundly transformative, that it makes the philosophers in any way more solicitous or more generous men.

Nor is it likely that the philosophers are moved by the same consideration that sways the good and decent men of Book 1, namely, the desire to avoid being ruled by worse men. For, first, Socrates expects his current argument—and not some earlier one—to be effective: "Do you suppose our pupils will disobey us when they hear *this?*" (520d).[9] And second, the good and decent men of Book 1, so far as we know, have not scaled the heights of philosophy or savored its incomparable pleasures—but the philosophers of *Rep.* 7 have. What is intolerable to the good and decent men, namely, being ruled by their inferiors, might therefore be quite acceptable to the philosophers—so long as they can continue to live the philosophic life. (For

---

own firmly held view that those who see the Good love whatever is good for its own sake. So, too, Kraut (1997, 213). Annas (1981, 267), Cooper (1977, 155), Waterlow (1972–73, 35), and Denyer (1986, 29) think the philosopher pursues the impersonal good, not valuing his own good above that of others. White (1978, 195) goes further than the others, attributing a measure of altruism to the philosophers. Yu (2000, 136–37) is one scholar who pretends neither that the philosopher wishes to rule nor that he is psychically just.

9. Sedley (2007, 280) seems to think that once the founders are no longer in the picture the compulsion could no longer take the form it takes when they are. But why couldn't the philosophers who are already ruling present to the next generation the argument that was presented to them? They wish, after all, to leave behind "other like men" in their place "as guardians of the city" (540b).

further discussion of the nature and motivations of the good and decent men of Book 1, see the addendum to this chapter.)

It would be odd, too, for the philosophers to feel compelled to rule because of some law that requires it, particularly in light of the fact that the text speaks of no such law. The only law mentioned is the one that approves the founders' use of persuasion and compulsion to ensure the happiness of the city (519e). Because the law's primary concern (*melei*) is the city's harmonious well-being it permits the founders to infringe on the happiness of the philosophers, to cause them, as Glaucon puts it, "to live a worse life when a better is possible for them" (519d). It is the founders, then, who conform their actions to the law (or to its spirit), when they say and do what they must to induce the philosophers to rule. And if they succeed in convincing the philosophers to rule, the philosophers, in ruling, obey the founders—not the law. Indeed, the question Socrates poses to Glaucon immediately following the argument he presents to the philosophers is "Do you suppose our pupils [*trophimoi*—lit., nurslings, those who have been nourished and nurtured by us] will disobey *us* (*hēmin*)?" (520d); and Glaucon's response is "Impossible. For surely *we* shall be imposing [or "ordering"—*epitaxomen*] just things (*dikaia*) on just men" (520e, echoing Socrates' earlier "we will say just things to them"—520a). There is no suggestion that the founders enact a law to which the philosophers then submit.[10] The word "law" vanishes after 519e.[11]

Most misguided is the attempt (by Miller 1986) to project onto the philosophers of *Rep.* 7 all the qualities that attach to Socrates qua philosopher. If for Socrates the moral life is best, surpassing even the contemplative, then *Rep.* 7's philosophers are not like him at all. If Socrates' pedagogic practice expresses his overflowing goodness and generosity (Miller, 190–91), then theirs is geared toward the training of their replacements: they "leave others behind to take their place," educating specifically "other *like* men" so that they themselves can then "go off to dwell on the Isles of the Blessed" (540b). Moreover, unlike Socrates, who is politically engaged even

---

10. Also, as Robert Heinaman notes in an unpublished paper, if the argument from justice with which Socrates confronts the philosophers suffices to justify a law that would require them to rule, what need is there for the law?; the argument itself should compel.

11. The next mention of law comes at 537d2, where Socrates speaks of the practices "established by law."

"in the far-from-just-setting of Athens" (192 n. 34), these philosophers resist rule even in a city that has nurtured them and solicits their enlightened
governance.

There can be no mistaking the contrast between Socrates' willing descent and the reluctance of *Rep.* 7's philosophers to rule.[12] The *Republic*
opens with Socrates announcing "I went down" (*Katebēn*) (1.327a); but in
Book 7 he has to command the philosophers to do the very same thing:
"So you must go down (*katabateon*)" (520c).[13] Philosophers who need to be
ordered to rule show themselves to be not only less generous than Socrates
but also shamefully more selfish than philosophers who would rule so
long as they could preserve their moral integrity and secure the people's
support—the philosophers of Book 6.[14] Book 7's philosophers, despite facing no adverse conditions—no danger of corruption, no belligerent subjects—indeed, despite having been cared for and educated by their city,
are unwilling to do the city's business; they have no intention of giving up
a life that approximates or replicates life on the Isles of the Blessed (519c).[15]
If even at the very end of their journey, after they have seen the Form
of the Good, they have to be compelled to order city, private men, and
themselves, using the Good as a pattern, if even at that point they regard
ruling not as a way of practicing something noble (*ouch hōs kalon ti* . . .
prattontas—540b) but as a kind of "drudging" (*epitalaipōrountas*—540b),
then they are not in the least like Socrates.

---

12. See Nichols 1984 and 1987 for the view that the philosopher-rulers of Book 7 are a "dra-
matic foil" for Socrates, from whom they differ radically. See, too, Chapter 4, section VII, for a detailed consideration of the many ways in which *Rep.* 7's philosophers are unlike Socrates.

13. Bloom (1968, 407) notices how odd it is that suddenly in Book 7 (at 519c), the *Republic*'s
philosophers have to be compelled to rule. He remarks: "Previously it appeared that the philosophers are anxious to rule and must persuade a recalcitrant populace. In the investigation of the
philosophic nature it has by accident, as it were, emerged that philosophers want nothing from the
city and that their contemplative activity is perfectly engrossing, leaving neither time nor interest
for ruling." In my view, it is not that some new truth about the old philosophers is "by accident"
now being disclosed, but rather that there are now new philosophers.

14. The philosophers of Book 6 are never said to look down with disdain on ordinary human
beings or to "pity" (*eleein*) them, the way the philosophers of Book 7 are (516c, 516d; 517c). Nor
are they ever said to be, as Book 7's philosophers are, unwilling to mind the business of human
beings (517c).

15. Wilson 1984, 187: "Even if the best city . . . persuades the philosopher to pay his debts and
share in rule, that return is against his developed inclination."

That the philosophers rule only reluctantly is manifest, too, in the concession or compromise implicit in Socrates' allowing them to take turns: "So you must go down, each in turn" (520c); they will "join in the labors (*sumponein*) of the city, each in his turn, while living the greater part of the time with one another in the pure region" (520d); they will "spend the greater part of their time in philosophy," but each, "when his turn comes," will do a stint at ruling, and, having done his part to train others to replace the current rulers, will eventually, when he dies, go off to dwell on the Isles of the Blessed (540a-b). From the age of fifty, then, and for another, say, twenty to thirty years, the philosophers live the contemplative life interrupted only briefly. Neither the philosophers of Book 6, should they chance to rule, nor Socrates enjoy (or require) a comparable reprieve. And even so, the philosophers of *Rep.* 7 have to be compelled.

Perhaps, however, being unwilling to rule is not a bad thing. Does Socrates not say three times (520d, 520e-521a, 521b) that unwillingness to rule is actually a prerequisite for being a good ruler?[16] Does he not think that those who rule willingly are likely to sow discord and disharmony? Does Socrates not declare that it is the city ruled by those "least eager to rule" (*hēkista prothumoi archein*—520d) that is "governed in the way that is best and freest from faction" (520d)?

Since Socrates certainly does say that a good ruler is one who does not wish to rule, it is critical to distinguish the various ways in which one might be said to wish to rule or to be willing to rule. (1) A person might be eager to rule, might even clamor for rule, in order to advance his own interests—to gain power, wealth, or prestige. (2) One might be willing to rule for the sake of the ruled—to benefit them. (3) One who is initially or by inclination unwilling to rule might eventually shed his opposition and agree, albeit reluctantly, to rule. Corresponding to these are the ways in which a person might be said not to wish to rule or to be unwilling to rule. (1') A person might not be overly eager to rule because he is not interested in attaining ruling's rewards. (2') He might not wish to rule because he is unwilling to take the trouble to benefit others. (3') One who is initially or by inclination unwilling to rule might remain that way. In the interest of

---

16. See Burnyeat 1985, 34: it is the philosophers' very unwillingness to rule "that makes them suited to rule."

securing Glaucon's assent to the idea that a ruler ought to be someone who does not wish to rule, Socrates obscures the distinctiveness of the various ways in which one might wish or not wish to rule.

In truth, only in the first sense of "wishing to rule" is yes the appropriate answer to the question, "Would not the worst ruler be someone who wishes to rule?" Clearly, the men who Thrasymachus in Book 1 assumes are most covetous of rule (345e), the sailors in the ship allegory in Book 6 who fight each other and would kill in order to rule (488b-d), and the men described in Book 7 as "beggars, men hungering for want of private goods, [who] go to public affairs supposing that in them they must seize the good," men for whom "ruling becomes a thing fought over" (521a) and who are "rival lovers [of ruling]" (*anterastai [tou archein]*—521b), are the most unsuited to rule. If sense (1) were the sense in which the philosophers of Book 7 wished to rule, they would indeed make bad rulers. That they do not seek the crass accoutrements of ruling is surely a point in their favor. In this way they resemble the philosophers of Book 6, who don't have the time to be "filled with" the "envy and ill will" that tends to infect human affairs (500c).

It should be evident, however, that when "wishing to rule" is taken in either sense (2) or sense (3), the correct answer to Socrates' question is no. To answer yes when "wishing to rule" is taken in sense (2) would be tantamount to maintaining that the worst doctors[17] are those who actually *want* to heal people.[18] Although we would, of course, be rightfully wary of doctors who are overly eager to be doctors, right to suspect that what they are really after is the prestige and money associated with the medical profession (that is, that they wish to practice medicine in sense [1]), why would anyone avoid a doctor who wants to benefit others by making them well? If Socrates would not view with favor a doctor to whom the very idea of healing another person is repugnant, how could he approve of a ruler who

---

17. Rulers are compared to doctors in Book 1, first by Thrasymachus at 340d-e, and then by Socrates at 341c-342d and at 346. See also 389b-d, 459c, 489b-c (the ship metaphor), 564c, and 567c. Justice is compared to the medical art at 332c-e, 333e, and 350a. Glaucon compares *in*justice to it at 360e.

18. One could subscribe to so bizarre a view only if one believed it unthinkable that anyone with a lick of sense could want to help someone else. Socrates appears to assert just that in Book 1 at 347d, but see the addendum to this chapter.

is repelled by the very prospect of making someone else more just? It may *seem* as if this is precisely what Socrates intends when he says that "the city in which those who are going to rule are least eager to rule is necessarily governed in the way that is best" (520d), but it is clear from the surrounding text that the kind of eagerness to rule that Socrates decries is the kind that leads to faction, the kind that drives men to fight over it (520c-d).[19] It is those who so desperately desire power that they would step on others in order to attain it who are unworthy to rule (521b). A good ruler will indeed "despise political offices" (521b), but that is hardly the same as spurning the job of caring for the ruled. On the contrary, the same ruler who despises political offices, who shuns the hubs of money, power, and influence, is the one most willing to rule "in the precise sense" (342d)—that is, to care for the souls of "the weaker." It is certainly not such men who arouse Socrates' anxiety and suspicion.[20]

Turning to sense (3), it is evident that it is this sense that best captures the condition of the philosophers of Book 7 (as well as, as we shall see in the addendum to this chapter, that of the "good and decent men" of Book 1). Surely if they are eventually willing to rule—or at least, more accurately, not, or no longer, not-willing[21]—their rule is to be welcomed. Their initial resistance does not mark them as bad rulers. Only the rulers who wish to rule in sense (1) are an unmitigated evil.

As for unwillingness to rule, Socrates indeed regards this as a good thing, but, again, not in every sense. In fact, only those who do not wish

<hr>

19. The expression "fight over," *perimachēton*, is the same one used in Book 1, where, in a city of good men, "there would be a fight [among the good and decent men] over *not* ruling, just as there is now over ruling" (347d). Although what these men fight over is not-ruling—like our philosophers of Book 7, they do not crave money and honor—nevertheless, insofar as they fight to spare themselves the trouble of caring for others, they exhibit the same selfishness as those who fight *to* rule. (See the addendum to this chapter.)

20. Socrates has nothing but praise for the guardians of Book 3, who are "entirely eager to do what they believe to be advantageous to the city" (412e). These men, he thinks, make the best guardians—and not because they have something better to do. They "save" their regimes by virtue of their courage and moderation (412a). They love (*philōn*) their city and are for that reason well suited to care for it (412c-d).

21. The philosophers of Book 7 are never said to be positively willing to rule. What is said of them is that they will no longer be permitted "not to be willing" (*mē ethelein*) to go down (519d), and that perhaps Socrates' argument will persuade them not to be "not willing" (*ouk ethelēsousin*) to join in the labors of the city (520d).

to rule in sense (1') are at all commendable. Rulers who do not wish to rule in sense (2')—because they would not wish to trouble themselves for anyone else—may be compared to physicians who would not want to take the trouble to heal people. Even if a craftsman who is not willing to use his craft to benefit others is not a worse *craftsman* than one who is, he is certainly a worse human being. Philosophers who have the skill and opportunity to rule yet would not be willing to use their ruling skill to help others even under favorable conditions are hardly worthy of praise; indeed, they are no better than anyone else. As Socrates tells us in Book 1, when ruling is viewed as an activity that benefits others rather than oneself, "*No one* wishes to rule willingly" (*oudeis ethelei archein hekōn*—345e; *mēdena ethelein hekonta archein*—346e): not wishing to care for others is the rule, not the exception.

It is likely that Book 7's rulers retain their distaste for rule even as they rule. If that is the case, then they are "not willing to rule" not only in sense (1') but in sense (3') as well: since "a better life" has been found for them (520e-521a),[22] they rule only reluctantly.[23] Although governance by such men is not undesirable, nevertheless the men themselves are, as men, scarcely better than those to whom sense (2') applies: they may consent to rule, but they are too enamored of the more satisfying life they lead to rule willingly, to serve others because they want to. It is true that Socrates says to Glaucon: "If you discover a life better than ruling for those who are going to rule, it is possible that your well-governed city will come into being" (520e-521a). But Socrates says this by way of responding directly—if somewhat belatedly—to something Glaucon had said. To Glaucon's earlier objection at 519d that "we are making them live a worse life when a better is possible for them," Socrates now in effect retorts: Well, if they in fact had no better life, they indeed would not make good rulers. Unless the life they have makes it possible for them to "despise political offices" they are not fit to rule.[24] It is those who are so in love with ruling (*erastas tou*

---

22. In the case of these philosophers their "better life" is indeed found *for* them; they do not, as we have seen, pursue philosophy on their own initiative.

23. See note 21 above. If at 1.347a, where it is said that "wages must be provided to a person if he is to be willing (*ethelēsein*) to rule" (also 347c), the "willingness" is at best grudging, how eager could *Rep.* 7's philosophers be to rule when it is said of them only that they are "not unwilling"?

24. So Socrates at *Ap*. 36b.

archein) that they would fight over it (521b) who are utterly unqualified to "go to it" (521b).

Although the philosophers of *Rep.* 7, then, are not the worst of rulers—they do not, after all, seize on ruling, as other men do, as a means by which to enrich or empower themselves—they are nevertheless far from ideal: like the general run of men, they do not care to benefit others. They are "not willing to go down again among those prisoners or share their labors and honors" (519d), they are "not willing to mind the business of human beings" (517c); at best they can be persuaded to "obey us" and no longer be "not willing" to "join in the labors of the city" (520d).[25]

II. Securing the City's Happiness

Since the philosophers do not wish to rule, is Glaucon not right to think that the founders, in compelling them to rule, "do them an injustice"? Is it not unjust to make the philosophers "live a worse life when a better one is possible for them" (519d)? In defense of the founders, Socrates argues as follows: The law is concerned for the happiness of the city; the city's happiness depends on each of its classes making its appropriate contribution to the whole; the philosophers are no exception (519e–520a). The city cannot permit itself to promote the especial happiness of any one group.[26] To do so would be to jeopardize the well-being of the whole. Therefore, whatever is necessary—persuasion or even compulsion (519e)—for the unifying of the city, for "binding it together" (520a), is warranted. As was made plain in Book 5, the "greatest evil" for a city is "what splits it and makes it many instead of one"; the "greatest good" is "what binds it together and makes it one" (462a-b).

The only happiness that is of any interest to the law (and hence to Socrates and the founders) is that of the city as a whole (see 3.369c, 389b, 412a, 412d-e, 413c; 4.420b, 420e, 421a, 421b, 434a, 434b-c; 5.464b, 466a, 473d; 6.487e,

---

25. We shall discuss in Chapter 4, section III, Socrates' willingness to undertake "labors" (*ponous tinas ponountos—Ap.* 22a).

26. Even the benefits that the law makes the citizens "share with one another" are brought "to the commonwealth" (519e-520a).

497a, 501e, 503a; 7.540e; 9.576e). Even the apparent exceptions to this rule in fact confirm it. At 421e, where it would seem as if Socrates fears that the craftsmen might "become worse" as a result of becoming wealthy or poor, what troubles him in fact is that they might become worse *craftsmen* and hence worse *for the city*. Similarly, at 459c the lies that are said to be for the benefit *of the ruled* are actually, as is clear at 462a-b, for the sake of the city: "Have we any greater evil for a city than what splits it and makes it many instead of one?"[27] The city's happiness always trumps that of its classes and citizens. At 421b-c, Socrates explicitly assigns to the guardians the task of ensuring the happiness of the city as a whole (*tēn polin holēn; sumpasēs tēs poleōs*). And at 519e he observes that faring exceptionally well is something the law "contrives to bring about [only] for the whole city." Socrates leaves it to nature to allot to each of the groups its share of happiness (421c).

It is likely, then, that when Socrates asserts that the law is not concerned "that any one class in the city fare exceptionally well" (519e), what he means is that the law is equally indifferent to the happiness of all classes. By saying that the law favors no *particular* class he counters Glaucon's supposition that it should: Glaucon is partial to the philosophers now just as Adeimantus had privileged the guardians earlier. At the start of Book 4 Adeimantus had complained that not only does Socrates fail to make the guardians—"those to whom the city in truth belongs," "men who are going to be blessed"—happier than others, but he actually makes them less happy. And Socrates responded to Adeimantus there precisely as he does to Glaucon here: "In founding the city we are not looking to the exceptional happiness of any one group among us, but as far as possible, to that of the city as a whole" (420b, 421b; repeated at 466a: "We were making the guardians guardians and the city as happy as we could, but we were not looking exclusively to one group in it and forming it for happiness").

Certain scholars are adamant that Socrates cares about the happiness of each of the classes, and that it is because he believes that the happiness

---

27. In the *Republic*, unification of the city is the end at which the legislator must aim in setting down the laws (462a). In the *Gorgias*, by contrast, the "one work of a good citizen" is to "lead desires in a different direction . . . toward the condition in which the citizens were to be better" (517b-c).

of the city ensures the happiness of the classes that he cares about the city's well-being.[28] What Socrates is loath to promote, they contend, is the special or greater happiness of any one group over that of the others. Some have looked to the statue-image Socrates presents at 420d for support.[29] In fact, however, the statue-image tells against the view that the happiness of the classes matters. For if a statue is to be beautiful each part must be painted in such a way that it contributes to the beauty of the whole: not only need no part be painted *especially* beautifully, but no part need be painted beautifully at all. By analogy, then, if the city is to be happy, not only is it counterproductive to have any one part be happier than the others, but there is no need for any part to be happy at all. Moreover, just as the beauty of the statue does not guarantee the beauty of any, let alone of all, its parts, the happiness of the city does not ensure the happiness of its classes (or citizens).

Socrates is well aware that there is a way to make the city happy by making its people happy: "We know how to clothe the farmers in fine robes and hang gold on them and bid them work the earth at their pleasure, and how to make the potters recline before the fire, drinking in competition from left to right and feasting, and having their wheel set before them as often as they get a desire to make pots, and how to make all the others blessed in the same way so that the city as a whole will surely be happy" (420e).[30] Of course, no one expects Socrates to approve of this foolish (and impracticable) way of making people, or cities, happy. But that he offers no thoughtful alternative for ensuring the happiness of individual citizens

---

28. See, for example, Reeve 1988, 205. Reeve maintains that all people, and all classes, will be happier—and believe they are happier—in Callipolis than in any other city. See also Morrison 2001. Kamtekar (2004, 142) speaks of "the benefit of the city or the happiness of the citizens" as if these are the same. Vlastos (1973, 14 and 26 n. 94) supposes Socrates must mean by the happiness of the whole the happiness of all.

29. See, for example, L. Brown 1998, 21: "Each of the constituent classes is to be made happy—oh yes!—but with the happiness which it derives from its place in the polis as a whole—compare the eyes, hands etc. of the statue"; and 24: "True *eudaimonia* for a member of any class is to live a life in which they contribute the most their nature allows to the polis." Also Kraut 1999, 244: "He [Plato] compares the moulding of a city to the design of a statue, and asserts that it is well designed only if its parts are structured in such a way that each is happy."

30. In the *Lysis* (207d-210d), even though Lysis's parents love him very much and want him to be happy, they do not let him do whatever he desires. The reason they don't, however, is not that doing whatever he desires won't make him happy but that it won't make him useful to others.

only serves to underscore his single-minded determination to make the city happy only as a whole, only as a collective—not in the aggregate or additively. It might be thought that the reason Socrates assigns people jobs for which they are suited is precisely that he cares about their individual happiness. After all, he says at 3.407a that when a man "has a definite job it would be of no profit [for him] to go on living if he couldn't do it."[31] But surely what Socrates means is that a craftsman could not survive without a job, without any means of earning a livelihood. His point is not that life is not worth living without the satisfaction derived from work, but rather that if a poor man can't work he is better off dead. Indeed, Socrates immediately adds that for a rich man there is "no such job at hand that makes his life unlivable (*abiōton*) if he is compelled to keep away from it" (407a). The reason Socrates recommends that people perform the tasks at which they are best is not so that their lives will be enriched but so that the city's happiness—not their own—will be secured.[32]

It is only with respect to the guardians of Book 3 that Socrates says: "It wouldn't be surprising if these men, as they are, are also happiest" (420b); "They'll live a life more blessed than that most blessed one the Olympic victors live. . . . The life of our auxiliaries now appears far nobler (*kallion*) and better (*ameinōn*) than that of the Olympic victors" (465d-466a). What these men attain, however, is the happiness appropriate to guardians: victories, public support, preservation of the city, prizes, and a worthy burial (5.465d-e)—whether or not these are the things these particular guardians actually desire.[33] For here, too, the happiness of the city as a whole

---

31. Heinaman (1998, 42 n. 64; 2004, 390) regards the passage at 406d-407a as the sole exception to Plato's general view in the *Republic* that the producers' menial labor is without intrinsic value and of no benefit to them. As I read the passage, however, its point is to assign worth not to manual work but to the manual worker's attitude toward sickness: unlike rich people, a poor person who has a job does not indulge or pamper himself when he is ill but, out of necessity, gets back to work as swiftly as possible.

32. See, for example, 374b: "So the shoemaker's art would produce fine work *for us*." Some scholars believe that aptitude and enjoyment usually go together. So Craig 1994, 8. Of the four passages Craig cites, three, however, fail to support his claim: 370a-c, 455b-c, 586d-e. Although the fourth, 486c, does have some merit (see Chapter 2, note 49), it implies only that one who is not good at something will not love it, not that one will love whatever he is good at.

33. See 466b, where Socrates regards any conception of happiness a guardian might have other than the "moderate, steady, and (as we assert) best life" as "a foolish adolescent opinion about happiness."

is paramount and supersedes the guardians' having "the most happiness" (421b). If the auxiliaries and guardians are to be "the best craftsmen at their jobs", they must be "compelled and persuaded" (*anankasteon . . . kai peisteon*) (421b-c) to see to the happiness of the city as a whole. And, as we have seen (Chapter 2, section III), they have to be kept away from the private property, secret storerooms, and gold and silver they clearly still crave (416d-417a).

However happy the auxiliaries and guardians are or are not, Socrates assures Glaucon (though his target audience is Adeimantus, the referent of "I don't know whose" [465e]) that the producers will be considerably less happy: "Is there any risk that it [the life of our auxiliaries] will in some way appear comparable to that of the shoemakers or any other craftsmen or to that of the farmers?" (466a-b). When Socrates says at 434a that it would hardly be a catastrophe if shoemakers and carpenters were to exchange jobs or if one man were to try to do both jobs, his insouciance reflects his confidence that the *city's* happiness will not be seriously compromised by these deviations from his plan. Socrates does not seem to care—indeed no one does—about how the shoemakers' and carpenters' happiness might be affected. The question never even comes up.

III. The Founders' Argument

Since the law is concerned with securing the happiness of the city, it sanctions whatever is needed to promote this end. The city can no more afford to allow the members of its ruling class to "turn whichever way each wants" (520a) than it can permit the city's other constituents to do as they please. If, therefore, the founders compel (*prosanankazontes*) the philosophers to do their part in the city, they do them no injustice. In fact, virtually anything the founders might say by way of persuading the philosophers to rule would count as "just things" (*dikaia*—520a). With the law's blessing, then, and with the considerable latitude it grants him, Socrates proceeds to devise an argument to convince *Rep.* 7's recalcitrant philosophers that it is their duty to rule.

The theme of justice is introduced indirectly. When philosophers arise in other cities, Socrates says, when they "grow up spontaneously (*automatoi*) against the will of the regime" (a clear nod in the direction of the philosophers of Book 6),[34] when their nature "grows by itself and does not owe its rearing to anyone" (520b; cf. 486d), *this* nature "has justice on its side when it is not eager to pay off the price of rearing to anyone" (520b). It may then be inferred that justice would not be on the side of men who refuse to rule when their regime does in fact "beget" them and educate them to philosophy. The same justice that absolves those philosophers who have come to philosophy on their own of any obligation to rule demands of those who have been born and bred by the city that they "pay off the price of their rearing" to it (520b-c). Moreover, since the birth and rearing the philosophers receive at the hands of the city is not for the city alone—so that they serve it as "leaders in hives, and kings"—but "for yourselves" as well (520b), the philosophers owe a debt to the city for something it has done for them: it has made them able to participate not only in the life of the city but also in the life of the intelligible realm ("in both lives") (520b-c).

The founders' argument further implies that the philosophers' competence, in addition to the debt they owe to the city, confers on them an obligation to rule. Once their eyes adjust to the darkness, once they "see ten thousand times better than the men there" and, "having seen the truth about fair, just, and good things," "know what each of the phantoms is, and of what it is a phantom" (520c), they must rule: "You have been better and more perfectly educated and are more able to participate in both lives. So (*oun*), you must go down, each in his turn, into the common dwelling of the others and get habituated along with them to seeing the dark things" (520b-c).

Despite the superficial legitimacy of the demands the founders make on the philosophers, a second, closer look at their argument shows it to be more slick than sound: none of its elements can be sustained from the perspective of strict justice. The argument's first element is the philosophers' purported obligation to repay a debt to the city that "begot" and educated them. Terence Irwin (1995, 314–15) rightly points out that this aspect of the argument is reminiscent of Cephalus's understanding of justice in Book 1. (See, too, Benardete 1989, 180.) But that in itself is not a decisive strike against it: there is in fact little reason to doubt that for Socrates justice includes a prima facie duty to repay one's debts. Repaying one's debts

---

34. See Vegetti 2000, 353. See Chapter 2, note 26.

may not capture the essence of justice and may not be what justice requires in all instances—in particular, when it causes harm[35]—yet it remains one of the most basic of obligations. In Book 4 Socrates includes it among the things that, according to vulgar standards (*ta phortika*), a just man is least likely to fail to do: "upon accepting a deposit of gold or silver, would such a man seem to be the one to filch it?" (442e). If the nurture and education the philosophers receive is a sort of deposit; how, then, could they, if they are just men, fail to return it?

Is it perfectly perspicuous, however, that the rudimentary standard of justice that requires of a person that he repay a debt (by returning goods that he either borrowed, took unjustly, or had faithfully entrusted to him) or even that he requite good with good applies to the case of the philosophers in relation to the city? In what sense can they be said to have incurred a debt that they must now discharge? They certainly didn't steal something they must now restore, nor did they borrow anything, nor did they in any ordinary way accept a deposit. Furthermore, although it may well be true that philosophers who are not nurtured by their regimes owe their regimes nothing, the inverse—that those who are, do—does not follow. The philosophers are taken charge of by the city when they are but children, and are forcibly put through a rigorous educational curriculum that may or may not be (and most likely is not) to their liking: indeed, if they are like their counterparts in the Cave allegory, then they are "distressed and annoyed at being so dragged" (515e-516a). Arguably, one is not obligated to repay a debt that was not willingly incurred or to return good for a good that was not wanted.

A further weakness in the founders' argument is that although it relies on the benefit the philosophers derive from the city—the education they receive does enable them to engage in the wondrous activity of philosophy—it recognizes, too, that they are not begotten only "for yourselves," are not educated solely with an eye to their own advancement or achievement. On the contrary, they are groomed to serve the city ("and for the rest of the city"). The good turn the city bestows on them is thus at least in part (and

---

35. One defect in the rule-following conception of justice is that the person with whom one interacts is a mere placeholder, an *x*. Once one raises the question, "Will I be causing harm?" one is forced to attend to the particular situation at hand and to the particular person affected by one's actions.

probably in large part) self-serving.[36] If it is not entirely evident that even a fully selfless favor obligates the recipient to "repay" (for, as we have seen, the benefit might be something neither asked for nor wanted), how can it be assumed that a self-serving "favor" does? So, although it is true that as a result of the special treatment the philosophers receive at the hands of the city, they are "more able to participate in both lives" (520b-c), nevertheless, one of those lives is the political life of the city. Considering that the philosophers did not ask to be educated, do not seem to like the course of instruction they are forced to undergo, and are not the sole beneficiaries of their studies, it is unlikely that they have in any straightforward way incurred an obligation to "repay." Moreover, the benefaction comes with strings attached: in return for their superior education, the philosophers are expected to rule; their education is anything but a free gift. And, in addition, it is not left to the philosophers to determine how *they* might wish to express their gratitude for the benefaction they received: why should what the benefactor wants to receive dictate what the beneficiary owes— especially when what the benefactor demands is the very thing for the sake of which he conferred the benefaction? Furthermore, the argument leaves unaddressed the matter of the need for commensurateness between good bestowed and good returned.

The philosophers, then, who have received a benefaction they did not seek, one they might well not have wanted, one that was not bestowed solely for their benefit, one that was anything but "free," one that came with a stipulation of precisely how it is to be repaid, and one that may not be equal in value to the payment demanded in return do not stand to the city in the way a debtor stands to his creditor or a willing beneficiary to his benefactor. Socrates uses language of debt repayment in order to add moral heft to what is arguably no duty at all.[37] Even the argument's third point, namely, that the philosophers are now competent to rule, is

---

36. See 520a, where Socrates says of the law that "it produces such men in the city . . . in order that it may use them in binding the city together." The philosophers could surely object that their becoming philosophers in their own right is no more than a side effect of the city's effort to provide itself with competent leaders.

37. The personified Laws in the *Crito* also seem to conflate arguments concerning repaying a debt with arguments from benefaction. And there, too, the arguments are rhetorically charged. See Weiss 1998, chap. 6.

insufficient to ground a duty or obligation. For justice does not ordinarily require of one who is able, that he put his skills to use for the good of the community. And if that is so, then no single element of Socrates' speech to the philosophers, nor all three of them taken together, makes ruling morally incumbent on them.

Now that we have seen the argument Socrates offers in hopes of persuading the philosophers to rule, it may be instructive to consider the arguments he might have offered but did not. Socrates might simply have invoked the argument of Book 4 according to which it is "the greatest harm to the city," "extreme evil-doing," and "injustice" for the classes to meddle with each other and for each to fail to do "what is appropriate" (434b-c). If justice requires that each class do its assigned part in the city, then justice requires that philosophers rule. Indeed, it is to this obligation that Socrates points in explaining to Glaucon why "we will not be doing injustice to the philosophers" (520a): he cites the law's concern that each part of the city do its part for the city (519e-520a). Why, then, when he turns to the philosophers directly, does he say nothing about their obligation to take their proper place in the city as everyone else must? Why does he not tell them that they must "do their fair share" (Kraut 1997, 213) or that they may not be "free riders" (Brickhouse 1981, 5)? Why does he tell them instead only that they have been privileged and must "pay off the price" of their *special* treatment? That Socrates does not produce the fairness argument suggests that he does not trust the philosophers—as members of a class—to be prepared simply to do what justice demands, namely, to put the good of the city ahead of their own private good. It is likely, of course, that no other class willingly does its part or puts the good of the whole first—but are the philosophers no better than the others? Even though ruling the city is a matter of political justice, that is, of the parts of the city doing their appropriate jobs, Socrates appeals to the philosophers not as a class but rather as individuals who are morally bound to requite good with good.

Socrates might alternatively have approached the philosophers as he did Thrasymachus in Book 1; he might have said to them: "Or else you have no care for us and aren't a bit concerned whether we shall live worse or better" (344e). But he does not. If Socrates knows full well that Thrasymachus has no concern for others but nevertheless appeals to him on altruistic grounds, the fact that he does not so much as hint at the possibility that caring for others would or should motivate the philosophers loudly signals his suspicion that in this regard they are no better—or are perhaps even worse—than Thrasymachus. It seems that if they are just at all, it is only as a result of their no longer craving the things that lead to injustice; it is not because other people's interests are of concern to them.

Socrates also does not assure the philosophers of *Rep.* 7 that ruling is good for their souls, that it will make their souls ordered and healthy. Nor does he tell them it will afford them the opportunity to bring down to earth, to share with the world, the overwhelming beauty they experienced above. These are clearly not considerations that Socrates thinks will move them. Socrates is furthermore unable to tell the philosophers that ruling will make them happy: since they derive no pleasure from helping others—or even just from doing the right thing—there is little reason that it should. Socrates indeed never denies that he is making the philosophers less happy than they might have been (519e-520a). The only time the philosophers are "happy" or consider themselves so is when, like the released prisoner, they dwell in the light and, recalling their time in the dark and what passed for wisdom there, see how lucky they are to have escaped (516c).

Socrates thus frames the philosophers' obligation as narrowly as possible: as the duty to "pay off a price," as something they *must* do. He perceives them and portrays them as remarkably self-centered and as caring little or not at all about the needs of others. They are hardened men, products of coercion. Even the vision of the Good leaves them cold. If they are to rule they must be made to; they agree to rule only because they have been persuaded or compelled.[38]

The argument Socrates presents to the philosophers is, as we have seen, far from perfect. Yet this slender argument is all that stands between the philosophers' unwillingness to rule and their grudging willingness—"Do you suppose our pupils will disobey us when they hear this?" (520d). There

---

38. The mark of moderation in *Rep.* 4 is that both the ruled *and the ruler* accept their role and do not "raise faction against" the ruler: "And isn't he moderate because of the friendship and accord of these parts—when *the ruling part* and the two ruled parts are of the single opinion that the reasoning part ought to rule and don't raise faction against it?" (442c-d). The philosophers of Book 7, insofar as they prefer not to rule, fail in this way to be truly moderate. It appears that the passage in *Rep.* 4 anticipates the resistance of the philosophers of *Rep.* 7. As Benardete (1989, 88) remarks, "Rulers rarely need to be told that they should rule." See Chapter 2, note 46, and corresponding text.

can be little doubt that Socrates sees the argument's weaknesses: he presents it in the form of an oration that is unexamined and not open to question; he knows—and says—that the philosophers must be compelled (519e, 520a, 521b, 540a-b). And he designs his argument not simply to persuade but to compel—not by physical violence, to be sure, but in some other way.

Socrates never quite spells out the nature of the compulsion the founders might need to resort to, should the "just things" they say fail to persuade. His expression, "[while] compelling [them] besides (*prosanankazontes*)," however, strongly suggests that the compulsion is embedded in the very "just things" he tells them (520a). In other words, the compulsion is in some way a feature of the argument; an implicit threat lurks beneath its surface.[39] Since the philosophers believe that they reside "even while they are still alive" in a colony on the Isles of the Blessed (519c)[40] and wish to live nowhere else, surely the only thing that could persuade them to rule is the promise of continued leisure to pursue the life of the mind—or, to flip the coin to its more sinister side, the threat of having that leisure curtailed.[41] Socrates is thus in effect offering them a rather grim choice: they can either "pay," by ruling, for the good they have received—that is, for

---

39. The founders' argument is menacing in the same way the Laws' arguments in the *Crito* are. In the *Crito*, those who are indebted to "us" ("us" being the personified Laws) and refuse to pay up, do so at their peril. Wilson (1984, 196) speaks of the "barely-cloaked compulsion" in Socrates' argument in *Rep.* 7, though he doesn't specify its nature.

40. At 519b-c the city faces one of two equally undesirable consequences, depending on the point at which the potential philosophers are left to their own devices. If the founders never set the philosophers on the upward path, the philosophers would "never be adequate stewards of a city" because they would lack direction: they would have no single goal at which to aim. If, however, the founders do educate them, if they lead them up the ascent all the way to the Good, but then permit them to remain outside the Cave, they would not be willing to rule because they would see themselves as dwelling right now—that is, while still alive—on the Isles of the Blessed. Translators tend to render the present participle *eōmenous* as "those who *have been* permitted"—as if there were philosophers in some vague past who were allowed to "spend their time in education continuously to the end" (519c). But Socrates is talking about the present philosophers whom he is crafting before our very eyes: if they are permitted to dwell perpetually in the light, they will not be willing to descend to the darkness.

41. E. Brown (2000, 4) thinks it cannot be the case that Book 7's philosophers have the same reason to rule as Book 1's good and decent men do, because Socrates is charged to defend justice without recourse to its "wages." Yet it is not for being just that the good and decent men of Book 1 are compensated; they are compensated for ruling, which strict justice does not require in their case (since their regime did not educate and nurture them). As we shall see, Book 7's philosophers are compensated as well, and they, too, for ruling. See section III of this chapter.

the opportunity to live the life of philosophy—or they can refuse to rule and forfeit that good. The city that supports them in exchange for their rule can cease to indulge them should they be unwilling to rule. In that event, the philosophers would have no alternative but to sustain themselves, and would no longer be able to "live the greater part of the time with one another in the pure region" (520d).[42] Like the good and decent men of Book 1, then, the philosophers of *Rep.* 7 rule in order to avoid a "penalty" (*zēmian*—347a5, 347a7). Knowing full well how desperately his philosophers want to avoid life in the Cave, Socrates tells them twice at 520c-d, and repeats the point at 540b, that, so long as they provide the leadership for which they were trained, they will have to do no more than take their turn.

The philosophers of Book 7, it seems, do all the things they do—go up out of the Cave, endure the rigors of their educational curriculum, go back down for fifteen years, go back up again to fix their gaze on the Good, and finally, order the city, private men, and themselves—because they are compelled. It would be most peculiar if the founders' argument were, then, free of coercion, if it contained no veiled threat.[43] But it surely does: there is more than a hint of "you had better" in Socrates' imperious *humas . . . katabateon oun*, "so you must go down" (520b-c). It is hardly likely, then, that it is because the philosophers' eyes have suddenly been opened to an obligation of which they were formerly unaware that they agree to rule. They rule—if they rule—because they must, because the city leaves them little choice.

The efficacy of Socrates' argument depends, then, not on its soundness but on the force of its threat. If the argument were a proper argument from justice, and if the philosophers it addressed were truly wise and just men, how would they have failed to think of it themselves? Attempts to excuse their moral obtuseness because either (1) the fifteen years they just spent in the Cave have dulled their moral sense (E. Brown 2000, 12) or (2) "*noesis*

---

42. Reeve (1988, 203) seems to think the philosopher comes to realize on his own that "he must, as it were, exchange some ruling for the food and protection he needs in order to spend much of his time doing philosophy." If, however, the philosophers determine on their own that they must rule if they are to survive, why must Socrates present an argument to compel them?

43. Bloom (1968, 407) observes that "compulsion is necessary since rhetoric could not deceive philosophers."

is always at the level of forms, not individuals," and so "the obligation to other people must be introduced to them from outside" (Dorter 2006, 218), fall flat. On the one hand, the fifteen years during which the philosophers dwell in the Cave before they ascend to the Good ensures that "they won't be behind others in experience" (539e). If anything, these years provide the time needed for their eyes to readjust to the dark (517d-518b) so that when they descend once again to the visible realm after having at last seen the Good, they can deal effectively with practical moral matters. On the other hand, it is surely not the vision of the Good that makes the philosophers *un*able to know what is right: is it not precisely seeing the Good that equips them, once their eyes have adjusted, to "see ten thousand times better" than those who reside permanently in darkness? Should they be incapable of appreciating so simple a duty as repaying a debt? Should they not know that it is unjust not to acknowledge a benefaction received? If not, how are they to lead others?[44]

Only Glaucon trusts that the philosophers are just men (*dikaiois*) who will respond to Socrates' argument as a call to justice. He confidently asserts that, as just men, they will do the "just things . . . we will order" (*dikaia . . . epitaxomen*   520e). "It is impossible," he says, that they would not now "obey us" but would continue to be "not willing to join in the labors of the city, each in his turn" (520d-e).[45] To be sure, he expects the philosophers to rule only as a "necessary thing" (520e): it is likely that he has not quite relinquished the view of justice he expressed (ostensibly in the name of the many) in Book 2, namely, that justice is undesirable in itself, that it belongs

---

44. A novel solution to the problem of the philosophers' apparent moral obtuseness is provided by Smith (2010, 95–98). Smith agrees with Brickhouse (1981, 7; contra E. Brown 2000, 1 n. 1; and Reeve 1988, 195) that the recalcitrant rulers have already apprehended the Good. According to Smith's timetable, the would-be philosophers first see the Good and are only then compelled to serve as "apprentice rulers" for a period of fifteen years. The reason they are unable at this time to appreciate their moral obligation to rule, Smith suggests, is that during this entire period the returners' eyes are not fully adjusted to the darkness. The text, however, at 539e-540b, leaves little doubt that the fifteen years of "adjustment" precede the vision of the Good: during those years the philosophers are said to rule in "all the offices suitable for *young* men" (539e) in order that they gain "experience." And it is only subsequently, when they are fifty years old, that they must "at last"—that is, for the first time—"be led to the end" (540a). They are thus compelled to return to the city both before and after their vision of the Good (539e, 540a-b). Surely by the second time they descend their vision should be sharp enough for them to know the moral basics.

45. The rhetoric that may well fail to persuade the philosophers (see note 43 above) may nevertheless sway Glaucon.

in the lowest category of goods, which contains things one does as drudgery (*epipona*) and only for the sake of desirable consequences (357c-358a). For the philosophers of Callipolis those consequences are that they will get to live "the greater part of the time with one another in the pure region" (520d; also 540b). Glaucon, from the very start, has been eager to learn what incentive—what "penalty"—would motivate the best sort of man to rule (1.347a). In Book 1 he got his first answer: good and decent men rule in order not to be ruled by worse men. He now has his second.

IV. Compulsion

One of the clearest indications that the new breed of philosopher does not wish to rule—and that consent to rule comes only with the greatest reluctance—is the pervasiveness of compulsion language (*anankazein* and its cognates) in *Rep.* 7. To insist, as many scholars do, that the philosophers rule willingly and gladly, happily doing what is just because they recognize how good being just is for them or for others, is either to ignore the ubiquity of compulsion in *Rep.* 7 or to explain it away or domesticate it as something else—as a moral requirement, as self-compulsion, as something necessitated by logic—thereby removing its sting.[46] But any attempt to muffle the persistent drumbeat of compulsion in Book 7, however well-meaning, serves only to obscure Socrates' clear intent.

The sheer frequency of the appearance in Book 7 of words deriving from the *anank*-root (515c6, 515d5, 515d9, 519c9, 519e4, 520a8, 520d4, 521b7, 525d6, 526b1-2, 526e3, 526e7, 529a1, 537b1, 593e4),[47] in conjunction with such terms as "by force" (*biāi*—515e5) and "drag" (*helkoi*—515e5; *helkomenon*—516a1), should leave no doubt in the reader's mind that when

---

46. The idea that the philosophers are somehow compelled to do what they really don't want to do meets fierce scholarly resistance. See, for example, Kraut (1973, 342–43), who, although he accepts that the philosopher's "love of the Forms exceeds his love of the polis," and admits therefore that the philosopher consequently needs to be "directed" or "prodded" by his "colleagues," denies nevertheless that compulsion entails "action against one's will." It is not the case, he asserts, "that the philosopher positively dislikes ruling, that he has no desire whatever to do so."

47. The *anank*-root appears many, many more times in *Rep.* 7, thoroughly saturating the book, but in these other instances it does not suggest external compulsion.

Socrates says compulsion he means compulsion—external compulsion. Just as "someone" (*tis*—515d-e) forces the prisoner to leave the Cave and drags him, despite his distress and annoyance, up the ascent, so, too, there is a "someone" (*tis*—521c2), a "you" (Glaucon—521b7), and a "we" (the founders collectively—519c),[48] whose task it is to coerce the philosophers every step of the way and to see to it that they are not permitted to "turn whichever way each wants" (*trepesthai hopēi hekastos bouletai*—520a).[49]

The most frequent weak reading of *anankazein* takes it in the sense of "necessitated." On this reading, once the philosophers come to appreciate that it is their duty to rule, they are necessitated to rule by ruling's very rightness.[50] Shields thus traces the compulsion to an agentless nomic modality of "metaphysical obligation" (2007, 39), that is, to the way in which

---

48. In response to Strauss's (1964, 124) contention that philosophers would never be willing to compel the people to compel them to rule, it should be said that Socrates' scheme seems to assign a rather wider role to the *founders* than Strauss supposes. The founders' first job is to persuade people to accept rule by philosophers—not an easy task, since those who remain in the Cave are prepared to kill anyone who threatens to release one of them and lead him up (517a). The people then nurture and educate the philosophers to rule; the founders, as their agents, train the first set of philosopher-rulers. The founders next persuade and/or compel the philosophers to rule. The philosophers then take it from there: they—not the people—persuade the next generation of philosophers to rule. One problem with this scheme is, of course, that founders who are not themselves philosophers in the requisite sense nevertheless lead the potential philosophers to the highest reaches of the transcendent realm.

49. The *Republic* contains other instances of doing "whatever one wants." At 2.359c the invisibility procured by turning the ring of Gyges "gives each, the just man and the unjust, license to do whatever he wants" (*poiein hoti an boulētai*); and at 360b-c and 362b the man who has such a ring can take anything desired from the market, have intercourse with "whomever he wants," slay and release from bonds "whomever he wants" (like a god [!] among men), take in marriage a woman from whatever station, give in marriage whomever he wants, contract and form partnerships with whomever he wants. In Book 8 at 537b the democratic regime is described as consisting of men who have license to do in it "whatever one wants." This expression reminds us of Polus in the *Gorgias* (466b-c), who so admires rhetoricians that he elevates them to the ranks of tyrants: "Do rhetoricians not, just like tyrants, kill whomever they wish, and confiscate possessions, and expel from the cities whomever they please?"

50. Irwin (1995, 299) is representative: "The relevant sort of necessity is not legal or physical compulsion imposed by the coercive powers of the rulers; for since the philosophers are just people, they want to do what justice requires and do not need to be coerced into doing it. They recognize that ruling is necessary if they are to fulfill the requirements of justice; this sort of necessity need not involve coercion." Dorter (2006, 218) holds a view similar to Irwin's. See, too, Ferrari ([2003] 2005, 29), who thinks the philosopher rules not unwillingly (*akōn*), but "is considering what means are necessary to achieve a certain aim." Eric Brown's notion of acquiescing to law was discussed above in section I.

the Form of the Good impinges on the philosophers' awareness (38). And Cathal Woods (2009, 4) says that "the so-called 'compulsion' takes the form of thoughts about justice." A second weak reading takes the compulsion to be self-compulsion:[51] perhaps the philosophers would prefer not to rule but, it is argued, when they come to see the impropriety of refusing to rule, they compel themselves to rule.

As we saw in Chapter 2, section III, however, one of the marks that distinguish the philosophers of Book 7 from those of Book 6 is precisely that those of Book 7 have nothing internal to propel them: just as they lack the erotic impulse that drives Book 6's philosophers upward, just as they have to be turned in the right direction and their ties to the material world severed, so do "just things" have to be said to them while "compelling them besides" (*prosanankazontes*—520a) to care for those who need them.[52] Although they see the Good, the philosophers of *Rep.* 7 "must be compelled"—by others—to order the city, private men, and themselves accordingly (*anankasteon . . . kosmein*) (540a-b). Everything that happens in Book 7 is therefore by design: the convergence of philosophy and political power is not left to happy coincidence (as it was at 5.473c); philosophic rule is not "necessitated *by chance* (*ek tuchēs*)" as in Book 6 (499b-c, 502a-b). On the contrary, promising young people are converted quite deliberately into philosophers and put in charge of their city.

---

51. See Rosen 2005, 230; Cooper 2000, 20. Strauss (1964, 128) doesn't rule out the possibility that compulsion is self-compulsion. Cf. Lampert (2010, 370), for whom the self-compulsion is driven not by moral considerations but by "the unique self-interest of the philosopher, the interests of philosophy. In the service of the rational, the philosopher goes down." Since, however, the argument that is presented to Book 7's philosophers in order to persuade them to rule is not of their own devising, it seems unreasonable to speak in their case of self-compulsion.

52. Scott (2007, 151) thus incorrectly supposes that it is *erōs* that makes philosophers (as it does tyrants) "asocial." It is in fact not the erotic philosophers of Book 6 but rather Book 7's nonerotic philosophers who don't care for others. Scott relies on 3.402e-403a to support an alleged Socratic association of *erōs* with hubris (141), yet in that passage it is not *erōs* but excessive sexual pleasure (*hēdonēi huperballousēi*) to which Socrates links hubris and licentiousness; Socrates actually commends the kind of *erōs* that is naturally proper or right as moderate and musical, orderly and fine, and regards it as "utterly distinct from licentiousness and madness" (403b). See, too, 402d, where the musical man, one who lacks harmony, would love (*erōiē*) those who are fairest, whereas moderation is wholly incompatible with indulgence in excessive pleasure.

None of this is to deny that *anankazein* and its cognates have many meanings. Shields divides its senses into four categories (2007, 27);[53] many more can be identified. The root appears some 270 times in the *Republic*, and its meanings are so wide-ranging as to resist neat compartmentalization or easy plotting along any sort of spectrum. Among *ananke*'s varied uses are, on one end, the goddess Necessity in Book 10 (616c, 618d, 621a) and the (hopelessly indecipherable) "necessity of Diomede" (493d) in Book 6, and, on the other, obvious cases of people compelling other people to do things they would rather not do. To be sure, in many instances in which *anankazein* is used, neither compulsion from outside nor opposition on the part of the party compelled is implied.[54] And on at least one occasion in the *Republic* it is an argument that is said to compel (611b9–10). But in the case of the philosophers there are specific people designated, namely, the founders, whose very job it is to compel them (519c): "We will say just things to them while compelling them besides" (520a). Socrates nowhere suggests that the philosophers of Book 7 compel themselves or feel themselves compelled by a justice argument of their own devising. What Socrates asks Glaucon at the conclusion of the argument he presents on behalf of the founders is whether the philosophers will disobey *us* (*hēmin*—520d), and Glaucon responds that their disobedience is impossible because *we* will impose (*epitaxomen*—520e) just things on them.

The compulsion the philosophers of *Rep.* 7 are subjected to involves, as we have seen, a suppressed threat embedded in the founders' speech as well as an explicit *order* in it to "go down." As such, the way in which these philosophers are made to rule is not only unlike the necessity involved in the ruling of Book 6's philosophers ("Some necessity by chance [*ek tuchēs*] imposes on those few philosophers who aren't vicious . . . to care for [*epimelēthēnai*] a city" [499b]; also 500d: "if some necessity *arises*

---

53. Shields's categories are: external and proper, external and improper, internal and improper, and internal and proper.

54. Two such instances are particularly interesting: 5.473d, where the coincidence (*sumpesēi*) of political power and philosophy—which is surely something that happens by chance—nevertheless necessarily (*ex anankēs*) excludes the one being present without the other; and 6.499b, where "some necessity" (*ananke tis*) "by chance" (*ek tuchēs*) imposes on the decent philosophers to care for a city—whether they want to or not." In the first instance the necessity supervenes on a chance occurrence; in the second the necessity is itself a matter of chance.

[*genētai*] for him"), but differs, too, from the "necessity" that induces the good and decent men of Book 1 to rule: they fear—on their own—being ruled by inferior men; in the absence of inferior men they won't rule. The philosophers of Book 7 are more like the poets of Books 2 and 3 who are coerced adventitiously: the agent of the compulsion is someone other than its target.

When in Book 8 Socrates describes the permissiveness with respect to rule that is a feature of the democratic city, he is clearly contrasting it with the coerciveness that marks Book 7's city. In the democracy, Socrates says, no compulsion is brought to bear on one who is competent to rule; he is free not to rule if he does not wish to. Similarly, no one who is incompetent is prevented from ruling: even when there is a law that would forbid one who is unfit to rule or to serve as a judge, there is no power to ensure its enforcement (557e-558a). Both the laxness in the democracy with respect to its people, and the compulsion in Callipolis with respect to all three of its classes, including the ruling one, are external.

The way in which the tyrannic nature discussed in Book 9 comes to be a tyrant also stands in marked contrast to the way Book 7's philosophers become rulers. It might happen, Socrates says, that one who possesses such a nature is "compelled by some chance" (*anakasthēi hupo tinos tuchēs*) to "tyrant" (*turanneusai*—579c). Here Socrates clearly does not envision a "someone" who deliberately ushers in this calamitous event. The tyrannic nature that comes to rule is in this respect just like Book 6's philosophers and decidedly unlike Book 7's. For in Book 7 the matter is not left to chance.

The philosophers of Book 7, then, who do not wish to rule, and have to be persuaded or compelled to do so, have little in common with the philosophers of Book 6, who do wish to rule under reasonable conditions, even though, insofar as they "grow up spontaneously against the will of the regime," they surely have no obligation to do so. Book 6's philosophers do not share Book 7's aversion to the human realm: on the contrary, their souls always "reach out . . . for everything divine *and human*" (486a).[55] The compensation that Book 7's philosophers receive (in advance) for ruling—that they are "begotten" and educated by the city and are thus able to (and permitted to) participate in the contemplative life—has no

---

55. See Chapter 1, note 21.

counterpart in Book 6. Whereas Book 6's philosophers are thus gener-
ously willing to rule   without compensation   for the sake of improving
the souls of others but are prevented from doing so by the corruption of
their cities' regimes, Book 7's are selfishly averse to ruling even when
their city has groomed them for just this task and eagerly awaits their
guidance.

The reason the philosophers of Book 7 have to be compelled to rule,
have to be commanded to do so (*katabateon*—520c)—just as they have to
be forced, as we saw in Chapter 2, section III, to ascend to the Good and
to order their own souls (as well as to leave the visible realm and to be
educated)—is that none of these activities is something they desire. (Compare Glaucon's "No one is willingly just but only when compelled [*ananka-
zomenos*] to be so" [360c].) The evidence provided, first, by the allegory of
the Cave, second, by how unambiguously and explicitly the philosophers'
unwillingness to rule is expressed (517c-d, 519c-d; cf. the Cave image:
516d-e), and, third, by the sheer frequency of references to compulsion,
heavily favors taking *anankazein* with respect to the philosophers of *Rep. 7*
in its strongest sense.

The alternative view, the view that Callipolis's founders do not make
the philosophers do what they would prefer not to do, would require
us to believe that (1) contrary to the implications of the allegory of the
Cave, the philosophers do not start out with a strong attachment to the
visible world from which they have to be forcibly wrenched and, if left
to themselves, would turn on their own toward the higher realm; and
(2) the repeated references to compulsion in Book 7 could just as easily
be replaced by the language of coming to hold an opinion or of being
persuaded by an argument. Yet, we have seen at 518c-519b, even apart
from the allegory, that the philosophers are appetitive by nature and
feel at home in the visible realm. They are made to ascend to a realm
for which they have extraordinary aptitude but no love (519b-520d;
540a-b). And when they come at long last to appreciate and prefer the
exquisite luminousness of the higher realm, they find the prospect of
returning to the darkness of the material realm repugnant (540b). If
they in the end take on the two tasks that are anathema to them—
ruling the city and ruling themselves—they can hardly be thought to
do so of their own accord.

V. Justice

We have seen that Glaucon regards the philosophers of Book 7 as just men.[56] They will "obey us" and not be unwilling to rule, he thinks, because, as just men, they will respond appropriately to the "just things" they are told, to the argument cast in terms of duty with which they are presented. (Glaucon, it appears, fails to detect either the logical weaknesses in Socrates' justice argument or the threat implicit in it.) Socrates, however, does not affirm the justness of these philosophers—either here or anywhere else in Book 7.[57] He may agree with Glaucon's assessment that they "will certainly approach ruling as a necessary thing" (520e), but does he share, too, Glaucon's opinion that they are just, that justice matters to them?[58]

From the information we are given we have no reason to think that justice counts as a consideration for the philosophers at all. Not only does Socrates have to urge them to be just at the most basic level—that of repaying a debt—but we never actually see them considering their options and choosing justice. We aren't told that they come to regard themselves as morally obligated to rule because they see ruling as required by justice. And Socrates seems to think they need an incentive to rule, something to compel them.

Nor is there any indication that it is important to the philosophers of *Rep.* 7 that anyone else be just. Yet, in his conversation with Polemarchus about justice in Book 1 (335b-335e) Socrates argues in effect—although he doesn't say so explicitly—that it is the business of justice and the just man

---

56. The question of whether *Rep.* 7's philosophers are just will be revisited in Chapter 4, section VII.

57. Commentators have tended to assume, with Glaucon, that the philosophers are just men. They have not noticed, or have not thought it significant, that it is not Socrates but Glaucon who thinks well of them.

58. That Socrates' agreement, "That's the way it is, my comrade" (520e), applies only to Glaucon's assertion that the philosophers will approach ruling "as a necessary thing"—not to his assumption that the philosophers will obey us because we will be ordering just men to do just things—is confirmed by what he goes on to say. Socrates develops at some length (520e4–520b10) the ruling-as-necessary point, arguing that a city will be well governed only if the rulers have a life they regard as better than the political; he says nothing at all, however, about how critical it is that the rulers be just.

to make human beings just. Socrates draws an analogy between cooling and wetting, on the one hand, and justice, on the other. Cooling, he argues, is not the work of heat but of its opposite, wetting not the work of dryness but of its opposite; it follows, therefore, that making others unjust is not the work of justice but of its opposite. (The argument replaces "making bad" or "making unjust" with "injuring," but it had already established that when people are injured they "become worse with respect to human virtue" and that "justice is human virtue" [335c].) Of course, the same argument can be put positively: if the job of cooling is to make things cool and that of wetness to make things wet, it follows that the business of justice and the just man is to make human beings just. Socrates' point is clear: justice is active; it, like cooling and heating, reaches out to others.[59]

If justice involves more than repaying a debt, if it means that the interests of others, particularly as concerns their moral rectitude, have a part to play in the choices one makes, then the philosophers of *Rep.* 7 certainly do not qualify as fully just.[60] They see nothing noble (540b) in ordering the city, private men, and themselves in accordance with the Form of the Good. Unlike Socrates, for whom justice belongs in the "noblest" of the three categories of goods that Glaucon presents at the start of Book 2 (358a), the philosophers—were they to give the matter any thought— might well place justice, along with ruling, in the lowest category. And so, instead of seeing justice as desirable both for itself and for its consequences, as Socrates does, it is likely that they would regard it as an unwelcome means to desired ends. Just as justice, from the perspective of the many is, as Glaucon asserts, a form of "drudgery" (*epiponou*) that "all by itself

---

59. Since Socrates' purpose in this section of Book 1 is limited to refuting Polemarchus's contention that justice involves harming enemies no less than helping friends (332a), he is content to have Polemarchus grant only the negative conclusion that "it is not the work of the just man to harm either a friend or anyone else, but of his opposite, the unjust man" (335d). Polemarchus, like Thrasymachus, thinks it's important to help, and to be able to help, one's friends. In the *Crito*, Crito would be ashamed to be thought indifferent to his friend Socrates' plight (44b-c); he also thinks Socrates should care for his family (45c-d). But what is most repugnant to Crito about Socrates' refusal to escape from prison is that he thereby furthers his enemies' ends (45c).

60. Yu (2000, 125) distinguishes two senses of just—practical and intellectual—thereby salvaging some sense in which the philosophers are "just": they have, he says, "intellectual justice." Yet, for Yu (136–37), although the philosophers "will not do something that is opposed to conventional justice," they are not altruistically just: they will not rule a city willingly.

should be fled from (*pheukteon*) as something hard" (358a), so, too, do the philosophers of *Rep.* 7 "drudge" (*epitalaipōrountos*) in politics (540b). Yet surely neither justice nor just rule should be viewed as the kind of good that is no more than a necessary evil; it certainly should not appear so to just men. Would a truly good man show no regard for the needs of others when he is uniquely positioned to help them? The founders care for the city; why don't the philosophers? When Socrates says of justice that it "ought to be liked by the man who is going to be blessed both for itself and for what comes out of it" (358a), is it not *Rep.* 7's philosophers whom he has in mind? Are they not the most blessed of men, men who "believe they have emigrated (*apoikisthai*) to a colony on the Isles of the Blessed while they are still alive" (519c) and who are destined for those same isles when they die (540b)?[61] And in saying not that justice *is* liked by the man who is going to be blessed but rather that it *ought to be* liked (*agapēteon*) by him, does Socrates not hint that those who are going to be blessed may not value justice as they ought? The philosophers, it seems, either give justice no thought at all or consider it to be, like ruling, necessary drudgery.[62]

One thing we do know, however, is that the philosophers cannot be trusted to give up what they prefer to be doing—contemplating the Forms—on their own, just "for the sake of the city"; if they could, the founders would not have to see to it that they don't "turn whichever way each wants" (520a), would not have to compel them to rule, would not have to forbid them to do "what is now permitted" (519d). However unlikely it is that the philosophers would commit an outright injustice of the kind to which ordinary men are prone, it is nevertheless doubtful that they would readily give up the life of contemplation in order to rule others. If they have to be prevented from turning whichever way they want, then the way they want does not include ruling.

There is but one passage in Book 7 that may seem to suggest that the philosophers do in fact place a premium on justice.

---

61. At 419a Adeimantus regards the guardians as those who are "going to be blessed." He complains that although these men are the ones "to whom the city in truth belongs," they are wrongfully deprived in Socrates' fair city of the appurtenances of the good life that are their due.

62. Burnyeat's view (1985, 34) is thus hard to sustain. Since ruling "can give [the philosophers] nothing they value," he says, they rule because their education in mathematics and philosophy "teaches them to know and love justice."

When the true philosophers, either one or more, come to power in a city, they will despise the current honors and believe them to be illiberal and worth nothing. Taking what is right and the honors coming from it as of greatest moment, and what is just as the greatest and the most necessary, and indeed serving and fostering it, they will provide for their own city. (540d-e)

A careful examination of this passage, however, reveals that justice is not the philosophers' own favored goal but is the virtue they both adopt for themselves and promote in the city once they have been compelled to take their turn at rule. It is true that they care nothing for the honors and prizes of the Cave, and that their indifference to such vulgar things makes them good rulers when they exercise rule. As we observed above in section I, they are not the worst sort of rulers, whose eagerness to rule derives from a desire for money and power; their deficiency lies in their lack of interest in ruling, in their disdain for the visible realm and its inhabitants. Nevertheless, in their role as rulers they indeed take "what is right" as of greatest moment and derive from implementing it the honors due them as judicious rulers, as well as the public memorials and sacrifices dedicated to them, no doubt, because they are also warriors (see 3.414a). They are memorialized and offered sacrifices as if they are divinities (*daimosin*) or at least as happy (*eudaimosi*) and divine men (540b-c).

It is striking that whereas the philosopher-rulers thus regard justice as "greatest" (*megiston*) and "most necessary" (*anankaiotaton*) for governing the city,[63] they are not said to regard it as either "best" (*beltiston*) or "most noble" (*kalliston*). The term "most necessary" as applied to justice recalls the sophists of Book 6, who call the necessary "just and noble" (6.493c). In the case of the sophists, it is because they lack knowledge that they apply to what is necessary the terms "just" and "noble": they have "neither seen nor are able to show someone else how much the nature of the necessary and the good really differ" (493c); "knowing nothing in truth" about the noble and shameful, good and bad, just and unjust, they can only follow

---

63. The expression "their own city" is used literally here to mean the city they govern. In Book 9 at 592a-b, however, the phrase "his own city" means his own soul. See the discussion of this passage in Chapter 5, addendum II.

the opinions of the multitude (that "great animal") and make their virtue-terms and vice-terms correspond to what the many like and dislike.[64] The philosophers, by contrast, know the good, just, and noble things, and thus have no comparable excuse for taking the just as "most necessary"; they should see the just as more than what must be done if the city is to flourish under their rule. Although the philosophers then do not, any more than sophists, distinguish in the human world between the necessary and the just, they do differentiate, as we have seen, between the necessary and the noble, insofar as they regard ruling as necessary but not as noble (540b). If, for the philosophers, the just is necessary but the necessary not invariably noble, it is likely that they do not think of the just as noble. They may recognize that justice is most important—even indispensable—if the city is to function as it should, but there is no indication that otherwise, that is, outside the political context, they have any particular admiration for it.

There is, finally, the matter of the way in which the philosophers plan to go about promoting the city's justice. Glaucon raises the question with a perfunctory "How?" (540e), prompting Socrates to outline an alarmingly monstrous procedure.[65] Though the philosophers' course of action is shockingly offensive, Socrates presents it as nonchalantly as if it were perfectly benign and as offhandedly as if he were merely repeating something Glaucon had already heard before. The philosophers, Socrates says, will send out to the country everyone who is older than ten, will impose their authority on the children who remain behind, and will erase all traces of the older generation's dispositions, substituting for these their own manners and laws (540e–541a). How can the reader fail to be horrified by the philosophers' plan[66]—particularly since its purported purpose is to promote *justice*? How can anyone think it just to banish an entire adult population—especially when it was these very grown-ups who did the nurturing and educating that prepared the philosophers to rule, and for which the philosophers are

---

64. On the sophists' view of the necessary, see Chapter 1, note 72.

65. Nichols (1984, 265) calls it "perfect horror."

66. Some seek to minimize the horrific nature of Socrates' proposal by pointing to the Athenian practice of establishing cleruchies, faraway colonies to which Athens deported its impoverished citizens. See Cohen 1983, 64–65. But population transfer is hardly the same as banishing the adult population—and only the adult population—of a city, and sending it "out to the country" (*eis tous agrous*—541a).

beholden to the city?[67] The manners and laws that the philosophers propose to implement—once they no longer need fear resistance or skepticism from the old guard—prominently include the design of the city that was announced in Book 5 and is about to be reviewed at the start of Book 8: "Women must be in common, children and their entire education must be in common, and similarly the practices in war and peace must be in common, and their kings must be those among them who have proved best in philosophy and with respect to war" (8.543a). The philosophers are to direct their efforts toward producing a city and regime that will "itself be happy and most profit the nation in which it comes to be" (541a).

In many respects the mode of rule implemented by *Rep.* 7's philosophers represents a radical departure from that of the philosophers of Book 6. First, the emphasis in Book 7 is on improving the city—as opposed to the citizens—with respect to justice (there is only the briefest mention of "ordering city, private men, and themselves" [540b]),[68] whereas in Book 6 it is the task of improving the citizens that takes center stage (with only a quick reference to the need to rewrite the laws of the city [501a]). Indeed, in Book 6, the philosophers' activity with respect to individual souls is described in some detail: they will replace the current state of individual souls with human dispositions that are dearer to the gods, "looking away in both directions, toward the just, noble, and moderate by nature and everything of the sort, and, again, toward what is in human beings" (501b), "rubbing out one thing and drawing in another again" (501c). Second, and most striking, there is no mandate in Book 6 to send anyone away. Whatever else rubbing out and drawing in, "mixing and blending the practices as ingredients" (501b), might mean, one thing it surely does not mean is exiling everyone over ten. As was noted in Chapter 1, section I.C, the whimsical image of philosophers scrubbing old dispositions clean and drawing fresh new dispositions in their place can be understood only metaphorically. Yet the concrete plan to send away everyone over ten can be taken quite literally—and, so taken, there is nothing in the least amusing or charming about it. In Book 7, the philosophers banish the bad dispositions (*ēthōn*) (541a); in Book 6, they fix all dispositions (*ēthē*—501a, 501c).

---

67. The philosophers' plan is only needed the first time around. See note 48 above.
68. See note 27 above.

Third, there is patent cruelty in Book 7's plan, a willful indifference to the plight of those deported—as well as to that of those left behind without parents and older siblings. Nothing remotely like it is found in Book 6:[69] in Book 6 those who have antipathy toward philosophy are to be "soothed" and their slander stopped by "pointing out [to them] whom you mean by the philosophers" (499e); they are not to be treated as pariahs to be cast out of the city. And fourth, whereas Book 7's aims are accomplished "most quickly and easily" (Glaucon concurs: "So it is by far [*Polu*]"—541a)— no matter that the cost is exiling all but the children—the process in Book 6 is laborious: "And that's hardly easy (*ou panu rhāidion*)" (501a).[70] It is apparently too much to ask of the philosophers of Book 7 that they tax themselves for the sake of others. Better to have them rid themselves of the problem than require them to address it.

The philosophers' act of sending parents away lest their dispositions rub off on their children is reminiscent of another reference in Book 7 to parents and children: the image of the changeling child (537e-539c). This image, invoked to explain why dialectic is best reserved for older men, depicts a child who, having learned that the people he thought were his parents really aren't, rejects them and takes up with his flatterers. It teaches that youngsters whose honored convictions are tested and refuted become susceptible to a life of flattery unless they find true beliefs to replace the traditional ones that could not survive scrutiny. The philosophers of Book 7, like the adopted child who learns the truth, and like the young men whose conventional beliefs cannot be sustained, have contempt for the old. They thus mercilessly banish the older people—along with their

---

69. The coldhearted practice of exiling all those over ten is reminiscent of Book 5's similarly callous plan to hide away "in an unspeakable and unseen place, as is seemly," infants who are of poor stock or deformed (460c). It reminds us, too, of Book 3's proposal that those who have chronically sick bodies be permitted to die, and those who have incurably sick souls be killed (410a). In the *Gorgias* the man who is incurably evil is said to be no better off living than dead (512a); and it is *only because* he has passed the point where anything can be done to profit him that in death he is put to use as an example to others, as a way to benefit them (525c). In the *Laws*, too, death puts an end to the bad state of incurable criminals' souls only on the assumption that "it is not better *for them* if they go on living" (862e). The *Republic*, however, kills incurables because to do so is best for the city.

70. Socrates says in Book 5 that the change from nonphilosophic to philosophic rule is "not, however, a small or an easy one" (473c). Note, too, Socrates' remark at 497d: "As the saying goes, noble things are hard." For further instances, see Chapter 1, note 56.

dispositions—from their city. The philosophers of Book 6, by contrast, though they, too, require a clean slate on which to etch their reforms,[71] do not callously toss out the older people but try to improve their souls along with the souls of the young. After all, not every adopted child who learns the truth no longer cares for his adoptive family; one who is "by nature particularly decent" is an exception to the rule (538c).

Remarkably—or perhaps not—Glaucon voices no objection to this malevolent plan; somehow, he is not aghast. On the contrary, he appears to like that it is quick and easy, and thinks Socrates has "stated well" how this beautiful city would come into being, "if it ever were to come into being" (541a-b). Glaucon prefers that the philosophers be burdened as little as possible. His early fear that they might be unjustly compelled to live a worse life when a better is possible reflects his belief that superior men should be left to themselves, free to do as they like. He conveniently "forgets" (519e) that they have a part to play in the city and that they are not at liberty to evade their duty. Glaucon is not puzzled or alarmed by their having to be told to pay their debts, by their having to be ordered to go down. He expects them to be selfish, to calculate their interest, to rule for a short time in exchange for benefits already received and for the opportunity to continue enjoying the contemplative life they favor.

And what of Socrates? How does he regard the philosophers of Book 7? If he thought well of them, if he saw them as just men, would not the substance and tone of his argument to them have been different? Would he have felt the need to say to them in effect: "In light of all we did for you, you now *must go down*"? There is no gentleness in his address, no appreciation of the supposed goodness of these men. There is certainly no expectation that these are men who would care about others, who, in discharging their obligation, would even notice others. The philosophers of Book 7 are simply not like those of Book 6. In Book 6 we saw men of sterling character; in Book 7 "a special guard" is needed to distinguish the bastard philosophers from the genuinely virtuous (536a). In Book 6 the philosopher is forced to isolate himself from the community for fear of corruption; in Book 7 the philosopher is compelled to relinquish his *preferred* isolation

---

71. They do not, then, as Socrates initially intimated they would, "preserve those [laws] that are already established" (484d), unless, of course, some of the already established laws are good ones that they see fit to enact anew. See Chapter 1, note 57.

and join a community for which he has disdain. In Book 6 the philosopher is useless but decent; in Book 7 the philosopher is converted from useless and harmful to useful and helpful: he is never decent; he would shirk his responsibilities if he could. But a truly just man would not find serving others disagreeable; he would regard justice as noble and good, even as desirable in itself.[72]

VI. Conclusion

Cicero has been famously critical of the *Republic*'s philosophers:

> And so there is reason to fear that what Plato declares of the philosophers may be inadequate, when he says that they are just, because they are busied with the pursuit of truth and because they despise and count as naught that which most men eagerly seek and for which they are prone to do battle against each other to the death. For they secure one sort of justice, to be sure, in that they do no positive wrong to anyone, but they fall into the opposite injustice; for hampered by their pursuit of learning they leave to their fate those whom they ought to defend. And so, Plato thinks, they will not even assume their civic duties except under compulsion. But in fact it were better that they should assume them of their own accord, for an action intrinsically right is just only on condition that it is voluntary. (*Off*. 1.9.28)

Cicero's reproach is surely on target—with respect to the philosophers of Book 7.[73] For it is the philosophers of *Rep*. 7 who do no injustice but assume their civic duties only under duress. As we have seen, however, these are not Plato's only philosophers. The philosophers by nature of *Rep*. 6, philosophers who rule willingly so long as they are not shunned or their lives endangered, make it possible to vindicate Plato and his philosophers

---

72. On this point I depart from my view in Weiss 2007, 112–13. As Aristotle says (*EN* 2.3.1104b), the mark of a man who has become virtuous is that he experiences virtuous activity as pleasant or at least not as painful.

73. Popper's notorious excoriation of the *Republic* as a totalitarian manifesto (1945, vol. 1) is similarly not without justification when applied to Callipolis as governed by Book 7's philosopher-warriors. See, too, Runciman (2010, 37–39), who defends Popper's view, taking the *Republic*'s utopia to task for its "repressive authoritarianism."

in Cicero's eyes. Only near the close of Book 6 does the sunny fantasy of willing rulers governing obedient subjects give way to the darker, more disturbing utopia of Book 7. It is, of course, far from certain that either of these cities could actually come to fruition. The first depends on the many's being persuaded that philosophers are admirable (499d-500a)—yet how can they appreciate philosophers if they themselves cannot be philosophic (494a)? The second depends on the founders' being able, first, to create philosophers out of men who have no natural yearning for wisdom, truth, and being and, second, to compel these philosophers to rule once they have seen the Good. Even if neither city is realizable in practice, only Book 6's represents any sort of Platonic ideal. It is Book 6's city that Socrates de-clares is best—if, as is not quite impossible, it can come to be (502c). We are all better off, however, if Book 7's city never gets beyond the blueprint stage.

Addendum: *Rep.* 1's Good and Decent Men

The philosophers of Book 7 most closely resemble the good and decent men of *Rep.* 1, men who are no more good and decent than Book 7's phi-losophers are "wholly noble" (in Glaucon's phrase—540c). The reader who greets Socrates' apparent adulation of Book 1's exemplary men with skepticism is best equipped to see through his seeming support for their philosophic doppelgängers in Book 7. Can Socrates really believe that a genuinely good and decent man would avoid at all costs taking the trou-ble to benefit another?

Good and decent men are introduced into the discussion when Socrates, exploiting Thrasymachus's notion of "ruler in the precise sense," casts him not (as Thrasymachus does) as the stronger man who knows his own ad-vantage and thus unerringly furthers it (1.340c-341a), but as one who looks out for the interests of the weaker men he rules. Comparing the political ruler and political rule to other "ruling" craftsmen and crafts—the pilot who rules sailors, the doctor who rules bodies, and the horsemanship that rules horses—Socrates contends that since craftsmen and crafts are not de-ficient (342a-b), they seek the advantage, not of themselves (342b) but of "what is weaker and ruled by" them (342d). That craftsmen earn money for their efforts is wholly irrelevant to their enterprise—"in the precise sense."

Reacting violently to Socrates' "driveling" (343a), Thrasymachus derides the idea that shepherds seek the good of the sheep rather than either their masters' good or their own.[74] Indeed, the very thought that rulers might consider "night and day anything else than how they will benefit themselves" (343b-c) prompts him to ridicule Socrates' naïveté with respect to justice: justice is always, Thrasymachus asserts, "someone else's good, the advantage of the man who is stronger and rules, and a personal injury to the man who obeys and serves" (343c). Thrasymachus mocks justice and the just man, holding up large-scale injustice as the source of power and freedom and as profitable and advantageous "for oneself" (344c).

Not to be outdone by Thrasymachus, Socrates ramps up his own rhetoric. Arguing, as earlier, that "every kind of rule, insofar as it is rule, considers what is best for nothing other than what is ruled and cared for, both in political and private rule" (345d-e), he now makes the further, stunning claim that "no one is willing (*ethelei*) to rule willingly (*hekōn*)" (345e), a claim that is designed to, and that indeed does, elicit a scornful snicker from Thrasymachus. Asked if he thinks that "those who truly rule, rule willingly," Thrasymachus replies: "By Zeus, I don't think it; I know it well" (345e).[75]

Socrates' defense of his new claim that all rulers, like all "ruling" craftsmen, rule only unwillingly begins with a notion that is familiar from an earlier phase of the debate, namely, that moneymaking is strictly separate from the specific art of the craftsman; it is now a distinct "art" (341c-342e), which he dubs "the wage-earner's art" (346b).[76] This art, he says, is practiced by all craftsmen in conjunction with their various specialized crafts, for the specialized crafts indeed bestow benefit but not on the craftsmen

---

74. Cf. Aristotle, *EN* 8.11.1161a: "The friendship of a king for those who live under his rule depends on his superior ability to do good. He confers benefits upon his subjects, since he is good and cares for them in order to promote their welfare, just as a shepherd cares for his sheep, and a father for his sons." For Aristotle, it is only the wicked tyrant who seeks his own advantage.

75. Socrates in Book 7 is well aware that wanting to govern is the rule rather than the exception. And in Book 1, too, he recognizes that men now do actually "fight over ruling" (347d). When Socrates says that no one rules willingly, what he means, of course, is that no one finds appealing that aspect of ruling that involves caring for others; when everyone "fights over" ruling, it is its perquisites of wealth, power, and honor that they seek.

76. Roochnik (1996, 143–44) rightly criticizes Bloom (1968, 333) for taking the wage earner's art too seriously and for seeing it not only as "ubiquitous" but as an "architectonic art" that is needed by all the others and completes them.

themselves; the only benefit that redounds to the craftsmen is the wage they earn (346d).[77] If that is the case, however, then surely no one, Socrates concludes, willingly chooses to rule (346e; first at 345e). Although Socrates might have said simply that craftsmen are entitled to payment because they provide important services that address human needs, he reaches for a more sensational conclusion, one that views craftsmen's wages as compensation for the craftsmen's benefiting others and not themselves. By insisting that no sensible person would wish to rule were it not for ruling's wages— because ruling benefits someone else and not oneself—Socrates in effect says about ruling what Thrasymachus had said about justice, namely, that it is "a personal injury to the man who obeys and serves" (343c). Socrates thus twists "benefiting others" into something necessarily repugnant, something that no reasonable craftsman could ever do willingly. He portrays all rulers as resentful of having to "straighten out other people's troubles" (346e). The money and honor most rulers demand for their trouble is now fit remuneration for the unwelcome burden they assume.

All rulers, then, Socrates maintains, require compensation of some kind for their loss. If money and honor are the "wages" of most men, there must be yet another sort of wage that compensates the better run of men, men who are "good and decent" (or, as they are called at first, "best" and "most decent"—347b[78]), men who are not motivated (or at least not outwardly so) by the desire for money and honor.[79] The wages of these men are a kind of penalty (*zēmian*—347a; twice more at 347c): able men rule lest they be ruled by lesser men than themselves.

---

77. Glaucon in Book 2 sees medicine as a moneymaking craft and places it (along with justice) in the lowest category of goods (357c). No one, he thinks, would want medicine (or any other moneymaking craft) for itself; in themselves these crafts are onerous (*epipona*) and are beneficial only because of their wages.

78. It may well be significant that Socrates swiftly downgrades these men to "good" and "decent" from "best" and "most decent." He surely regards them as neither.

79. These men may not be entirely free of the desire for money and honor. With respect to money Socrates says of them that "they do not want to take wages openly . . . and get called hirelings, nor secretly on their own to derive profit from their ruling and get called thieves" (347b). And although he declares that they are not lovers of honor, might not their concern with appearances, their concern lest they be *called* hirelings or *called* thieves, belie that pronouncement just a little? These are dignified and self-respecting men who would not demean themselves or besmirch their reputations by appearing to be moneygrubbing, and who do not pursue honor in the obvious and vulgar way some politicians do.

In declaring that even good and decent men require inducements to rule, Socrates appears to endorse Thrasymachus's unsentimental view of human beings. For if good and decent men[80] eschew ruling because they recognize that "a true ruler really does not naturally consider his own advantage but rather that of the one who is ruled" (347d), then good men are like all men. It is because all men that are equally selfish *no one* rules willingly (345e, 346e). Superior men, on this account, exhibit the very traits that Thrasymachus, as we saw, ascribes to all rulers: "Day and night they consider nothing else than how they will benefit themselves" (343c). Indeed, their concern is lest *they* be ruled by worse men—not lest this be the fate of others. Far from being more concerned about others than most men, far from having any sort of heightened awareness of people's need for moral guidance and being willing to address it, the only way good and decent men differ from others is in the type of "wage" that would be effective in persuading them to rule. Ruling is not a good thing in their eyes, not something they think would enhance their lives (*hōs eupathēsontes en autōi*), but something they regard as a necessity (347c-d). If there were someone better than themselves or even someone their equal they would gladly pass the job of ruling on to him (347d). Indeed, in a city in which all men are good, a city in which there are no men worse than themselves, good and decent men would fight each other to avoid ruling (347d).[81]

Has not something gone terribly awry when good and decent men would do just about anything to avoid helping someone else?[82] Are we

---

80. Socrates seems to be avoiding calling these good and decent men "just," though in conversation with Polemarchus Socrates had said without hesitation: "Yet the good men are just and such as not to do injustice?" (334d); and "And it's the just man who is good?" (335d). One reason that Socrates now avoids the term might be simply that Thrasymachus has just maintained that just men are *not* good or admirable. A second reason might be that Socrates can simply not bring himself to apply the term "just" to men who are so callously indifferent to the needs of others.

81. One reason not mentioned here that might persuade someone to rule others willingly—insofar as ruling others indeed entails improving them morally—is so as not to be surrounded by corrupt men at whose hands one is likely to experience harm. See *Ap*. 25d-e, where Socrates denies that he would corrupt his companions intentionally, since he is not so naïve as to fail to recognize that bad people do bad things to their associates. See also *Prot*. 327b, where Protagoras argues that since no one wishes to live among bad people, everyone makes it his business to teach virtue all the time. It is likely that the same point is being made at *Meno* 92a.

82. When the new, truly good and decent men make their appearance in Book 6, now as philosophers, their character is beyond reproach: they are no longer averse to ruling; their "uselessness" is blamed on those who don't—but should—use them.

not meant to see in this portrayal of good and decent men a grotesque
distortion? Are we to believe that in Socrates' view the mark of a good and
decent man is extreme selfishness, that a truly good man, a truly decent
man, would refuse to rule even when the cost to himself is minimal—that
is, when he would be ruling other good men[83]—just because under such
conditions there is no discernible "wage" to be earned?[84] Indeed, Socrates
compounds the absurdity of this result by saying next that "everyone who
knows (*gignōskōn*) would choose to be benefited by another rather than to
take the trouble (*pragmata echein*) of benefiting another" (347d).[85] Only a
fool, in other words, would willingly help someone else.[86]

It should be evident that Socrates does not actually subscribe to this
view, regardless of how forcefully he advances it.[87] For, besides the stark
implausibility and repugnance of the notion that good and decent and wise
men never act for the sake of anything but their own advantage, this idea
relies on the patently Thrasymachean view that men are ineluctably selfish and that another man's gain must be one's own loss. Indeed, Socrates
sharply reprimands Thrasymachus, in the passage immediately preceding
this one, for exhibiting just the sort of callous and uncharitable behavior
that Socrates now ascribes, seemingly approvingly, to good and decent

---

83. Unlike the philosophers of Book 6 (496c-e), who would shy away from ruling in a city of
beasts, where they would be in danger of being corrupted, the rulers in Book 1 refuse to rule in
a city of all and only good men, where there is little or no chance of their being corrupted. These
men simply do not wish to extend themselves on other people's behalf.

84. Irwin charitably misreads Socrates' point about the good and decent men. Socrates argues that since the only "wage" good and decent men would accept as compensation for ruling is
not having to be ruled by their inferiors, once there are no inferiors—when everyone in the city
is a good man—they lose their compensation, and so refuse to rule: they are, after all, not so foolish as actually to want to benefit someone else (347d). Irwin, however, thinks the just person rules
unwillingly in such a city only because he "finds the advantages to be gained from ruling so unappealing" (1995, 299). It is not, however, because just rulers eschew the usual rewards associated
with ruling that they prefer not to rule in a city of just men, but because in such a city they stand
to gain nothing from ruling.

85. If the philosophers of Book 7 have seen the Good, would they not be the *most* knowing?
Would they not, then, in accordance with Socrates' characterization of knowing men in Book 1,
be the most selfish?

86. As we know, Thrasymachus regards the just man as simple, innocent, and naïve—that is,
as a fool (343c). He will reaffirm this view twice more, at 348c and 349b.

87. For a similar analysis of 347a-d, see Altman 2009, 93–95. For an opposing view, see Lampert 2010, 264: "The best rule to the advantage of themselves and their like. Thrasymachus [in
Socrates' opinion] is not wrong."

men. "You have no care for us," Socrates scolds him, "and aren't a bit concerned whether we shall live worse or better as a result of our ignorance of
what you say you know" (344e). Is it not clear that Socrates would expect
of a good and decent—and knowing—man the kind of care for others
that would include a willingness to take the trouble to set them straight,
to share with them for their sake what he thinks he knows—particularly
when the matter at hand is in what way human beings may achieve "the
most profitable existence,"[88] that is, how they are to live well? Realizing
on second thought that Thrasymachus is not a good man, not a man who
would help others without compensation, Socrates offers him the only incentive that is likely to work: he assures him that if he benefits his audience
it will be worth his while. "But, my good man," he says, "it wouldn't be a
bad investment for you to do a good deed for so many as we are" (345a).
Thrasymachus, after all, is the man who had earlier refused to give his
"other and better" answer to the justice question until he was paid a fee.
Socrates' friends, pledging payment on Socrates' behalf, then demanded
that Thrasymachus speak "for money's sake" (337d).

    Although the next chapter of this book is devoted to Socrates, it is per-
haps worth noting here that Socrates, as he says in the *Apology* (30b-c),
never took wages for his efforts to encourage his fellow citizens to embrace
a life of virtue; he never "got something out of this." Could Socrates then
think well of those who would not deign to benefit another human being
without adequate compensation? Moreover, when Socrates explains why
he hasn't entered politics, he doesn't say of himself: "Surely you don't think
me so stupid as to take the trouble to benefit someone else when I might be
the one benefited." The reason he gives is that he knew he would benefit
no one—neither others nor himself (*Ap.* 31d, 36c). And since he couldn't
be of benefit as a politician, he found another way to be of use. Indeed,
he calls himself a "benefactor" (36d) who sought to "perform the greatest
benefaction" (36c). For Socrates, "acting in a manner worthy of a good
man" is equivalent to "coming to the aid of the just things and, as one
ought, regarding this as most important" (*Ap.* 32e). Anyone who puts his

---

88. For Socrates, "profitable" is not restricted to profitability "to oneself." "Profitable" (*lusiteloun*) is just another of the terms alongside "advantageous" (*sumpheron*) in the long list of
synonyms—"inanities"—that Thrasymachus forbids Socrates to use to define justice (336c-d).

own well-being above serving justice can clearly not be a terribly good or decent man in Socrates' estimation.

Let us pause for a moment and ask why it is that Socrates would claim that even a good man, even a decent man, would not rule were it not for fear of incurring a "penalty." Why does he not simply say that good and decent men, unlike greedy and honor-loving men, would rule for the sake of the ruled even in the absence of compensation? Why would he not contend that what sets good and decent men apart from other men is that they alone would willingly take the trouble to benefit others?

The answer to this question lies no doubt in the far more illuminating question that we might pose in its place. For indeed more important than why Socrates makes his outrageous claim is why Glaucon does not object to it, why Glaucon is not offended by the suggestion that good and decent men, would, just like all men, avoid helping others at nearly all costs. Surely Socrates paints the picture of the good and decent man in ever more garish colors in an attempt to provoke Glaucon, to stir him to protest this unwarranted vilification of the good and decent man.[89] And yet, he fails to elicit from Glaucon so much as a hint of disapproval. Since it is certain that Glaucon counts himself among the good and decent men, the fact that he does not object to Socrates' characterization of them as utterly self serving suggests that he regards this as a fair—even flattering—representation of himself. It is not as if Glaucon is shy: he does not hesitate to interrupt, raise questions and objections, or speak at length, as he sees fit. As Socrates will soon say, "Glaucon is always most courageous in everything" (2.357a). That he is silent now suggests, therefore, that he sees no incompatibility between being good and decent, on the one hand, and caring for no one but oneself, on the other. What is Socrates to think but that Glaucon is, at least in this respect, hardly better than Thrasymachus? It is this same Glaucon who worries in *Rep.* 7 that it might be unjust to require philosophers to rule—that is, to put the needs of the ruled ahead of their own desires.

---

89. On Socrates' general interest in provoking Glaucon, see Miller 1986; also Strauss, 1964, 85.

4

SOCRATIC PIETY

The Fifth Cardinal Virtue

> Socrates also universally avoided all ostentation. And when persons came to
> him, and desired to be introduced by him to philosophers, he took them and
> introduced them; so well did he bear being overlooked.
>
> —Epictetus, *Enchiridion* 46

Despite the *Republic*'s extensive and expansive consideration of a whole host of philosophers and philosophic types, scant attention is paid to Socrates as philosopher or philosophic type. Although he serves as narrator of the *Republic*, Socrates says very little about himself—and very little is said about him by others. Only Thrasymachus speaks of Socrates directly; indeed, he has a few choice words for him in Book 1. Registering a complaint about what he calls "that habitual irony of Socrates" (337a), Thrasymachus charges that Socrates will do anything to avoid answering questions or teaching; instead, by way of gratifying his "love of honor" (336c), he will only ask but not answer; he will have recourse to his usual ploy (*eiōthos diapraxētai*) and will refute other people's arguments, or will learn from them without giving proper thanks (337a-338b).

At the same time, however, that Thrasymachus berates Socrates for his ironic posturing and dissembling, he comes at, him, too, from the opposite direction, faulting him for his naïveté. Calling him "most naïve (*euēthestate*) Socrates" (343d1), Thrasymachus aligns him with all other "truly naïve and just men" (*tōn alēthōs euēthikōn te kai dikaiōn*—343c6–7), men who are "ruled," that is, taken advantage of, by unjust men. Glaucon, too, thinks of Socrates as naïve. Although he does not explicitly say so, he clearly has Socrates in mind when he speaks of the man who is "simple and genteel" (*haploun kai gennaion*—361b),[1] one who wishes not to seem but to be just yet is nevertheless reputed to be unjust. Surely it is because he sees in Socrates the embodiment of justice that he turns to him for its defense. Indeed, no one better fits Glaucon's description of the just man than Socrates does: "Doing no injustice, let him have the greatest reputation for injustice. . . . Let him go unchanged until death, seeming throughout life to be unjust although he is just" (361c-d). Neither Thrasymachus nor Glaucon (at least when he's playing devil's advocate) holds the just man in high esteem. Rather, Thrasymachus lauds *in*justice as *euboulia* (good counsel—1.348d), and Glaucon admires the unjust man as a "clever craftsman" (360e).

I. Socrates on Socrates

Although generally reticent in the *Republic* with respect to himself, Socrates does provide one quick self portrait, or, to be more precise, he describes a little band of philosophers among whom, for a moment, he includes himself.[2] As we saw in Chapter 1, section I.B, Socrates in Book 6

---

1. At *HMi.* 364c-e Hippias describes Odysseus as *polutropos* (wily or crafty), and Achilles as *haplous* (simple). From Socrates' point of view, *euēthes*—though not *haplous*—appears to be a term of derogation. At 3.404a and 10.598d Socrates uses *euēthes* to mean "being gullible or easily fooled"; at 4.425b and 7.529b it means "foolish"; and at 3.400e Socrates distinguishes the folly "that we endearingly call *euētheia*" from the *euētheia* that is the product of understanding (*dianoian*), rightly trained. He also contrasts an opinion of Glaucon's that might be noble or worthy (*kalōs*) with his own that might be *euēthikō* (529b). In the *Theaetetus*, Socrates takes note of the popular disparagement of the philosopher as *euēthes* (175e). But Socrates calls the god *haplous* at 2.380d and 381c, and traces the origins of timocracy to the aristocracy's wise men's having lost their simplicity (*haplous*—8.547e) and to the felt need to replace them with "simpler" men (*haplousterous*)—even though the replacements are to be men of spirit. See, too, 3.404e, where simplicity (*haplotēs*) in music is said to produce moderation in souls.

2. On one earlier occasion Socrates suggests—obliquely (and humorously), to be sure—that he himself is a philosopher suited to rule. At 5.474c, after asserting that it is by nature appropriate for some men to engage in philosophy and to lead a city, and for the rest to forgo philosophy and to follow the leader, he instructs Glaucon to "follow me here," to which Glaucon responds: "Lead." Socrates does not, of course, proceed to rule; he leads Glaucon as they think through the question of the nature of the philosopher.

at 496a-e speaks of a very small group whose members, by various quirks of fate, are barred from entering politics, and so "remain to keep company with philosophy in a way that is worthy" (496b). Having stayed with philosophy—for whatever reason—these men are now privileged to "taste how sweet and blessed a possession it [philosophy] is" (496c) and are able, too, to discern clearly the vileness of politics. The political arena, they now see, is a den of savagery in which a decent man would quickly surrender either his decency or his life. In order to preserve both his life and the purity of his soul, each of the members of this little band of philosophers elects to "keep quiet and mind his own business," taking shelter from the threat of corruption or death as others protect themselves from the dust and rain blown about in a windy storm (496d).

Socrates is, to be sure, very much like the philosophers among whom he includes himself.[3] As the *Apology* confirms, he, too, is held back from entering politics and, having resisted, is able to see why entering politics would not have been a good or wise thing for him to do. Like the other philosophers described here, Socrates wants to come to the aid of justice, but he realizes, as they do, that politics is a dirty business, that when one fights for justice amid beasts one fights alone, and that when one fights alone one is either corrupted or killed and hence of no use to oneself, one's friends, or one's city. Indeed, the very language Socrates uses in the *Republic* to express the small band's reluctance to become politically engaged echoes almost to the word the expressions he uses in the *Apology* with respect to his own abstention from politics. In the *Apology* he says that as a politician in the present political climate he could not "come to the aid of

---

3. For Popper, the worthy philosophers Socrates describes at 496 include Plato and perhaps some of his friends (possibly Dion), but, Popper thinks, they are the antithesis of the sort of philosopher Socrates represents. Alluding to the passage in which Socrates observes that they regard politics as no place for a just man, Popper says (1945, 1:154): "The strong resentment expressed in these sour and most un-Socratic words marks them clearly as Plato's own." These "sour" words, however, are virtually identical to the words Socrates uses in the *Apology* to characterize his perception of politics in Athens. Popper also sees the prideful Plato in the philosophers of the earlier ship allegory, who will rule only if the ruled come to them; Plato regards himself, Popper says, as their "natural ruler," the true "philosopher king," who *may* rule if the people approach him and insist on it (1:154–55). But as was pointed out in Chapter 1, note 40, although Socrates does not think the would-be ruler should beg to rule the people, he does not require that the people beg to be ruled. Both in *Rep.* 6 and in the *Apology* Plato's intention is to represent not himself but Socrates, probably as he understands him and certainly as he wishes his readers to.

justice" (*Ap.* 32e; cf. *Rep.* 496c-d), would fail to be of "benefit to myself or to others" (*Ap.* 31d, 36c; cf. *Rep.* 496d), and would therefore do well to guard himself against doing anything unjust or impious (*Ap.* 32d; cf. *Rep.* 496e).

Yet in addition to the similarities Socrates notes between himself and the decent philosophers of Book 6, there is one quite stunning difference that he neglects to mention: whereas they retreat from the city to protect their souls, he does not; whereas they "stand aside under a little wall," he does not.[4] Despite the fact that Socrates and the other worthy philosophers are averse to politics for the very same reasons and are equally aware of its dangers and futility, he alone does not shy away from engagement with others.[5] As he says in the *Apology*, "I did not keep quiet during my life" (36b; also 38a: "It is impossible for me to keep quiet"). What Socrates does when bereft of an ally with whom to "go to the aid of justice" is "come to the aid of the god" (*Ap.* 23b)—by himself; in this way he acts in "a manner worthy of a good man (*andros agathou*)" (32e). Confronting the very same circumstances faced by *Rep.* 6's small band of philosophers, Socrates chooses not politics per se but a certain form of political life, a life of being "a busybody in private."[6] That Socrates includes himself among the philosophers of Book 6—the very best of the philosophic types the *Republic* considers—yet at the same time ascribes to them a mode of conduct, a way of life, that he himself spurns, suggests that his philosophic practice is better than theirs, indeed that he exhibits a virtue greater than theirs.

How are we to categorize the virtue that sets Socrates apart from the philosophers of Book 6? The *Republic* names four virtues—justice, temperance, courage, and wisdom—as marks of the "perfectly good" city (*polin*

---

4. Brann (2004, 167) contends that Socrates, in locating himself among the philosophers who live and die in private and thus fall short of "the greatest [achievements]"—one of which is ruling in a suitable regime (497a)—"is commenting on his own limited success in Athens." On the contrary, however, although Socrates indeed has only limited success, he embraces politics, if only on his own terms.

5. The *daimonion* does not shield Socrates from all harm, for it generally permits his elenctic activity, intervening only in certain of his speeches (*Ap.* 40b). It is triggered when Socrates is about to betray his own convictions. When he is of one mind, as he is in the case of his elenctic activity, it is silent. See Chapter 1, note 44.

6. It is possible to regard the *Republic*—and specifically the passage at 496d-e where the reader cannot help but be struck by the difference between Socrates and even the best philosophers—as a vindication of Socrates and his life, as a new *apologia Socratis*, as it were. The term *apologia* appears in the *Republic* nine times: 419a, 420b, 453c, 488a, 490a, 607b, 607d, 608a.

teleōs agathēn—4.427e7) and, by extension or analogy, of the perfectly good human being. Do these virtues, however, capture what is unique about Socrates? Or does Socratic virtue somehow outstrip them?

II. The Suppression of Piety

A fifth virtue, one that is conspicuously absent from the *Republic*'s list, is piety. Yet piety or holiness is investigated in the *Euthyphro*; it is vitally important in the *Apology*, where Socrates must defend himself against the charge of impiety; it is included quite naturally and without fanfare among *five* cardinal virtues in the *Protagoras*[7]—justice, temperance, holiness, wisdom, and courage;[8] in the *Gorgias* (at 507b-c), the perfectly good man (*agathon andra teleōs*—507c2–3) is the moderate man who is also just, courageous, and pious;[9] and in the *Laches* (at 199d), someone who has courage and hence wisdom with respect to what is good and what is bad in the past, present, and future, will also not be lacking in any virtue—not in temperance, justice, or holiness.

It appears that piety is deliberately suppressed in the *Republic* from the very start. Although Cephalus early in Book 1 speaks of the importance

---

7. The Greeks apparently had no fixed set of "cardinal" virtues, despite the too-quick assumption by some scholars that they did: see Nettleship 1955, 146; Barker 1959, 116. As Annas asks and observes (1981, 110), "What is so 'clear' about the claim that goodness or virtue is found in precisely these four forms? . . . Some commentators refer to a standard or well-known doctrine of the 'four cardinal virtues'; but far from appealing to common sense Plato seems to be innovating." And, as J. Sachs remarks (2007, 121 n. 61), "That complete human goodness must include the four virtues named would have been a prevalent opinion. That no fifth virtue was regarded as having that same 'cardinal' status is less likely." Bloom (1968, 373) notes: "Nothing has been done to establish that these four—and only these four—virtues are what makes a city good." Also see Adam (1969, 1:224): "This part of the *Republic* has an independent value in the history of Ethics as the first explicit assertion of the doctrine of four cardinal virtues." According to Adam, then, the notion of four cardinal virtues originates with Plato in the *Republic* at 427e.

8. When Protagoras contends that justice, moderation, holiness, "and the rest of civic virtue" are taught by all people in civilized places to all other people (*Prot.* 327c-e), Socrates follows up by asking "one little thing": how are the various virtues—justice, moderation, piety, wisdom, and courage, five in all—related to one another (329c-330b)? He thus makes explicit that wisdom and courage constitute "the rest of civic virtue."

9. The virtue of wisdom appears to drop out in the *Gorgias*. Perhaps that is because Socrates' interlocutors in the *Gorgias* praise immoderation and injustice. What these men then most need to be shown is not that wisdom is one of the virtues, but that immoderation and injustice are the choice of the *un*wise.

of leading "a just and holy (*dikaiōs kai hosiōs*) life" (331a), and takes care
lest he cheat or lie or depart this life owing sacrifices to a god or money to
a human being (331b), Socrates asks only about "this very thing, justice"
(331c).[10] It is likely, of course, that Socrates is not interested in the piety of
offering proper sacrifices,[11] but, even so, he could have inquired into the
nature of genuine piety had he wanted to. The *Republic*'s omission of piety
is made all the more evident by Glaucon's reminder to Socrates at 427e, *just
before the four virtues of wisdom, courage, temperance, and justice are enumerated*, that it would be, as Socrates himself had recognized in Book 2 (at
368b-c), *not pious* (*oud' hosion*) of him not to come to the aid of justice.

There are a number of ways in which piety's neglect might be explained. Perhaps piety is omitted because its inclusion would further undermine the already precarious project of discovering individual virtues
by first beholding their magnified counterparts in the city: maybe a city
has no virtue of piety; maybe its piety does not readily transfer to the individual; or, maybe, individual piety is no different from civic piety, in which
case Socrates would end up not with analogous versions of piety in city
and soul but with the same one.[12] Alternatively, one might attribute piety's
neglect in the *Republic* to its assimilability to one of the other four virtues,
justice being the most likely candidate.[13] It will be argued here, however,
that by excluding piety Plato calls attention to the fact that none of the
Republic's rulers exhibit it—not the guardians described early on (they are

10. Mara (1997, 49) observes that Socrates focuses on the justice question while "ignoring or
submerging the equally plausible" piety question.

11. The *Republic* opens, of course, with a prayer to "the goddess" and a festival in honor of
the goddess Bendis. But the all-night religious spectacle, which was to begin with a novel torch
race on horseback at sunset, is replaced with a nightlong conversation about justice in the home
of Polemarchus and Cephalus.

12. Annas (1981, 111) thinks that since virtue in the *Republic* is internal, and since piety for
Socrates is a matter of the performance of conventionally sanctioned actions with respect to the
gods, there is no place in the dialogue for piety. Yet, as Nichols points out (1987, 208 n. 32), there is
for Socrates a sense in which piety is reverence and awe (see *Euthyph.* 12a-c)—and in that sense it
is certainly internal. Nichols's view is that piety is out of place in the *Republic*'s city because its citizens fit perfectly in the class to which they are assigned, and so have "no desire in their souls" that
"leads them to a divinity beyond political life" (89).

13. In the *Protagoras* Socrates argues that justice and holiness are the same (330c-331e), in
order to test Protagoras's assertion that the virtues are distinct from one another in the way features of a face are. Socrates' larger goal, however, is to show that all the virtues are the same or at
least mutually implicating. In the *Euthyphro*, Socrates eventually situates holiness within a larger
category called justice, but nevertheless allows it to retain its distinctive character. See section VI.

courageous and moderate), not the members of the ruling class of Book 4 (they are noted for their wisdom), not the philosophers of Book 6 (they are wise and are said to be endowed as well with every moral and personal virtue but are never called pious), and not the philosopher-warriors of Book 7 (they are distinguished by being smart and steady). Why is it that even the presumably most exemplary of the ruling types—the philosophers of Book 6—lack piety? If piety is for Plato an estimable virtue, then the possibility must be entertained that there is some other "ruler" that he prefers to any of those outlined in the *Republic*—a pious one.

Who else but Socrates fits this bill? It is Socrates who, because he is well aware that he falls far short of divine wisdom, devotes himself, both reverently and at considerable personal cost, to the political activity of examining himself and others. Yet, despite his prominence, even dominance, in the *Republic*, the kind of philosopher he is is not discussed. He is the left-out philosopher just as piety is the left-out virtue. Still, he is the only character in the *Republic* aside from Cephalus to speak of piety and to have it figure in his choices: "For I am afraid it might be not even pious (*oud' hosion*)," he says, "to be here when justice is being spoken badly of and to give up and not bring help while I am still breathing and able to make a sound" (2.368b-c).

III. A Man on a (Divine) Mission

It is arguable that one of the more serious sources of Socrates' fellow citizens' dissatisfaction with him, a resentment that led them eventually to convict him and sentence him to death, was his refusal to participate in politics.[14] Particularly in democratic Athens, Socrates' having remained aloof from the political realm, his having insisted on publicly "minding his own business" ("In doing my own business, I never begrudged anyone who wished to hear me, young or old"—33a) while being "a busybody" only "in private" (*Ap.* 31a-c, 36b), would have been deemed an inexcusable and unforgivable dereliction of civic duty. As Pericles declares in his Funeral Oration, "For we alone regard one who does not take part in politics not

---

14. According to the *Apology*, Socrates performed the public service required of him by law (32b)—but no more. See *Gorg.* 473e-474a: "I am not one of the political men, and when last year I was by lot a member of the council and my tribe was presiding and I had to put a question to the vote, I gave people a laugh and didn't know how to put the vote."

as a non-meddler (*apragmonta*) but as someone useless (*achreion*)" (Thucy-dides, *Hist.* 2.40.2).

To defend his avoidance of the political arena Socrates offers in the *Apology* at least four distinct explanations or justifications. First, he has something more important and more pressing to do, namely, to improve souls at the behest of the god—and he hasn't the time to do both that and politics (23b). Second, he simply does not care for the same things the many do: moneymaking, household management, generalships, popular oratory, and the other offices and conspiracies and factions that come to be in the city (36b). Third, politics is a corrupt and corruptive business, and no place for a just man (31e-32a, 36b-c).[15] And fourth, as a just man, he wouldn't survive long enough in politics to do himself or anyone else any good (31d-e, 36b-c).

Of these four reasons it is the first that sets Socrates decisively apart from the worthy philosophers of Book 6. For whereas each of these philosophers remains loyal to philosophy for one reason or another, none of them is said to have been sent by the god to practice philosophy. Yet Socrates in the *Apology* repeatedly calls attention to the divine source of his mission, to his having been the god's gift or servant or messenger (22a, 23b, 23c, 28d, 30a, 30e, 31a, 33c). Although he does speak in the *Republic* passage of the *daimonion*, the divine voice that prevents him from pursuing the political life, it is not the *daimonion* that inspires his philosophic activity: its role is purely dissuasive, keeping him away from harmful and bad things (*Ap.* 31d, *Theag.* 128d, *Theaet.* 151a, *Phaedr.* 242b-c, *Euthyd.* 272e), among which is politics (*Ap.* 31d).[16] The *Republic* is silent, however, about the Delphic oracle, which, according to the *Apology* (20e-21a), is responsible for Socrates' "wandering" (*planēn*) and for the "labors" (*ponous*) he endures in examining others.[17] It tells us nothing about Socrates' elenctic

---

15. In the *Gorgias*, the skill needed to avoid suffering injustice is identified by Socrates as one that requires not only flattering those in power but being like them; in other words, the only way to avoid suffering injustice is to commit it (510e).

16. On the *daimonion*, see note 5 above and Chapter 1, note 44.

17. Socrates' "wandering" recalls Odysseus; the "labors" he undertakes are reminiscent of Hercules. See Cicero, *Fin.* 2.118: "Scan the contents of your own mind, deliberate thoroughly, and ask yourself which you would prefer: to enjoy continual pleasure . . . or to be a benefactor of the whole human race, enduring the labors of Hercules to bring it aid and succour in its hour of need?" In the context of the *Apology*, where Socrates must defend his life's work or die, he can perhaps be forgiven this bit of hubris—though arguably it hurt rather than helped his cause.

occupation, undertaken by him initially for the sake of "refuting" (or, per-haps, "testing"—*elenxōn* [*Ap.* 21c]) the god, but ultimately as a form of di-vine service. Socrates in the *Republic* says not a word about the "oracles and dreams" and other forms of "divine allotment" (*theia moira*)[18] through which he was ordered by the god to undertake his special mission (33c). By pointing in *Rep.* 6 only to the *daimonion* as what sets him apart ("My case—the daimonic sign . . . has perhaps occurred in some one other man, or no other, before"—496c), Socrates deflects attention from the uniquely divine origin, featured so prominently in the *Apology*, of his philosophic practice.

Just as Socrates suppresses in *Rep.* 6 his determination to practice philos-ophy rather than cower by a sheltering wall, so, too, he conceals the divine source to which he traces his philosophic activity. Yet on both these counts he stands apart from the philosophers of *Rep.* 6. Moreover, these two dif-ferences are clearly related to one another. For to regard one's philosophic mission as divine makes all the difference in how one comports oneself in relations with others. What Socrates shows us in Book 6 is how philoso-phers who are just act—and are right to act—under the grievous circum-stances they face, having had no calling to supererogation. The pilots of the ship allegory, Socrates makes clear, do no wrong in not begging to be permitted to rule; by right, those in need of rule should "go to *their* door." As he explains, there is something disturbingly amiss when a benefactor must implore those in need of benefaction to permit him to provide it. (We see how disgraceful it is when those unsuited to manage the ship never-theless beg the shipowner to permit them to do so; and although it is not comparably shameful for someone fit to rule to beg to do so, still there is something "not natural" [489b] about it.) The counterparts of these pilots, the worthy philosophers of 496, would, as we have seen, come to the aid of justice if they could; it is only once they recognize that they cannot do so

---

18. In the *Meno* (99b-100b) it is *theia moira* that enables poets, politicians, and others to utter truths and promote the prospering of cities despite their lack of knowledge. (See, too, Socrates' de-scription at *Ap.* 22b-c of divine inspiration as the source of the "noble things" poets say.) Something similar appears in the *Republic* at 499b-c: a city might come to be perfect if kings or their sons are imbued by "divine inspiration" (*theias epipnoias*) with an erotic passion for philosophy. Also in the *Republic* (at 493a) divine dispensation is identified as the best hope for saving people from their otherwise inevitable undoing in corrupt regimes; and at 492a Socrates says that if the philosophic nature does not chance upon the proper nurture and education, it will come to vice "unless one of the gods chances to assist it." In Socrates' case the divine influence is experienced as a divine com-mand or duty, as a mission.

safely and effectively that they choose to tend instead to their own souls. Although they don't try to find a way to serve justice under unfavorable conditions, they nevertheless, strictly speaking, have not shirked their duty. If anything, the members of the small band of philosophers described in Book 6 are willing to exceed their strict duty. For, as Socrates will say in Book 7 (520a-b), "it is fitting" for those who "grow up spontaneously against the will of the regime" "not to participate in the labors of those cities." Thus these good men of Book 6, who don't owe the rearing of their nature to anyone, "have justice on their side when they are not eager to pay off the price of rearing to anyone" (520b). After all, in its most basic sense, justice requires only that one do no injustice.[19] But Book 6's philosophers not only refrain from committing injustice; they also care about justice. Indeed they care enough to want to come to its aid in the city, even though they owe the city nothing. They are surely just, then, not in the term's narrowest sense but in a broader one. It would seem that the true love of wisdom that characterizes the philosophers of Book 6 disposes them to rule—to come to the aid of justice—at least under not unfavorable conditions.[20] As we have seen, the only thing that causes them to shy away from politics is the dearth of fellow fighters for justice in their cities and the prevailing corruption there.

That Socrates alone does not take refuge beside a little wall puts him in a class by himself: only he manages to carve out for himself, under discouraging circumstances, a way to serve justice and thereby serve the god. Socrates may say that his "whole care" is "to commit no unjust or unholy deed" (*Ap.* 32d), but in truth he also seeks to foster justice: he is "someone who really fights for the just" (32a)—even under difficult conditions.[21] Whereas the *Republic* conjoins "minding one's own business" with "not being a busybody," Socrates in the *Apology* links "minding one's own business" (*ta emautou prattontos*), with which he credits himself ("If anyone, young or old, desires to listen to me when I am minding my own business"

19. See 1.334d and *Crito* 49b.

20. See Mara 1997, 57: "Yet the practice of philosophy, which includes the teaching about the necessity of avoiding injustice, may also appear as a very positive kind of justice. It makes others better instead of merely keeping its possessor pure."

21. On justice, philosophy, and truth, as things needing to be fought for or defended, things that will either be victorious or go down in defeat in the contest with their opposites, see *Ap.* 28–29, 32a; *Gorg.* 503a, 505e, 521a; *Meno* 86b-c; *Phaedo* 89a, 89c; *Rep.* 335e, 427e, 453a, 534c, 583a-b, 608b, 612b-d, 613b-614a; *Laws* 731a.

[33a]), with "being a busybody in private" (*Ap.* 31c).[22] Although he minds his own business—that is, he avoids political intrigues and stays out of affairs not his own—he nevertheless "always minds *your* business, going to each of you privately,[23] as a father or older brother might do, persuading you to care for virtue" (*Ap.* 31b).[24] He "delights in" (*aspazomai*) and loves the men of Athens (29d).[25] Not content to protect his own soul's purity, Socrates descends into the trenches, and seeks to improve souls one by one; his approach to each is customized.[26] The *Republic* indeed opens with his "going down" (*katebēn*) to the Piraeus.[27] In the *Gorgias* Socrates sees as the proper role of the citizen-statesman making the citizens as good as possible (513e), improving individual souls by taking them "in a different direction" (517b-c); he therefore proclaims himself virtually the only Athenian to "put his hand to the true political art and practice the political things (*ta politika*)" (521d).[28] And in the *Laches* Socrates says (200e): "This

---

22. See *Gorg.* 526c, where Rhadamanthus sends to the Isles of the Blessed the soul that has lived "piously and with truth," a soul mostly found in "a philosopher who has minded his own business and has not been a busybody in life." Although minding one's own business is frequently paired with not being a *polupragmatos*, in Socrates' case the former is also joined with "busybodying" (*polupragmonō*) in private; he says of himself that he "minds *your* business" (*to humeteron prattein*). For discussion of the ways in which "minding one's own business" (*hautou prattein*) is, and is not, commendable, see Chapter 1, note 45.

23. Socrates has a funny way of "going to each of you privately." His conversations tend to take place before an audience, usually in a quite public place. His exhibitions are witnessed, as he admits, by young people, who then go on to do their own examining of others (*Ap.* 23c). In the *Theaetetus*, Socrates observes that if an unjust man is made to give and take an account "in private" (*idiāi*) of the things he disparages, he will fail to satisfy even himself (177b); whether or not he will change as a result of his failure, Socrates doesn't say.

24. In the *Protagoras* and the *Meno*, Socrates assumes fathers wish to have their sons become virtuous. See *Meno* 93c-d, where Socrates says to Anytus about Themistocles: "Or do you think he grudged virtue to him and deliberately didn't pass on the virtue he himself had?"

25. Socrates thus feels toward his fellow citizens the way the philosophers described at the end of Book 5 feel about "what is."

26. See Saxonhouse 1992, 105: "Socrates, through his care for the education of the citizens as individuals, transforms the city from . . . an abstract unity of equals to one made up of diverse citizens to whom he must go in private. . . . The city, as an abstract unit with its laws engraved in stone, tries to educate all at once and to punish according to its principles without attending to the peculiarity of each individual."

27. Cephalus complains that Socrates has not "come down" (*katabainōn*) for a while and ought to do so more often (328c).

28. In the *Euthydemus* as well (291c-292c), Socrates understands the kingly art (*hē basilikē*) or the political art (*hē politikē*) to be "that by which we make others good." Moreover, those whom we improve will, in turn, do the same for others.

would indeed be a terrible thing, Lysimachus, to be unwilling to join in someone's zeal to become as good as possible." Socrates seeks to benefit others with respect to their virtue, and so finds a way—being a busybody in private—that will enable him to stay alive for at least some time ("if he is to survive for even a short time" [31e-32a]). As he says in the *Apology*, "no man will survive who genuinely opposes you or any other crowd and prevents the occurrence of many unjust and illegal happenings in the city. A man who really fights for the just must lead a private, not a public, life" (31e-32a). Socrates will "go down," then, but, as he says in the *Apology*, he will not "go up": "I do not dare to go up (*anabainōn*) before your multitude to counsel the city." If Socrates cannot risk being a conventional politician, he will be political in his own way. He will choose a course that honors both the admonitions of the *daimonion* and the demands of the oracle. He will preserve his virtuous character as the "decent" philosophers of Book 6 do (Socrates, too, is "decent": "I hold that I myself was really too *decent* to survive if I went into these things" [*Ap.* 36b-c]—that is, into politics), but, unlike them, he will avoid the trap of thereby rendering himself "useless."

It is clear that from Socrates' point of view merely preserving one's own soul is far from best. When Adeimantus says of the self-protective philosopher: "Well, he would leave [this life here] having accomplished not the least of things," Socrates immediately counters that such a man would have accomplished "not the greatest things (*ta megista*), either" (497a). The greatest things—"growing more and saving the common things along with the private" (497a)—can be accomplished, Socrates says, only through philosophic rule in a suitable regime.[29] Yet despite the fact that the regime in which he lives is not a suitable one and that, moreover, there is no regime that is—asked which of the current regimes is suitable for philosophic rule, Socrates replies: "None at all" (498a)—Socrates resists retiring to the sidelines to save himself; he alone among the worthy philosophers refuses to settle for a state of affairs so far from optimal. Instead, he finds a way both to further his own growth and to save (or try to save) his community, a middle path between the grand ideal of ruling in a suitable regime and the

---

29. The personal growth the philosophers are promised here is a by-product of their caring for others. "Saving the private" means saving not oneself but others—though individually (also at 495b, 500d, 501a). At 5.465d the reason the guardians are said to be happier than Olympic victors is that their triumph entails "the preservation of the whole city."

insufficiently ambitious goal of guarding one's own soul from injustice and unholy deeds. He seeks to improve souls privately, one at a time.[30]

If the philosophers of Book 6 are not unjust, if they are, indeed, positively just, how are we to characterize Socrates, who surpasses them in caring for others? Since the virtue justice, even in its more expansive sense, asks no more than that one preserve one's soul from injustice and unholy deeds when the alternative is to participate in a government that is corrupt and vicious and threatens one's good character and one's life, then the virtue that demands still more is not simple justice but piety. It is piety that Socrates exhibits in his devotion to others, in his coming to the aid of the god by coming to the aid of justice, in his laboring for the people's sake under unfavorable conditions and despite potential harm to himself. If the philosophers to whom Socrates is most akin seem to fall short in some way, it is only because they are being measured against him; it is only because their justice is being measured against his piety.

None of this is to say that Socrates is completely selfless—only that he is remarkably unselfish. He does not disregard his own well-being, but neither is his first thought "What do I stand to gain from what I am about to do?"[31] Unlike the good and decent men of Book 1, who would not rule without remuneration (*misthon*) of some kind—they rule so as not to be ruled by worse men (347c)—Socrates gives no thought to compensation, to "wages," and indeed receives no compensation for his exhortation of

30. Socrates thus avoids extremes. See 10.619a-b.

31. I rely heavily on the *Apology* and the *Gorgias* for a sense of how Plato's Socrates understood himself, namely, as unselfish and as caring deeply for the welfare of others. It might seem that *Charm.* 166c-d suggests otherwise: Socrates says there that in refuting Critias he acts chiefly (*malista*) for his own sake. In context, however, Socrates' intent is to spare Critias embarrassment and to avoid making his ignorance manifest. It must have occurred to Socrates that Critias did not appreciate his first attempt at appeasement, in which he specified that he refutes Critias, as he examines himself (*emauton diereunōimēn*), primarily (*malista*) so that neither of them imagine that he knows something of which he is actually ignorant. (Critias surely would have caught Socrates' intimation that Critias's estimation of his own wisdom is inflated.) Also, Socrates specifies that pursuing the argument chiefly for his own sake is something he does *now* (*nun*): it is not, then, his standard procedure. Moreover, no sooner does Socrates say "for my own sake" than he adds "and perhaps in some degree also for the sake of my other friends." And in the end, Socrates gives the following as his reason for refuting Critias: "For would you not say that the discovery of things as they truly are is a good common to all mankind?" Socrates, then, ultimately leaves no doubt that the good he pursues is one that is good for everyone—not only for himself and his friends but for all mankind—and thus, by implication, for Critias as well.

others. "If I were getting something (*ti*) out of this," he says in the *Apology* (31b), "and if I were receiving wages (*misthon*) while I exhorted you to these things," then, he supposes, his neglect of his own affairs would perhaps seem reasonable. But under the circumstances, that is, considering that he never takes or asks for compensation of any kind (31c), the only explanation for his caring for others even at his own expense is that he is "given to the city by the god" (31a-b). Although he is poor (23c, 31c), he nevertheless seeks and receives nothing in return for his service; he serves men in order to serve the god. Socrates might have chosen to be quiet, might have tested his own views without directly challenging those of others, might have done his own but not "your" business (31b).[32] Had he elected to take this isolationist path, however, he would not have been of benefit to anyone but himself; he would not have been the Athenians' "benefactor" (*euergetēs*—*Ap*. 36d), toiling at the behest of the god who sent him "in his concern for you" (31a). All he would have been is safe.[33]

Philosophic examination is, to be sure, a good common to all, and so a good thing for Socrates no less than for others. As he says in the *Apology* (38a), "This even happens to be the greatest good for a human being—to make speeches every day about virtue and the other things about which you hear me conversing and examining both myself and others." Indeed, so worthwhile an occupation is examination that "the unexamined life is not worth living for a human being" (38a). Still, Socrates' practice of examination and refutation is generally unwelcome; the people on whom Socrates confers this great benefit are often unreceptive if not outright hostile. Virtue, too, one might argue, is a good, perhaps even the greatest good, for a human being; yet the exhortation to virtue is regularly resisted and repulsed. For Socrates the activities of examining, refuting, and exhorting are labors (*ponoi*—*Ap*. 22a), and difficult and dangerous ones at that. As he says, "But to persuade you [of the worthlessness of an unexamined life] is not easy" (*Ap*. 38a).[34] And, as he notes at the end of the *Apology* (41d), his

---

32. Contra Nehamas 1992.

33. As Mara (1997, 58) rightly observes, "Socrates' own example is the clearest illustration that this sort of justice [of making other people more just] is not without its personal and public dangers."

34. On the matter of ease and difficulty in the *Republic*, see Chapter 1, note 57 and Chapter 3, note 56.

life is not free of troubles (*pragmata*), even if troubles need not be a bad thing: "There is nothing bad for a good man, whether living or dead, nor yet are the gods without care for a good man's troubles" (41c-d).[35] Indeed, Socrates is a supremely happy man. So serenely does he sleep in the days before his execution that Crito is moved to remark: "And though I have of course often previously through your whole life counted you happy in your way (*tou tropou*), I do so especially in the currently occurring calamity, so easily and gently do you bear it" (*Crito* 43b). And in the *Phaedo* Phaedo observes that, on the very day of his death, Socrates "appeared happy, both in manner (*tou tropou*) and words" (58e). Having served the god well, having taken the trouble to care for others rather than only for himself, he can depart serenely from this life and be at last "released" from those troubles (*apēllachthai pragmatōn*—*Ap.* 41d).

The *Republic* is remarkable in part because it is a conversation in which Socrates' interlocutors not only solicit his contribution but sustain their interest in it throughout;[36] it is an occasion on which those who need to be instructed by him go, as it were, to his door. Indeed at one point (368c), Glaucon and the others even "beg" Socrates not to abandon the argument. Yet, on most occasions, in most dialogues, Socrates at some point takes the initiative, imposing himself on unsuspecting interlocutors who quickly resent having to answer his often humiliating questions. In fact, even in the *Republic*, Socrates manages to frustrate and infuriate at least one interlocutor, the initially brazen and overconfident Thrasymachus. In the *Apology* Socrates tells his jurors that he has watched himself becoming hated (*Ap.* 22e-23a, 28a; also 21d, 21e); the hatreds he incurs will in the end cost him his life.

IV. Socrates' God

That Socrates describes himself as serving the god through his philosophic practice might, but need not, signify that he takes the god who sends him to

---

35. Since Socrates says in the *Apology* of his present troubles that they "have not arisen of their own accord" (41d)—implying that the god is their source—troubles cannot be simply bad. Cf. *Rep.* 10.613a-b: "For, surely, gods at least will never neglect the man who is eagerly willing to become just and, practicing virtue, likens himself, so far as is possible for a human being, to a god."

36. Even Thrasymachus remains to the end (450a-b, 498c-d).

be literally a god, some sort of divine being.[37] Indeed, for every "religious" reason Socrates offers in the *Apology* for the choices he makes he supplies its secular counterpart. The *daimonion*'s warning against politics (*Ap*. 31c-d) is immediately glossed as Socrates' own understanding that politics is no place for a just man (31d). (Note, too, that the other worthy philosophers of *Rep*. 6—even without a *daimonion*'s warnings—come to appreciate "the madness of the many" and the dangers of politics.) Socrates refuses to keep quiet not only because to keep quiet is to disobey the god (37e) but also because there is no better life for a human being than the examined one (38a). And although Socrates says that it is the *daimonion*'s silence that guides his conduct at his trial (40b), he remarks, too, that he "much prefers to die having made my defense speech in this way" (38e).

To be sure, Socrates insists that he has received his divine orders by way of oracles, dreams, "and in every way that any divine allotment ever ordered a human being to practice anything at all." But when he adds, "These things . . . are both true and easy to test (*euele-kta*)" (*Ap*. 33c), he goes on to show not how these decidedly *un*confirmable private experiences might be verified but rather how his preceding assertion—that he is no one's teacher and hence no one's corrupter—might be proved. Moreover, insofar as what the god orders Socrates to do is to practice philosophy, to examine himself and others (*Ap*. 28e, 33c), or, in other words, to "obey nothing else of what is mine than the argument that appears best to me upon reasoning" (*Crito* 46b), one might say that Socrates' god renders himself superfluous. Socrates' devotion to this god, then, his conviction that he was sent by this god, need entail no more than an acute consciousness on his part of having a "higher" mission, of being called on to serve truth and justice— or, in the *Republic*'s terms, the Good Itself. Although he speaks of being the god's servant and of doing the god's bidding, his god may well be the truth and justice and goodness he serves.[38] By attributing his activities on behalf of these ideals to a god, he implies in effect that what any gods worthy of the name *would* want from human beings is not prayer and sacrifice but goodness and truth born of critical reflection. Indeed, what such gods would ask

---

37. See note 52 below.

38. Since Socrates is on trial for impiety—for not believing in the gods of the city—it is hardly unreasonable for him to speak of the gods conventionally. See Weiss 1998, chap. 2, the section entitled "Gods and 'The God.'"

of their most devoted servants is that they encourage in others the pursuit of these ends. Although it might be thought that to ascribe religious views such as these to Socrates is wholly anachronistic, it is hardly unreasonable to expect a philosopher to be ahead of his time. (Xenophanes, for example, was, in his theological views, clearly ahead of his.) Indeed, to be a philosopher is, as Callicles says with respect to Socrates in the *Gorgias* (481c), to "turn the life of human beings upside down." If a message is to be delivered effectively, however, it must accommodate itself to the usage of the time. To speak of divine matters in an age of belief in gods one must speak of gods.

When piety is a matter of devotion to a literal god or gods, the line dividing the pious man from the just one, and holiness from justice, is sharp and clear. But when piety is instead a deep and abiding reverence for justice, truth, and the good, for those things that sanctify human existence and infuse it with transcendent meaning and worth, that line becomes blurred and indistinct. One way to see and to secure the distinctiveness of the pious man even in the latter case is to attend closely to the ways in which Socrates differs from the valued philosophers of Book 6, among whom he includes himself. For just as Socrates is a member of this small band of philosophers but nevertheless surpasses them, so too is holiness at the same time both a part of justice and superior to it.

V. Levels of Justice

Justice manifests itself at several levels. Those who are just at the lowest level (level one) refrain from committing injustice—they do not deliberately harm others[39]—but their motivations are less than noble: fear of men or gods or a desire for the "wages" of justice, such things as respect, good marriage prospects, choice offices. What distinguishes a man who is just in only this most narrow and restricted sense from one who is just in any of the more robust senses is that justice is not his preference: were he not afraid, or were he able to secure the good things he desires by merely

---

39. Socrates certainly does think that people deliberately commit injustice: he regards some men as just and others as unjust, some as good and others as wicked. As I argue in Weiss 2006, what Socrates means by his paradox, "no one does wrong willingly," is only that when a person does wrong he brings upon himself a state of wretchedness that no one—including him—wants. See, too, *Laws* 9; and Weiss 2006, chap. 7.

seeming just, he would readily commit injustice.[40] Such a man is not governed by principle. Cephalus, at least late in his life, is just in this minimal sense.[41] So, too, is the "just" man described by Glaucon in Book 2: this is the man who, if he had the ring of Gyges and could make himself invisible, would behave no differently than the unjust man (359c-360d). Another such man is described in Book 10 (619c-d) as one who, because he is virtuous by habit but not by philosophy, foolishly and gluttonously chooses the life of a tyrant for his next incarnation.[42] Despite the fact that these men evade wrongdoing for all the wrong reasons, they are nevertheless to be preferred to the unjust man—that is, to the man who intentionally commits injustice.[43]

---

40. For Aristotle it is even inappropriate to call someone who dislikes acting justly a just man (*EN* 1.8.1098a19-20).

41. Reeve (1988, 9) surprisingly sees not much difference between Socrates' and Cephalus's character: "His [Cephalus's] character is already as good as Socrates'." Yet Cephalus is hardly a man of exemplary character: the reason he values justice is that it can shield him from the terrors that await the unjust in the afterlife. Cephalus is at this time an old man; although we are not explicitly told what kind of man he was when he was younger, it is not easy to avoid the suspicion that his current chastity, piety, and justice stand in sharp contrast to former excesses. Tales that he dismissed as nonsense—laughed at—when he was young (330e), stories about the punishments the unjust will suffer after death, now suddenly both frighten him and spur him to righteous action. He is glad to be wealthy: he can repay his debts and offer his sacrifices. But how did he make the money he didn't inherit? We are left, again, to our suspicions. See Blondell 2002, 170, 173.

42. Even such a man, one who is virtuous only by habit, qualifies as just; after all, he descends from heaven (10.619d), which is the destination of the just. He chooses the tyrant's life because, on the one hand, his embrace of justice is not philosophical—he fails to appreciate its true worth—and, on the other, he has not been subjected to the punishments the unjust are made to endure. In the *Phaedo*, those who are virtuous by habit without philosophy are deemed happiest and are said to be destined for the best place, returning in their next lives as social and gentle animals or as measured (*metrious*) men (82a-b); they certainly don't become tyrants: in the *Phaedo* the soul more or less replicates or replays its previous life. In the *Republic*, by contrast, where the soul gets to choose its next life, it seeks to compensate in this new life for the deficiencies it perceives in the one most recently lived. Interestingly, in the *Phaedo* the philosopher or lover of learning will dwell in the company of gods when he dies, but in *Rep.* 10, those who "philosophize in a healthy way" (619e) will journey between worlds by way of the smooth heavens rather than the rough underworld. The fate of philosophers in Book 10's myth of Er thus differs from that of the philosophers of Book 7, who, when they die, simply go off to dwell on the Isles of the Blessed (540b). See this book's conclusion for a discussion of the myth of Er.

43. A man who has committed no injustice is also "happier" than an unjust man insofar as his soul is not excessively disordered and diseased. Indeed, according to Socrates in the *Gorgias*, the man who is justly punished is "second happiest" (*Gorg.* 478d-e). Socrates explains, expressing his point somewhat less provocatively, that the most wretched man is he who does injustice and is not punished for it; somewhat less wretched is he who does injustice and is punished; least wretched—indeed happy—is he who never does injustice at all (*Gorg.* 479e and 509b). Perhaps a

It is true that when Socrates attempts to delineate what justice is he tends to emphasize what justice forbids and what a just man would therefore never do. In his conversation with Polemarchus in *Rep.* 1, for example, Socrates says that "it is not the work of the just man to harm either a friend or anyone else. . . . It is never just to harm anyone" (335d-e). In the *Crito*, Socrates says: "One must in no way commit injustice . . . surely there is no difference between doing bad to human beings and doing injustice" (49b-c). In the *Gorgias* he says at 460c: "The just man will never wish to do injustice." And in the *Apology*, in seeking to establish his own credentials as a just man, Socrates points to his having placed not committing unjust or impious deeds above all else (32d; cf. 37b, where he declares that he has never done injustice to anyone; cf. also Gorg. 521d, where Socrates declares that if he is brought before a court, "some base man will be my prosecutor—for no worthwhile person would prosecute a human being who does no injustice"). Furthermore, in the *Republic* Socrates observes that the vulgar standard by which the just man is measured is whether he is least likely to be guilty of injustices: filching a deposit of gold or silver, robbing, stealing, betraying, violating oaths or agreements, committing adultery, neglecting parents or the gods (4.442d-443a).

And it is with good reason that Socrates settles for so minimal a condition when defining justice. For the fact is that he is often up against views according to which justice requires far less: in the *Crito*, Crito initially thinks it is just to harm one's enemies (45c) and probably, too, to return injustice for injustice (49c-d); in the *Gorgias*, Polus maintains that it is worse to suffer justice than to commit it (469b), and Callicles, that it is both worse and more shameful to suffer justice than to commit it (483a-b); and in the *Republic*, Polemarchus maintains that justice entails harming one's enemies no less than helping one's friends (331d-336a), and Thrasymachus, that justice is the "advantage of the stronger" (337c). Moreover, it would hardly do for Socrates in the *Apology* to boast of his benefaction before establishing that he commits no injustice. Nevertheless, would a truly just man be on guard lest his own justness go beyond not harming another, lest he actually help someone?

---

simple analogy will serve to elucidate the point. A garment is best if never stained, second best if stained and properly cleaned (though having been stained and then cleaned can never be quite the equal of never having been stained; there is no such thing as "good as new"), worst if stained and not cleaned. Cf. *Laws* 1.628d.

On the next step up the justice ladder (level two) stands the man who refrains from injustice because he is moderate. His soul is free of the rapacious greed and destructive envy that are responsible for most wrongdoing. He is the man described in the *Gorgias* at 507c-e, as well as in the *Republic* at 4.442d-444a. Perhaps the "good and decent men" of Book 1, who do not rule for the sake of money or honor, qualify as just at this level—though, as was noted (Chapter 3, note 80), Socrates does not call them just. And so, too, the good father of the timocratic man at 8.459c, "who lives in a city not under a good regime, who flees the honors, ruling offices, lawsuits, and everything of the sort that is to the busybody's taste, and who is willing to be gotten the better of so as not to be bothered." Unlike those who are just at the first level, those at the second level can fairly well be trusted not to do wrong even when they can be certain that no one can see them. Yet what even they lack is care for others.

Sadly, few people rise even to level two. Glaucon can scarcely imagine a man who, despite having license to do injustice without fear of retribution, would nevertheless "never be willing to do injustice" and would indeed never do it, one who would not "lay his hands on what belongs to others" (2.360d). If there were a man who actually wants to be just, Glaucon says, he would seem to those who were aware of his genuine antipathy toward injustice "most wretched . . . and most foolish too" (361b).

At the next level (level three) stands the man whose justness derives from his regard for others, someone to whom the interests of others actually matter. (Socrates does not supply any obvious examples of this type.) At neither of the first two levels need there be concern or even basic respect for the other: the agent is primarily self-interested. Indeed, the reason Cephalus's conception of justice—telling the truth and returning what is owed (331a-c)—fails is that, because those who adhere blindly to rules needn't care about or even see the person on the receiving end of their deeds, they cannot accommodate any special circumstances that might arise. And Book 1's good and decent men, we recall, are at best indifferent to the needs of others, grudgingly consenting to rule only to spare themselves the intolerably worse fate of being ruled by their inferiors. Socrates does not call these men just and, as was argued in the addendum to Chapter 3, he is far from fully sincere even in calling them "good and decent," let alone "best and most decent."[44] A truly good and decent—and just—man would

---

44. See Chapter 3, note 78.

be mindful of how his deeds affect others, and would avoid doing anything that is likely to cause injury or harm. Yet even such a man could not be relied on to "take trouble" (1.347d) on behalf of others; he would not hurt them, but neither would he go out of his way to help them.

Climbing still higher (level four), we find those who wish to promote justice in others. As early as *Rep.* 1 we find allusions to such an ideal. Implicit both in Socrates' notion of a "ruler in the precise sense," that is, a ruler whose goal it is to improve the moral condition of those in his charge, and in his reprimand to Thrasymachus for failing to care at all about whether his companions live well or fail to do so, is the idea that a just man does indeed seek to help others lead lives that are better—that is, more just. As we noted earlier, improving the souls of others is the task that is identified in the *Gorgias* as "the work of a good citizen" (517b-c). The men in the *Republic* who are most obviously just at this level are, of course, the philosophers of Book 6, those who are first compared to pilots of a ship and later described as remaining loyal to philosophy "in a worthy way." These philosophers commit no injustice and, because of their love for what is (500b-c), have no wish to do so. Moreover, other people matter to them; as Socrates explains, they are useless only because others have contempt for what they have to offer or because the regimes in which they find themselves are hopelessly corrupt. What they would do if they could is "go to the aid of justice"; they would encourage those they rule to be more just. Lamentably, men such as these, men who reach rung four of the justice ladder, compose only a "very small group" (496a).

VI. Piety: The Risk Factor

Piety is a species of justice, perched on the justice ladder's highest rung (level five). In what might be called its negative aspect, piety excludes injustice. Socrates can therefore accuse of *impiety*—and not just of injustice—those judges who would pervert justice by doling out favors to defendants whose emotional pleas they find gratifying (Ap. 35c-d): no matter how orthodox their views of the gods or how punctilious their ritual practice, such judges could never qualify as pious in Socrates' eyes. In its positive aspect, piety involves tending to the souls of others and fighting for the cause of justice. Socrates indeed speaks of his own activities on behalf of justice as ways in which he "serves the god" (see, for example, *Ap*. 23b, 28e, 29d, 30a-b, 30e 31a, 31a-b, 33c, and 37c). Although refraining from injustice, on the negative side, and helping others and fighting for justice, on the positive, are important components of piety, they are not quite the whole of it. They don't take us beyond justice's level four.

The idea that piety is a part of justice is one that appears in the *Euthyphro*, where Socrates compares the relationship between holiness and justice to that between reverence and fear, or that between odd and number: wherever there is reverence there is fear, but it is not the case that wherever there is fear there is reverence (*Euthyph*. 12c); wherever there is odd there is number, but it is not the case that wherever there is number there is odd (*Euthyph*. 12c). Reverence, then, is a specific kind of fear, as odd is one kind of number—and, analogously, holiness is a particular sort of justice. In each pair, the former may be said to be a proper subset of the latter: it (or all of its members or instances) is (are) included in the latter, larger, set, but not the whole of the latter, larger, set (or all of its members or instances) is (are) included in it.

When Socrates asks Euthyphro to specify "what part of the just is holy (*hosion*)" (12e), Euthyphro asserts that the part of the just that is pious (*eu sebes*) and holy (*hosion*) concerns "the tendance (*therapeian*)" of the gods, while the remaining part of justice concerns the tendance of men (12e). Euthyphro thus divides justice into two parts, one of which is holiness and the second of which remains unnamed. Socrates leaves utterly unexplored Euthyphro's second part of justice, proceeding instead to examine his notion of holiness as tendance of the gods. Should we assume, therefore, that Socrates agrees with Euthyphro that justice is one part tendance of the gods and one part tendance of men? Does he, too, think that holiness is best confined to relations between men and gods, and that relations between men and other men are properly consigned to another realm entirely?[45]

---

45. Socrates does indeed say that what Euthyphro proposes "appears noble" to him (12e). Yet, Socrates often commends an interlocutor's response, even when, as soon becomes evident, it strikes him as worthless. See, for example, *Lach*. 190e and *Charm*. 160e. When Socrates compliments Euthyphro (at *Euthyph*. 7a) on his suggestion that "what is dear to the gods is pious, and what is not dear is impious," saying: "Altogether noble (*Pankalōs*), Euthyphro. You have now answered just as I was seeking for you to answer," he immediately adds: "Whether it is true, however, I don't yet know." When Socrates tells Euthyphro at 13a that he is "still in need of a little something" (*smikrou tinos eti endeēs eimi*), we are reminded of the "one little thing" Socrates says is

It seems that it is up to the *Republic* to revisit Socrates' proposal in the *Euthyphro* that the holy is part of the just, to raise the question anew of what Socrates might have meant—as opposed to what Euthyphro did—by this idea. We note that he offers in the *Euthyphro* two different illustrations of the proper subset relation: reverence and fear, on the one hand, and odd and number, on the other. He thus provides two alternative models for construing it. On the second model, that of odd and number, number is evenly divided into two subsets, odd and even, each of which has a feature the other lacks: the even is isosceles and not scalene (12d); the odd is scalene and not isosceles. On the first model, that of reverence and fear, however, when reverence is present it adds "at the same time" (*hama*) a second emotion, namely, dread of reputation for villainy (12b-c), to the one that already attaches to "diseases and poverty and many other such things" (12b). Just as reverence colors fear, adding a further dimension to it, so does holiness raise regard for other people, which is essential to all of justice, to the level of divine service. Holiness, as a subset of justice, concerns, as does all of justice, relations between men and men.

It is likely that from Plato's perspective no one but Socrates has ever occupied justice's highest level; no one but he is truly pious. Socrates does not simply "do no injustice to anyone" (*Ap.* 37b) and seek to improve souls, but, "having no fear of death or of any other thing whatsoever" (*Ap.* 28e-29a), he puts himself in harm's way for justice's sake, for the Athenians' sake. Even while knowing that he is running great risks—"incurring many hatreds" (*Ap.* 23a, 28a; cf. 21d, 21e, 24a)—he "awakens and persuades and reproaches each of you, and . . . does not stop settling down everywhere upon you the whole day" (*Ap.* 30e-31a).[46] What holiness does—certainly

---

missing from Protagoras's great speech (*Prot.* 329a). Protagoras's careless clumping together of the virtues, attending neither to their individual natures nor to their relationship to virtue as a whole, proves his undoing in the ensuing discussion.

46. In the *Gorgias* myth, the soul "that has lived piously and with truth" belongs "mostly" to the philosopher, "who has minded his own business and not been a busybody in life" (526c). In the very same dialogue, however, Socrates describes himself as one who "puts my hand to the true political *technē*" and "alone of the men of today practice politics" (521d): only he has done "the one work of a good citizen," "leading desires in a different direction and not yielding, persuading and forcing them toward the condition in which the citizens were to be better" (517b-c). If it is the philosopher who lives piously, and if Socrates is the quintessential philosopher, then the man who "minds his own business" and "is not a busybody" is the very one who attempts to improve the moral condition of his fellow citizens. To encourage virtue in others *is* his business.

in Socrates' case—is raise regard for other people to the level of divine service, so that even under adverse conditions those who are holy persist in doing the god's work of fostering justice. Although justice at both the fourth level and the fifth goes beyond not harming others to the attempt to bring them closer to justice, only holiness—justice at the fifth level—carries on with its sacred task even when real danger and difficulty loom.

VII. Socrates and the Philosophers of *Republic* 7

Whereas the philosophers of Book 6 have much in common with Socrates—they, too, are willing to promote justice (although they ask at least to be given a fighting chance)—Book 7's philosophers resemble him not at all. Indeed, nowhere does Socrates affiliate himself with Book 7's philosophers as he does explicitly with Book 6's at 496c; on the contrary, in *Rep.* 7 he is consistently and exclusively one of the founders. As a founder, he is well aware of the kind of philosophers he has produced: they regard ruling as a distasteful but necessary task and not as anything noble (*ouch hōs kalon ti*); they must therefore be compelled to rule; and when they rule they "drudge" (*epitalaipōrountas*) (540b) Whereas Socrates willingly "goes down" to the Piraeus and, in response to the mildest of arm-twisting, stays all night to converse with the others about justice,[47] the philosophers of Book 7 are not

---

47. Whereas Glaucon is the one who at the opening of the *Republic* readily agrees that he and Socrates must stay, Socrates puts up no fight at all: "Well," he says, "if it is so resolved, that is how we must act" (328b). And although Socrates declares at the beginning of Book 2 that he is done with the argument (357a), by 358d he is saying that "there is nothing an intelligent man would enjoy talking and hearing about more again and again than justice in itself." When Glaucon and the others beg Socrates to help justice and not to abandon the argument, he does indeed "speak his opinion" (358c). In Book 4 Socrates appears to wish to relinquish the argument to others (427d)—just when the time has come for justice to be defined—but he immediately takes charge when admonished. And despite his complaint in Book 5 (450a) that he was "arrested," he is hardly an unwilling captive. He speaks at 450b of having "passed by" a "swarm" of arguments "so as not to cause a lot of trouble," but eventually addresses these awkward issues in Book 5 itself and in Book 6 beginning at 502d. It is noteworthy that all the participants, Thrasymachus included, become intrigued by Socrates' discussion of justice. Glaucon even comes to think that for an intelligent man the "proper measure of listening to such arguments is a whole life"—a rather Socratic thing to say (see *Ap.* 38a). In the *Phaedo*, too, despite Socrates' talk about the philosophic yearning for death, he gladly spends his last hours in conversation with his friends. On the significance of the *Republic*'s opening with Socrates' descent (*Katebēn*, "I went down")—it is the dialogue's first word—see Miller 2007, 317, 334.

willing to "go down" (517c, 519d) and must be compelled to do so (520a, 540a). Moreover, these philosophers must be subjected to coercion, even though in Callipolis people presumably (1) actually see value in philosophic rule, (2) are willing to be ruled by philosophers, and (3) create the conditions that make the joys of philosophy possible for their rulers during their time off. As we saw in the previous chapter, it is Glaucon—not Socrates—who thinks (520e) that Socrates' argument at 7.520b-d will persuade these philosophers to rule. It is he who thinks they are just men who will respond to a just argument. What Socrates believes is that the founders, while saying "just things" to the philosophers, will need to compel them besides (520a); indeed, by the end of Book 7 (540a) only compulsion remains. As we have seen, despite the considerable and frantic efforts scholars devote to softening or even discounting Socrates' bold assertion that these philosophers do not wish to rule, the fact remains that they do not.

Where, then, do Book 7's philosophers stand on the justice ladder? It is quite certain that they do not commit the usual sorts of injustice. Indeed, having been turned away from the delights of the earthly world and toward those of the transcendent, they lose interest in the material goods for the sake of which ordinary people lie, cheat, and steal. Moreover, it is not because they fear punishment or reproach that they refrain from unjust action, nor is it because they crave the rewards of being—or appearing—just. They thus qualify as just not only by the most basic measure but by that of the second level as well: owing to their having lost interest in the things of the world and their wishing instead to spend their time in philosophy, they have no *desire* to commit injustice. It is true, as we have seen, that it is not by their natures that they are disposed to be just, as the natural philosophers of Book 6 are; indeed, had their ties to the realm of Becoming not been severed, they would have sunk into the deepest abysses of moral turpitude (7.519a). Nevertheless, once they are forcibly turned to the realm of Being, they can be trusted to refrain quite willingly from injustice—at least until they have spent sufficient time back in the visible realm for them to become once again susceptible to its charms.

Yet Book 7's philosophers certainly do not reach even level three. They have no real regard for other people; the needs of others figure not at all in the way they conduct their lives. And since they do not love justice and have no particular wish to promote it among the unjust, they fall far short of level four. Like the other two classes in Callipolis, the philosopher-rulers must be made to share (*metadidonai*) with the rest of the commonwealth the unique benefit they are able to bring to it (519e-520a). And even when, as rulers, they promote justice, they do so neither out of devotion to justice nor out of care for other people. In their eagerness to evade their responsi-bilities, in their "always educating other like men and leaving them behind in their place as guardians of the city" (540b), they remind us of Thrasy-machus, whose first impulse is to head straight for the door once he's had his say (1.344e-345a). (He evidently has a change of heart, because, as was noted earlier [note 36], he stays for the duration of the conversation.) And as Cicero says of them, "While they steer clear of the one kind of injustice [viz. doing injury to others], they fall into the other; they are traitors to so-cial life, for they contribute to it none of their interest, none of their effort, none of their means" (*Offic.* 1.29)—except under duress.

In the final analysis, the philosophers of Book 7 are utterly self-interested; the contrast between them and Socrates could hardly be more pronounced. The "labors" that Socrates willingly endures for the sake of others (*Ap.* 22a7) under conditions far less ideal than those the philosophers of Book 7 face are the very "labors" that these philosophers are unwilling to undertake until they are persuaded or coerced (519d, 520b; cf. 520d). Unlike Socrates, who, because of his service to the god (*Ap.* 23b c), has "no leisure worth mentioning either for the affairs of the city or for my own estate," the philosophers of Book 7 take turns, each serving the city for a short time, while spending the bulk of their time in contemplation of the Good (540b). Even if Socrates had leisure, he would use it, as he tells the jurors at his trial, to carry out his unpopular mission of exhorting people to embrace virtue (36d). Whereas the philosophers of *Rep.* 7 see ruling as drudgery, Socrates takes on the care of the Athenians as a father or older brother would (*Ap.* 31b). And just as for some parents caring for children is an unwelcome chore while for the best parents it is good both in itself and for what comes from it,[48] so, too, is ruling regarded differently

---

48. Socrates appears, perhaps perversely, to be a far less devoted parent to his own children than to the Athenians: in serving the city, he says, he has "endured that the matters of my fam-ily (*tōn oikeiōn*) be uncared for" (*Ap.* 31b). Yet here the object of his neglect may well be not his children's nurture but the family finances: at 23b he associates his inattentiveness to his family with the "ten-thousandfold poverty" to which his devotion to the god has led. At worst, it seems, Socrates, in approaching *everyone* as "a father or an older brother might do" (*Ap.* 31b), educates all alike without privileging his own. It is true that in the *Crito* (48c) Socrates is contemptuous of

by rulers who are forced to rule and have no real care for their subjects, on the one hand, and by rulers who rule willingly out of genuine concern for the ruled, on the other.

Insofar as *Rep.* 7's philosophers take what is just as "greatest and most necessary" (540d-e) but not, as was noted in Chapter 3, section V, as best or most noble, it is to be expected that they, like the many and unlike Socrates, assign justice to the lowest of Glaucon's three categories. Whereas Socrates thinks justice "belongs in the most noble (*kallistōi*) kind, which is to be liked both for itself and for what comes out of it by the man who is going to be blessed," the philosophers of Book 7 probably consign it, as the many do, to the class of goods that involve drudgery (*epiponou*) (358a; cf. 357c). They fail to find justice appealing "both for itself and for what comes out of it."

One final striking difference between the philosophers of *Rep.* 7 and Socrates is perhaps worth noting. It concerns the manner in which they each practice philosophy.[49] Socrates, as Plato depicts him, is what Gregory Vlastos (1991, 177, 253) famously calls a "street philosopher," one who draws others into often public philosophic conversation. For Socrates, philosophic conversation represents "inconceivable happiness" (*amēchanon . . . eudaimonias—Ap.* 41c); rarely do we see him engaged in any sort of transcendent contemplation.[50] By contrast, contemplation of the Forms is, "for the most part," what *Rep.* 7's philosophers do: it is in this way that each of them "spends his time in philosophy" (540b). It is this activity

---

"spending of money and reputation and nurture of children" as unworthy concerns of the many, but what troubles him in this instance is that the many permit considerations such as these to take precedence over justice. If escape is unjust, Socrates will not escape; the greatest harm he could do to his children is to teach them that it is more important to stay alive than to do what is right. At the *Apology*'s very end (41e-42a), and so at his own, it is his children's moral welfare that is uppermost in his mind: the way he will attain justice at the hands of those who voted against him, he says, is if they punish and pain his children for valuing money or anything else above virtue.

49. I omit one other rather obvious difference: Socrates does not share *Rep.* 7 philosophers' love of gymnastic and the hunt (535d). The only battles he fights on his own initiative are verbal ones.

50. Socrates does fall into a trance on the way to Agathon's party in the *Symposium* (174d ff.; cf. 220c ff.). As Mara points out (1997, 17), however, he is not like the philosopher depicted at *Theaet.* 174b, who does not know how to get to the agora or whether the creature next to him is even a human being. "It seems," Mara observes, "that it is difficult for Socrates to find his way out of the agora" and that he indeed knows quite a bit about Theaetetus even before he begins to converse with him. Socrates merely reports the common perception of the philosopher; he does not endorse it.

that they are most reluctant to relinquish, and it is on account of it that they regard themselves as dwelling on the Isles of the Blessed even while they are still living.

Socrates represents, then, it would seem, a third type of philosopher, distinct from the two types adumbrated in the *Republic*. He is not the decent but useless philosopher of Book 6 who huddles by a wall, protecting his own soul. Nor is he the useful but coerced philosopher of Book 7 (to whom the term "decent" is, tellingly, never applied). He is, instead, the decent, useful, and willingly just and pious man, who, in his own idiosyncratic way, seeks to improve the moral condition of others, privately, despite the risks and hardships involved.

VIII. Piety: The Humility Factor

For a man to qualify as truly pious, however, it is not sufficient that he be prepared to undertake missions that are difficult and possibly dangerous; he must also approach his sacred tasks with humility. Turning once again to the *Euthyphro*, we see how wide of the mark Euthyphro's conception of holiness is. In his arrogance Euthyphro takes himself to be an expert on holiness and relies on his thoroughgoing knowledge of the gods' likes and dislikes to worm his way into their good graces (4e-5a).[51] In his eyes, the gods are his superiors only in power. They are therefore not to be served and obeyed but flattered and appeased.[52] Socrates seeks to effect a change in Euthyphro's understanding of holiness by getting him to relinquish his notion of holiness as *therapeia* (tendance) and to replace it with *hupēretikē* (service) (12e-14a).[53]

---

51. Euthyphro is so emboldened by his hubristic belief that he knows the gods intimately that he dares to prosecute his own father.

52. A striking feature of Socrates' piety is that he asks nothing of the god but wishes only to serve. For this reason, too, Socrates has no need to believe in literal gods; he is not looking to them to provide the things he needs or wants. Euthyphro's piety is deficient in part because he gives to the gods in order to receive; cf. *Lach.* 199d-e, where Nicias approves of the courageous man, who, in Socrates' description, knows how to "associate correctly" with "both gods and human beings," and whose knowledge equips him to elude the terrible things and "to provide himself with the good things."

53. As Socrates says in the *Apology*, "In fact, the god is wise, and . . . human wisdom is worth little or nothing" (23a). Socrates seeks to introduce *eusebeia*, a reverence for what is higher, into

Therapeia, as Socrates explains to Euthyphro, is something a superior does for an inferior to benefit him. For example, the person who tends horses and cattle directs his skill to benefiting and improving the animals in his care. Since, however, as Euthyphro concedes, human beings cannot benefit or improve the gods, the conception of piety as *therapeia* cannot be sustained. Euthyphro then suggests that pious human beings serve the gods in the way in which slaves serve their masters; to this kind of service Socrates attaches the name *hupēretikē*. On this model, the gods are like the doctor, shipwright, house-builder, or farmer, each of whom produces a certain valued product; the pious man is the counterpart of those who assist them. Although an assistant is certainly skilled, his skill is not that of a doctor or architect but that of a technician, who can put the doctor's or architect's plan into effect. The term *hupēretikē*, even if it resembles in form the terms used for the tendance of horses, dogs, and herds—*hippikē*, *kunēgetikē*, and *bolatikē*—does not, as they do, imply expertise at a craft.[54] The skill of the *hupēretēs* is that of executing the vision of another—not that of taking the initiative and setting the goal.

It is indeed essential to Socrates' characterization of the pious man that he lack the gods' expertise: an assistant in possession of the craftsman's

---

Euthyphro's conception of *to hosion*, holiness. Socrates initially frames the "What is *x*?" question he puts to Euthyphro in terms of *eusebeia* and *asebeia* (5e), immediately shifting, however, to *to hosion* and *to anosion*. Yet Socrates revives *eusebeia* at 12e and again at 13b, placing it alongside *to hosion*: if holiness involves assuming a posture of reverence and awe before a superior, then piety excludes human "tendance" to the gods.

54. Although *hupēretikē* might be thought to be shorthand for *hupēretikē technē* and thus to suggest that those who possess it are indeed experts at some craft, the *Euthyphro* makes clear that it is the gods, and not their human assistants, who are the counterparts of doctors and shipwrights. In the *Gorgias*, *kolastikē*, flattery, though it has the same form as *hupēretikē*, is explicitly said by Socrates not to be a *technē* at all. And Socrates denies to *rhētorikē* the status of *technē* as well (462b; even if by the *Gorgias*'s close he appears to relent [511b-c]: he finally ends up calling not only rhetoric but cookery, too, a *technē*, despite the fact that as late as 500b he regards cookery as the counterfeit counterpart of the genuine *technē* medicine). Socrates also uses the term *hupēresia* (at 14d6; also at *Ap.* 30a7), perhaps to indicate that this sort of service need not be seen as a *technē*. Moreover, even if *hupēretikē* is a *technē* of sorts, it is at some point supervised or directed by an expert. Wildberg (2003, 21 n. 31) thinks his view that those who have *hupēretikē* are experts of some kind is not reconcilable with mine; but my view is not that *hupēretikē* excludes technical ability. I maintain only that in the *Euthyphro hupēretikē* is the skill not of the master craftsman but of the technician who assists him or helps produce his product. From Versényi's perspective (1982, 104), *hupēretikē* is service that is "slavish, ignorant, and entirely submissive." He errs perhaps in the other direction, denying to the *hupēretēs* any skill whatsoever.

knowledge could and would be a craftsman himself.[55] Thus the question
Socrates poses to Euthyphro is, What is the "altogether noble work" (*to
pankalon ergon*—13e) that the *gods* produce, using us as servants? Although
Euthyphro is unsuccessful in specifying the product that the gods produce
through human assistance (13e10–11),[56] it is clear that, whatever that product
is, piety will be the province not of the wise expert, but of his dutiful servant.[57]

If the philosophers depicted in the *Republic*, those who ascend into the
light of Being, achieve the highest form of wisdom, divine wisdom, what
Socrates calls in the *Apology* "wisdom greater than human" (*Ap.* 20e), they
cannot then possess the virtue of piety. They cannot be the humble servants
of the gods, because, in knowing *ta megista* (the most important things—
that is, the moral things—*Ap.* 22d[58]), they are themselves, though surely not
gods, nevertheless virtual gods. As "craftsmen" of demotic virtue (500d), as
"painters who use the divine pattern" (500e), they cannot humbly regard
their skill as human wisdom "worth little or nothing" (*Ap.* 23b). Moreover,
having already become as orderly and divine "as is possible for a human
being" (500d), they can no longer be, as the pious are, merely "eagerly willing" to become as like the god "as is possible for a human being" (10.613a-b).[59]

But what of Socrates? Has he not seen the Good? Has he not been out
of the Cave? Socrates in the *Republic*, no less than elsewhere, professes
his ignorance of the important things: he does not know the truth, he
says, but is "in doubt and seeking" (*apistounta . . . kai zētounta*—5.450e;
cf. 1.337e). Although he is widely believed by commentators to be the one

---

55. Since in all cases the primary beneficiary of a craft is a third party—the patient, for example, in the case of health—it is other human beings who benefit from the gods' product: not
the gods themselves, who, in any event, cannot be benefited by human beings (13c-d), and not the
gods' servants, who are merely assisting them.

56. Socrates implies that were a satisfactory specification to be made, the desired definition of
holiness would have been discovered. It is likely that the unnamed product is human virtue. See
Weiss 1994, 274.

57. Socrates argues in the *Phaedo* (61c-62c) that suicide is forbidden because human beings are
possessions of the gods. If in fact we are the gods' servants or assistants, helping them to produce
something they cannot produce alone (human virtue, perhaps), we would indeed be doing them a
disservice by resigning prematurely from their employ.

58. In the *Republic* to know *ta megista* (450e) is to know about "fine, good, just, and lawful
things," or "fine, good, and just things in laws" (451a).

59. Cf. *Theaet.* 176b: "Becoming like a god is becoming just and holy with intelligent judgment." This is not to say that gods are holy, but only that when a person strives to "become like a
god as far as is in one's power," he must live as justly and piously as he can.

who releases and leads the prisoner out of the Cave, the text is not explicit on the matter. But even if he is its intended referent,[60] there are no grounds for assuming that the one who does the dragging has himself scaled the heights: in the Cave allegory the dragger leads the prisoner only out into the light; from that point on, the prisoner is ostensibly on his own (515e–516c). Indeed, although the philosophers who finally see the Good at 540a (cf. 519c) are led to it and are compelled to look at it, there is no implication that the founders who do the leading and compelling have themselves mastered the studies along the way, nor indeed that they are as capable as their charges are of "lifting up the brilliant beams of their souls" to see the Good (540a). Since it certainly cannot be assumed that two of the founders, Glaucon and Adeimantus, have completed the educational curriculum devised for the philosopher-rulers or have in some other way attained the vision of the Good, there is no warrant either for assuming that the third founder, Socrates, has. The founders' task is to compel the original group of philosopher-rulers to ascend to the vision of the Good—that is, they must set the curriculum and enforce it.

There are, to be sure, places in the *Republic* (6.506, 7.533) where it is said that Socrates will not, though not for any lack of eagerness on his part, take Glaucon any farther. One might reasonably infer that these are instances in which Socrates has *knowledge* that is beyond what Glaucon can grasp. Yet Socrates does not even on these occasions take himself to have anything more epistemically advanced than opinions. At 6.506b Glaucon wants to know what the Good is, yet, at 506d, Socrates says: "for it looks to me as though it is out of the range of our present thrust to attain the *opinion* I now hold about it (*tou ge dokountos emoi ta nun*)." Socrates is consequently willing to present only an image, the image of the Sun, the "child of the Good," something "similar" to it (506e). At 7.533a, where the nature of dialectic is at issue, again Socrates can take Glaucon no farther than an image; in particular, he cannot take him to the truth itself, "at least as it looks to me. Whether it is really so or not is not worth insisting on any further. But that there is some such thing to see must be insisted on." Here, too, Socrates deprecates his own epistemic state with respect to the nature of dialectic as

---

60. One reason to think the person who releases the prisoner is Socrates is that he "compels the man to answer his questions about what they [each of the things that pass by] are" (9.515d). The man is then "at a loss" (*aporein*), just as Socrates' interlocutors often are.

being "the truth at least as it looks to me" (*ho ge dē emoi phainetai*). Socratic piety depends on his having opinions and not knowledge about the Good.[61] What distinguishes him from the multitude is his recognition that there is a Fair Itself, besides the many fair things, an "*X* Itself" besides the many particular *x*'s (533a; cf. 6.493e-494a).[62]

Socrates, then, cannot do what even the philosophers described in Book 6—those who have seen the divine and orderly and who thus become orderly and divine (6.500c-d)—can. He cannot look "in both directions, toward the just, fair, and moderate by nature, and everything of the sort, and, again, toward what is in human beings" (6.501b) and shape human souls in accordance with these perfect Forms. He can, however, implement a practice that does for the soul what the doctor's "cutting, burning, reducing, and choking, giving bitter draughts, and making hungry and thirsty" does for the body (*Gorg.* 521e-522a). Socrates can "fight with the Athenians so that they will be as good as possible, as a doctor would do" (*Gorg.* 521a). He can ask questions that shatter his interlocutors' old answers, and he can encourage them to replace those answers with better ones.[63] In this way he

---

61. In Book 1 Socrates thinks his *opinion* (*houtō doxeien*) that the just is the needful, beneficial, profitable, gainful, or advantageous (336d) is worthy of being expressed and being heard, even though he "does not know (*eidōs*) and does not profess to know (*eidenai*)" (337e). Yet, in his exchange with Adeimantus in Book 6, Socrates unmistakably disparages opinions—even true ones—saying that, in the absence of intelligence (*aneu nou*), they are ugly or blind (506c). Cf. *Meno* 97b-d, where Socrates argues that true or right opinions are just as good and beneficial, practically speaking, as knowledge, so long as they are true. Plato highlights the difference between the *Meno* and *Rep.* 6 by using in both the metaphor of traveling the right road. In the *Phaedo* at 85c-d Simmias, sounding very Socratic, advocates adopting and relying on the best and least refutable opinions if one cannot learn the truth or discover it. It is likely that the reason Socrates degrades true opinion in the *Republic* is that if he were to maintain here that it is as valuable as knowledge, he could not establish that only philosophers who have knowledge of the Good are qualified to rule.

62. If Socrates is indeed the someone who drags the prisoner out of the Cave, that he leads him no farther than into the light (515e) may indicate that Socrates can do no more than point out to others *that* there are such things as the "things themselves."

63. Socrates may be the implicit target of his own censure at 539b, for he develops in young people, in "puppies," a taste for argument at the same time that he deprives them of their moral anchor, their confidence in the beliefs in which they were raised. He is guilty, too, of "sharing arguments with whoever chances by and comes to it without being suited for it" (539d). At *Ap.* 23c Socrates acknowledges the deleterious effect his elenctic activity has on the leisured and wealthy young; and at 30a he confirms that "I will do this [examine, test, and reproach] for whomever, younger or older, I happen to meet, both foreigner and townsman." Not all Socrates' interlocutors are receptive to or appreciate his brand of argument, and not in every case will they come away from an exchange morally improved. Neither, of course, will the spectator.

is able to come close—as close as is possible for someone who has not seen, but believes in, the things that truly are—to "wiping the slate clean" and drawing in a new image. Socrates lacks the divine wisdom with which to remake people, but he can try to get them to reevaluate their moral beliefs and to consider reordering their priorities.[64]

Socrates is, to be sure, an erotic man—and in this way again resembles the philosophers of Book 6 (see 490b). He boasts in the *Symposium* (177d-e) that "love is the one thing in the world I understand." He describes himself in the *Gorgias* as passionately in love with (*erōnte*) two things: Alcibiades and philosophy (481d; also 487b8-d9, 513c4-d1). It seems, however, that the philosophy he loves is its practice: more than *Rep.* 6's philosophers, he appears to want to spend his time reflecting on, discussing with others, and seeking the truth concerning the nature of justice and the rest of virtue. In the *Republic*, at the end of Book 1, Socrates even chides himself for seizing on every question that comes along. In the *Theaetetus* he describes his *erōs* for sparring in speech as being terrible (*deinos*—169c) and a disease (*noson*—169b). His fondness for speech and conversation is surely attributable in part to his harboring no illusions with respect to his attaining wisdom that is divine. He is convinced that such wisdom will elude him so long as he is in human form.[65]

Whether or not Socrates is the man who leads the unwilling prisoner out of the Cave, he certainly *is* the "someone" described at 6.494d-e who takes it upon himself to disabuse a promising young man of his inflated self-assessment and to set him on the path toward wisdom. For who but

---

64. In the *Gorgias* Socrates observes that if statesmen had succeeded in improving the people, the people would not have turned against them (515e-516e). Although Socrates is executed, he can nevertheless boast that at least none of his close associates find fault with him: neither the young people with whom he interacts nor their families are among his accusers, and none stand up at his trial to berate him or to complain of any corruptive influence he has had on them (*Ap.* 33d-34a). No Strepsiades steps forward in the *Apology* to complain that Socrates has corrupted his Pheidippides.

65. Perhaps philosophers who see the highest realities are for Socrates mere fictions. He observes, for example, at 500c-d, that even the philosopher who keeps company with the divine and orderly remains human, becoming orderly and divine only "to the extent possible for a human being." And, of course, the oracle Socrates quotes in the *Apology*—"That one of you, O human beings, is wisest, who, *like* Socrates, has become cognizant that in truth he is worth nothing with respect to wisdom" (*Ap.* 23b)—implies that human wisdom never exceeds the awareness of one's own ignorance. As Nichols (1987, 56) observes, "The complexity of man, his combination of body and soul, makes perfect knowledge impossible."

Socrates would gently approach a young man and inform him that "he has no intelligence in him although he needs it, and that it is not to be acquired except by slaving for its acquisition" (494d)? Who else would then be set upon and prevented by all available means from doing his "persuading" (494e)? And who else would end up, for all his trouble, the target of "private plots and public trials" (494e)? Only Socrates so loves wisdom that he would put himself at risk to encourage a young friend to think. Not regarding himself, however, as a knower or expert, Socrates would not presume simply to dictate to the young man just what he should think.

IX. Conclusion

Just as Socrates is left virtually undescribed in the *Republic*, so, too, is his virtue of piety. For if piety is the virtue of those who are humble before the gods, of those who recognize the incompleteness of their merely human wisdom, then the philosophers of the *Republic* who have seen the Forms, and particularly the Form of the Good, cannot be pious. Socrates' business may strike others as "not human" (*Ap.* 31b),[66] but Socrates is painfully aware of how very human his practice of examination and refutation is. He does not see himself as the "pilot," the philosopher who has attained true wisdom and is thus in a position to tell others what they must do and how they must be. Indeed, whereas "begging" may be beneath the dignity of the pilots and the doctors, and of the rulers who are compared to them, he himself is not unwilling to beg: he begs (*edeomēn*) even Thrasymachus to share his wisdom with him (344d). And under Socrates' influence "Glaucon and the others" do some begging (*edeonto*) of their own (338a).

Furthermore, if piety is the virtue of risk, then, again, no one but Socrates has it. Only he willingly incurs danger and difficulty for the sake of promoting justice. Indeed, only he makes coming to the aid of justice, makes

---

66. The reason Socrates' enterprise strikes others as "not human" is that Socrates cares for others as a father or older brother would when he is not in fact related to them. Fathers and older brothers are expected to be concerned for the virtue of their sons and younger brothers and even to go out of their way to ensure it: see *Ap.* 20a-b; *Prot.* 320a, 325b-e; *Meno* 93c-d. If strangers advance the morality of others it can only be, it is thought, because they themselves stand to benefit (*Ap.* 19e-20b; *Prot.* 327b; *Meno* 91b) or because doing so does not require very much effort (*Ap.* 19e; *Meno* 92e).

serving the god in this way, the central mission of his life. It is Socrates'
pious service that we witness in the *Republic* itself, where Socrates defends
justice because, as he says, it would not be *pious* (*hosion*) of him not to, to
be silent when justice is being slandered (2.368b-c). That Socrates regards
a refusal on his part to defend justice as a breach of piety rather than of
justice indicates that in his view the task is not an easy one, that it is both
fraught with peril (as his eventual execution attests) and exceeds his abilities (as he insists it does in the *Republic*—2.362d-e, 368b). As we shall see in
Chapter 5, Socrates knows he is not up to the task of defending justice—at
least not within the parameters set for him.[67] Glaucon's defense of *in*justice
was, in his words, "already enough to bring me to my knees and make
it impossible to help justice out" (2.362d). Nevertheless, he persists. Despite his reservations (362d, 368b), and because it would be not holy not to
(368b), he pleads justice's cause "as I am able" (368c).

---

67. As we shall see in Chapter 5, Socrates' task is to show that justice is profitable for the
just man.

5

Justice as Moderation

It is proper to justice, as compared with the other virtues, to direct man in his
relations with others. . . . The other virtues perfect man in those matters only
which befit him in relation to himself.

—Aquinas, *Summa Theologica*, question 57, article 1

In the previous chapters, justice was conceived in conventional terms as
the virtue that shows proper regard for the interests of others. Indeed, in as-
sessing whether and to what extent the philosophers of Books 5, 6, and 7—
and Socrates—are just, we considered only how much or how little their
preferences and choices were guided by the concerns of those they were
in a position to help or harm. The reader may well wonder what became
of justice as it was innovatively defined earlier in the *Republic*, specifically
in *Rep.* 4. There Socrates had urged the adoption of a new understanding of justice as internal—that is, as the concord achieved in city and soul
when their respective parts perform their appropriate jobs and no other.
Yet it is Socrates himself who all but abandons this novel conception of
justice after Book 4.[1] The critical question then is, Why does the *Republic*

---

1. For example, in Books 5, 6 and 7, the unified and efficient city that is free of internal strife
is no longer a just one; it is now "happy." For the marginalization of Book 4's conception of justice
in Books 8, 9, and 10, see addendum II.

proceed from Book 5 on oblivious to its arguably most important philosophical breakthrough?

I. City and Soul: The Search for Justice

Rep. 4's conception of justice as internal derives from what has come to be known as the city-soul analogy. On the assumption that justice is the same wherever it is found and whatever its size (368c-d), Socrates turns to the city where justice is "bigger"[2] to help him to discover justice in the individual where it is smaller and therefore presumably harder to discern. Since only those who are sharp-sighted are able to make out individual justice directly,[3] and since Socrates and his companions are not clever men, they are surely better off adopting the "easier" course (369a),[4] and looking at the magnified version of justice—in the city.

Two suppositions, then, anchor Socrates' proposed procedure: (1) that justice in the individual is hard to see, and (2) that it is easier to see justice in the city. Yet both are questionable. With respect to the first, Book 1 offers a fairly straightforward account of individual justice. For Socrates, the just man is one who commits no injustice, harms no one, and, as is likely, has no desire to take advantage of, cheat, get the better of, or succeed at the expense of other people (335d-e, 349b-350c).[5] Thrasymachus concurs:

---

2. 2.368e; cf. 4.434d. Socrates also imagines that justice is easier to see in the city because the city contains "more justice" (*pleiōn . . . dikaiosunē*—368e).

3. Sharp-sightedness is a recurring theme in the *Republic*. See Chapter 1, note 15.

4. On the matter of ease, see Chapter 1, note 56; Chapter 3, note 70; Chapter 4, note 34.

5. Some—e.g., Smith (1999, 46–47)—have reasonably thought that Book 1 defines justice as the virtue by which the soul performs its function, that of living, well (as Socrates argues at the book's end at 353d-354a). Although Socrates no doubt takes this conception of justice seriously (the idea that a person cannot live well without the soul's proper virtue is a point Socrates makes to Crito in the *Crito* [47e], and to Polus and again to Callicles in the *Gorgias* [478d-e, 507c]), Socrates' argument for it in *Rep.* 1 is fatally—and comically—flawed, as it equivocates on the notion of "living well." See Robinson (1970, 35–36), who cites *Gorg.* 507c, where Socrates by a similar equivocation argues that the moderate man must be blessed and happy, since "the man who *does well* must be blessed and happy" and the moderate man "must *do what he does well* and nobly." Annas (1981, 54–55) dismisses as insignificant the equivocation on "live well," as does Dorter (2006, 50), who notes that for Socrates the virtue of the soul "includes also performing the other functions well—caring, ruling, deliberating." Yet these functions of the soul mentioned by Socrates at 353d are just a distraction; the argument clearly turns on the soul's function of *living*. Even if, to be sure, a bad soul will rule and manage badly, and a good soul will perform these tasks well, Socrates'

he, too, believes that just men don't take advantage of others (339a, 343c), though he thinks them weak for not doing so, and fools for not wanting to (343c-344c). Nor is justice elusive at the beginning of Book 2. Glaucon recognizes that the truly just man is one who not only deals fairly with others but also wishes to (361b-d).[6] When he and Adeimantus ask Socrates to provide an account of justice, what they want to know is why justice is beneficial for the person who has it and injustice detrimental, why justice is a better thing to have than injustice (358b-d, 361d, 366e-367a, 367b, 367d, 367e, 368c). It is precisely because they well understand that justice essentially involves concern for the interests of others that they need to have someone explain to them why any man who can successfully avoid justice would nevertheless deliberately choose it.[7]

With respect to Socrates' second supposition, it turns out to be no simple matter to see the bigger and purportedly easier-to-read justice in the city. Socrates and his friends not only have first to construct the city in which they will see justice but, even once they do, none of them seems able to detect it.[8] To Socrates' question "Where in it, then, would justice and injustice be; along with which of the things we considered did they come into being?" (371e), all Adeimantus can say is "I can't think,

---

point is that a just soul and a just man will also *live* well (*eu biōsetai*—353e10; *eu zōn*—354a1), because living, too, is one of the soul's *erga*, and justice, the soul's virtue, enables the soul to perform well its *ergon* of living. (The plural, *ta erga*, at 353e1 signifies that each of the functions of the soul is distinct from the others. It is by virtue, then, of one's soul's performing well its particular *ergon* of living that one's soul and one "live well"; by its performing well its particular *erga* of ruling and managing, the soul, as Socrates explicitly says, "rules well" and "manages well.") Socrates' argument is funny.

6. The brothers' contention that no one is willingly just (358c, 359b, 360c, 366d) is hyperbolic; Glaucon indeed discusses the just man who would not wish to be unjust even if he could get away with it (360d, 361b-d), as does Adeimantus at 366c-d.

7. It is because justice is thought to benefit others (and to be a detriment to oneself) that it alone triggers the profitability question. No Greek gentleman would wish to be found lacking in wisdom or courage, although the many and presumably some sophists—Polus and Callicles in the *Gorgias* are examples—hold immoderation and licentiousness in high regard. On Glaucon's embrace of moderation, see section IV; on Adeimantus, see note 64 below.

8. Socrates' account of the city coming into being and with it, somehow, justice, is surely meant to rival Glaucon's account of the origin of justice (2.358e-359b). In Glaucon's account, justice arises out of people's mutual fear and suspicion; in Socrates' city, it is economic necessity that gives rise to cooperation.

Socrates; unless it is somewhere in some need these men have of one another" (372a). Indeed, the exercise of looking for justice in the city proves a most difficult one: in the healthy and true city (Glaucon's "city of sows"—2.372d) justice is either absent[9] or invisible; and when justice in the city finally does appear in Book 4, it is still the virtue whose nature is least evident, the fourth and last of the city's virtues, the one "left over" after the other three are found.

Indeed, all of the other virtues—wisdom, courage, and moderation—are remarkably easy to discover. Wisdom reveals its nature quickly and effortlessly: "So we've found—I don't know how—this one of the four" (429a). And with respect to courage Socrates says that "it isn't very hard to see" (429a). In the case of moderation—even of moderation in the individual[10]—Socrates knows immediately that it is "surely a certain kind of order and mastery of certain kinds of pleasures and desires" (430e). It is only in the matter of justice that Socrates tells Glaucon that they must, "like hunters, now station ourselves in a circle around the thicket and pay attention so that justice doesn't slip through somewhere and disappear into obscurity" (432b).[11] Socrates says of the place where they are to "hunt," the place that was supposed to have made seeing justice so much easier, that it is "hard going and steeped in shadows," "dark and hard to search out" (432c). And despite how much less clever they purportedly needed to be in order to see the enlarged version of justice, they nevertheless remained, Socrates says, in a "stupid state" (432d). Not only were they not better able to see the big-print justice, but they missed it even though it was "rolling

---

9. See Bloom 1968, 344: "It is an easy place: there is no scarcity, and justice takes care of itself." Note that the city that Socrates calls "true" and "healthy" is not one he ever calls "just."

10. In the case of moderation, Socrates reverses his normal course of discerning a virtue first in the city and only then turning to the individual. See note 51. It is likely, however, that not only moderation but all the virtues are personal first and political only derivatively, so that the *Republic*'s account, insofar as it proceeds from the city's virtues to those of the individual, distorts both. See Aristotle, *Pol.* 7.1.1323b34–36: "Moreover, the courage, justice, prudence, and moderation of a city have the same capacity and form that belong to a human being who is called courageous, just, prudent, and moderate."

11. Socrates knows it will be difficult to find justice in the city. That is why from the outset he expects to discover it not in itself but as what remains after the other three virtues come to light. See section III.

around at our feet[12] from the beginning" (432d):[13] somehow it was right there, but they must have been looking elsewhere (432d). The city-soul analogy, then, though proposed ostensibly to provide a shortcut to justice (435d, 504b), turns out to be neither quick nor particularly useful.[14]

If the view of justice that Socrates advances in Book 4, the view that derives from the city-soul analogy, is neither one he starts with (in Book 1) nor one he stays with (after Book 4), and if justice is actually difficult to see in the city, we must wonder why he goes to considerable lengths to construct the analogy and to infer from it his conception of justice as internal. The reason he does so is, no doubt, that he must satisfy interlocutors for whom profitability is the sole measure of worth (444e-445a). Glaucon (359a, 360c) and Adeimantus (364a, 367c) both fear that it is injustice that is profitable (as Thrasymachus had held) and justice not. The good things injustice yields are, after all, easy to enumerate: money, lucrative partnerships, material possessions, adulterous liaisons, influence, and the favor of men and gods.[15] The only way justice can be defended, therefore, is if it can be shown to be more profitable still[16]—a tall order indeed considering that the good things that come from being just are not quite so easily identified. Good things do, of course, come from *seeming* just, but how is one to deny

---

12. "Rolling around" appears in the *Republic* only once more. The many's beliefs are said to "roll around" between full being and complete nonbeing (479d). The notion of a truth being "at our feet" is found in the *Theaetetus* at 174a, in the anecdote about the witty Thracian servant-girl who mocks Thales for being so absorbed in the heavens and so neglectful of what is "at his feet" that he falls into a well. This caricature implies that the philosopher is worthless when it comes to practical matters, when, for example, he must appear in a courtroom or some other place where he must discuss the things "at his feet and in front of his eyes" (174c). The philosopher is also berated for investigating such abstruse questions as what the nature of a human being is and what is appropriate for such a nature, while not even knowing his next-door neighbor (174b). See, too, *Theaet.* 200e-201a, where Socrates urges himself and his interlocutor to persist in tracking the idea that knowledge is true judgment, on the chance that what they are after will come to light "at our feet." See Chapter 4, note 50, for a consideration of how ill suited to Socrates the *Theaetetus*'s caricature of the philosopher is.

13. Socrates says several times (432d, 433a, 433b-c) that "what justice is" was there from the beginning. But cf. *Euthyd.* 279d: "It is ridiculous, when something has been lying before us all this time (*palai*), to lay it before us again and to say the same thing twice."

14. Socrates is not satisfied with what he achieves by way of the city-soul analogy. See 7.504b-d and Chapter 2, section VI.

15. See Aristophanes, *Clouds* 1071–74.

16. Socrates consistently takes his task to be to demonstrate the profitability of justice: 392c (echoing Adeimantus at 367d), 444e-445a.

that only bad things are in store for those who are just but do not seem so? In what way, then, Glaucon and Adeimantus wonder, can it benefit a man to have justice in his soul?[17] What good is it if it isn't visible, if it is "not noticed by gods and human beings" (366e, 367e; see also Socrates at 4.427d)? For, as Adeimantus contends, the gods, no less than men, judge a man only by his "seemly exterior" (366b). The task Socrates' interlocutors set for him is to persuade them that justice is a valuable asset to its possessor, whether anyone sees it or not.[18] When they inquire as to why justice is beneficial in itself apart from its consequences what they want to know is that justice itself—not seeming just but being so, not only justice that is seen but even justice that is unseen—has benefits. They want to be assured—and this is the challenge of Gyges' ring—that injustice is detrimental to a man even when it is not witnessed. The city-soul analogy, as we shall see in section IV, enables Socrates to address his interlocutors' concerns about justice in a way he could not do otherwise.

II. Moderation

Before attempting to slake Glaucon's and Adeimantus's thirst for a justice that is profitable, Socrates offers an account of moderation (*sōphrosunē*) that is unusual and surprising in its own right. One peculiarity in his account of moderation concerns *where* he locates it in the city and the soul. The reader, having just learned that wisdom is to be found in the ruling class

---

17. Although the brothers speak of justice as being "in the soul" (358b, 366e), it is not quite accurate to say of them, as Reeve does of Glaucon (1988, 25), that they "presuppose that being just is primarily a property of a *psyche*." When Glaucon discusses, for example, the origins of justice, he isn't speaking of justice in the soul; and when he contends by way of Gyges and his ring that the "just" man is indistinguishable from the unjust, he considers what each would *do* when no one is looking. It is probably fair to say that for Glaucon a truly just man is a man who behaves justly whether he can be seen or not—and does so because he wants to (361b). It is in the just man's wanting to be just—that is, in his inclination or disposition to treat *others* justly—that the psychic aspect of justice is located. That Glaucon and Adeimantus speak of justice as a feature of the soul does, however, ease Socrates' transition to a very different conception of justice as a feature of the soul's internal relations.

18. Cf. *Gorg.* 527b: "More than everything, a man must take care not to seem to be good but to be so." In the *Theaetetus*, Socrates regards the notion that one should practice virtue and avoid vice in order to seem good as "the babbling of old women" (176e). One wonders how impressed he actually was with the brothers' challenge to justice. On "babbler," see Chapter 1, note 34.

(428e-429a) and in reason (442c), and courage in the auxiliary class (429b) and in spirit (442c), expects moderation to be the virtue of the city's producer class and of the soul's appetitive part.[19] Instead, however, Socrates locates moderation in all parts of city and soul, and characterizes it as "more like a kind of accord and harmony than the previous ones" (430e), such that it is not to be found in any *one* part of the city and soul.[20]

This move disappoints. A more elegant and satisfying schema would have assigned wisdom to the smallest part of city and soul, courage to the midsize part, moderation to the part that is largest (431c-d, 442a), and, finally, justice to the whole city and soul. Yet Socrates elects to deprive the lowest class of a virtue of its own, and to allow moderation to jostle justice as both seek to occupy and pervade the entire city and soul. Socrates thus forgoes a pleasing symmetry in favor of an awkward and unbalanced distribution of the virtues.[21]

Nothing in the dialogue up to this point prepares the reader for moderation's distribution throughout the soul.[22] In Book 3, for example, Socrates asks: "Aren't these the most important elements of moderation *for the multitude*: being obedient to rulers, and being themselves rulers of the pleasures of drink, sex, and eating?" (389d-c).[23] If indeed moderation consists in obedience to rulers (a kind of political moderation) and control of the animal appetites (personal moderation), should it not reside in the producer class of the city and in the appetitive part of the soul?[24]

Also odd is *how* Socrates defines moderation. Even after he suggests that *sōphrosunē* is different from wisdom and courage and is "a kind of accord

19. In a short book that attempts to summarize the *Republic* briskly, moderation is mistakenly, though understandably, presented as the virtue of the third class in the city and of the appetites in the soul. See Evans 2010, 13–15.

20. The notion of moderation as harmony appears earlier (3.410e-411a), where the guardians' souls are said to be "moderate and courageous" when their spirited and philosophic natures are harmonized (*hērmosthai*).

21. As Benardete notes (1989, 88), "The city thus seems to be complete without any room for justice."

22. In Book 1, Cephalus means by moderation what everyone means: moderation of appetites (329c-d). And, as we shall see in addendum II, in the later books of the *Republic* moderation reverts to its ordinary sense as the opposite of licentiousness.

23. At 390b3 moderation is referred to as self-mastery—*enkrateian heautou*.

24. If the appetitive part of city and soul were moderate, the entire city and soul would be, too, for the spirited part would not then have occasion to take the side of appetite in opposition to reason. See Chapter 2, note 56.

or harmony," he proceeds, for a short while at least, to describe it in familiar terms. Socrates begins by saying that "moderation is surely a certain
kind of order and mastery (*enkrateia*) of *certain kinds of pleasures and desires*"
(430e). He then goes on to say that moderation is self-mastery, which, he
explains, is a matter of the better part's being master (*enkrates*) over the
worse, both in the individual and in the city (431a-b). Next, he refers to
"the simple *and moderate* desires, pleasures, and pains" (431a-b). And finally, he observes that in the moderate city the desires of the common many
are mastered by the desires and prudence of the more decent few (431c-d).
These passages strongly suggest that moderation is the condition of a city
or soul in which the appetitive element is properly restrained, and hence
that it is the virtue most suited to the producer class in the city and the desiring part of the soul. Moreover, it seems that a city should qualify as moderate if its appetitive class is temperate, just as it is thought wise on account
of the sagacity of its ruling class and courageous on account of the bravery
of its spirited class ("the one making the city wise, the other courageous"—
432a1–2)—and so, analogously, in the case of the soul. One might object, of
course, that since moderation involves more than one part of the city and
soul—in the moderate city the producers are mastered by the rulers, and
in the moderate soul, the appetites by reason—moderation cannot reside
in the producers or appetites alone. Yet, the auxiliaries in the city and the
spirited part of the soul also yield to the authority of, respectively, the rulers and reason (429c, 441e, 442a), but are nevertheless not on that account
denied a virtue of their own, courage.[25]

Although, then, as it seems, there is nothing to prevent Socrates from
granting the lowest parts of the city and soul a virtue of their own, he
still chooses not to. Not only does Socrates diffuse moderation throughout
the soul; he also radically alters its character. At 431d-e, a moderate city
is no longer said to be one in which the worse elements are mastered by
the better; instead, it is suddenly one in which "the rulers and the ruled
hold the same opinion (*sundokein*) about who should rule." And when, at
431e, Glaucon responds to Socrates' question of whether it is in the rulers

---

25. Each of the virtues as Socrates describes it is systemic: in a wise city and soul the ruling
part oversees the others; courage is spirit's submissiveness to reason and its siding with reason in
reason's conflicts with appetite; and justice is the cooperation of all parts with each other, each
doing its own job.

or in the ruled that moderation resides, venturing that it resides in both, Socrates takes as confirmed their earlier "divination" that moderation is "a kind of harmony." It is, Socrates continues,

> unlike courage and wisdom, each of which resides in a part, the one making the city wise and the other courageous. Moderation doesn't work that way, but actually stretches throughout the whole, from top to bottom of the entire scale, making the weaker, the stronger, and those in the middle . . . sing the same chant together (*parechomenē sunadontas . . . tauton*). So we would quite rightly claim that this unanimity (*homonoian*) is moderation, an accord of worse and better, according to nature, as to which must rule in the city and in each one. (431e-432a)

What is distinctive about moderation as compared with wisdom and courage is that it must be exhibited by all parts of city and soul. Whereas with respect to courage Socrates explicitly says: "I don't suppose that whether the other men in it are cowardly or courageous would be decisive for its [the city's] being this or that" (429b), with respect to moderation he insists on having all parts "sing the same chant together"; all parts must affirm that it is the wise who should rule in the city, and reason in the soul.[26] In this second surprising turn of events, moderation is no longer the mastery of pleasures and pains (as it was at 389d-e), but rather the new and unfamiliar accession of all parts to the opinion that wise men or reason must rule.

The third surprise is that, as a result of the shift in the meaning of moderation, each of the higher and smaller parts contains two virtues—both its own virtue and the common virtue of moderation—but the lowest and biggest part contains only the common one. And yet a fourth is that moderation, as a consequence of now being stretched throughout all the parts of city and soul, is destined to collide with the similarly elastic justice.

A fifth curiosity is that moderation is not only found in each and every part of city and soul but is also an accord or harmony, or "unanimity" (*homonoia*). As an accord or harmony of shared opinion, moderation is not, strictly speaking, in any of the parts but in all of them taken collectively: "And isn't he moderate because of the friendship and accord (*philiāi kai*

---

26. The notion that it is specifically philosophers who must rule awaits the "third wave" of Book 5. See Chapter 1, section IV.

sumphōniāi—442d1) of these parts—when the ruling part and the two ruled parts are of the single opinion (*homodoxōsi*) that the reasoning part ought to rule and don't raise faction against it?" The singing of the chant—the acceptance of the opinion that the wise should rule—is the parts' moderation; the moderation of the whole is the harmony or accord produced by the parts' all singing the *same* chant, by their holding the *identical* opinion. Despite the appreciable difference between the two moderations, they are permitted to retain the same name.

III. Justice Springs Internal

The search for the nature of justice begins in earnest following Glaucon's and Adeimantus's challenge to Socrates in Book 2, and from the start it is fraught with suspense. As we have seen, no one can find justice in the healthy city; and in the luxurious city there is no mention of justice or even of injustice (despite the evident injustice involved in our "cutting off a piece from our neighbors' land" [2.373d]).[27] Moreover, the guardians who are to govern and defend the new city are distinguished by their courage and moderation[28]—not by their justice. Even the lists containing the virtues the poets and craftsmen are to instill in the guardians, and the vices they are to discourage in them, make no mention of justice and injustice. The vices enumerated are bad disposition, licentiousness, illiberality, and gracelessness (401b); the virtues, moderation, courage, liberality, magnificence, and all their kin (402c).[29]

When Socrates at long last turns his attention in Book 4 to justice, the virtue for the sake of whose discovery the entire enterprise of defining the virtues is undertaken (430d, 376c-d; see, too, 369c, 371e, 372e), the account he offers sounds oddly, and disturbingly, familiar. In fact, much that

---

27. Clay (1988, 25) observes that "it is left to Plato's readers to discover that Kallipolis is founded on an act of injustice."

28. The guardians' moderation is a gentleness or tameness that counteracts their savage tendencies; these tendencies are a matter of concern as early as 2.373a-376c and continue to be so throughout Books 2 and 3.

29. Justice (and injustice) appear specifically in connection with judges: (1) a city educated properly should not need judges (405a-c); and (2) judges, unlike doctors, should not themselves have experienced the ills they are to cure (409a-e).

Socrates says about justice he has already said about moderation: first, that it extends throughout city and soul, and is not confined to one particular part (443d, 434c); second, that it is a harmony among the parts (443e); and third, that it is a feature of both parts and wholes—in the parts, it is minding one's own business (433a, 433c, 443d), and in the wholes, the harmony or accord that arises when parts mind their own business (443d-e).[30] Indeed, in the individual it is all but indistinguishable from moderation. Justice "in truth," Socrates says, is *not* "a man's minding his external business." On the contrary, the just man minds his business

> with respect to what is within, with respect to what truly concerns him and his own. He does not let each part in him mind the others' business or the three classes in the soul meddle with each other, but really sets his own house in good order, and rules himself; he arranges himself, becomes his own friend, and harmonizes the three parts, exactly like three notes in a harmonic scale, lowest, highest, and middle. And if there are some other parts in between, he binds them together and becomes entirely one from many, moderate and harmonized. (443d-e)

The *justice* that results when each part does "its own," not meddling in the business of the others (443a-d), differs scarcely at all from the moderation that results when all the parts share the same opinion as to who should rule (442c-d).[31] Indeed, were one to compare the description of moderation at 431e-432a, quoted earlier, to the just-quoted description of justice, one would be hard-pressed to see any difference at all between them. The earlier passage had said of moderation that it "stretches throughout the whole, from top to bottom of the entire scale, making the weaker, the stronger, and those in the middle . . . sing the same chant together. . . . So we would quite rightly claim that this unanimity is moderation, an accord of worse and better, according to nature, as to which must rule in the city and in each one." And the current passage says that the just man "harmonizes the three parts, exactly like three notes in a harmonic scale, lowest,

---

30. The ambiguity in justice—its being both minding one's own business and harmony or accord—is discussed again at the end of addendum I.

31. Considering that Socrates has to differentiate justice from moderation in some way, it is noteworthy that the line he inserts between them is so fine. He nowhere elaborates on the distinction between agreeing to do one's own job and actually doing it, nor does he return to it or so much as mention it in later books.

highest, and middle . . . and becomes entirely one from many, *moderate and harmonized*" (443d-e).[32] Both passages employ musical metaphors—this represents a fourth way in which Socrates brings justice and moderation together. Yet a fifth is that the just man is actually said to become "*moderate and harmonized*." And sixth, just as moderation had most recently (just one Stephanus page ago) been defined as "the friendship and accord of these parts" (442c), the just man is now said to "become his own friend."[33]

There is in addition a seventh and decisive way in which Socrates indicates that justice in the soul *is* moderation. In the continuation of his consideration of what justice is in the soul, he characterizes it as the condition in which the naturally inferior part of oneself is ruled or mastered by the superior part of oneself—in his words, "a relation of mastering (*kratein*), and being mastered by (*krateisthai*), one another that is according to nature" (444d). This is, of course, precisely how Socrates defined moderation initially at 430e-431a, that is, as "being stronger than oneself," or, in other words, as "when that which is better by nature is master (*enkrates*) over that which is worse."[34] Indeed, the same characterization of moderation appears in the *Gorgias,* where Socrates famously seeks to convince Callicles of the value of ruling oneself (*Gorg.* 491d-e). It is true that in the *Gorgias* Socrates speaks quite casually of moderation and justice together as if they were the same (504d, 504e, 507d-508b, 519a);[35] but, in the *Republic*, unlike

32. Justice/injustice and moderation/immoderation are linked through the notion of faction (*stasis*). Compare 442d, where moderation is present "when the ruling part and the ruled parts . . . don't raise faction (*stasiazōsin*) against it [the reasoning part]," with 444b, where injustice is defined as "a certain faction (*stasin*) among those three."

33. Book 1 also associates friendship and accord with justice. See addendum I.

34. Is Leontius being *unjust* when he struggles internally and is finally "overpowered" (*kratoumenos*) by the desire to see the corpses of men slain by the public executioner (439e-440a)? Is it justice that a man exhibits when his reason and spirit are set over the desiring part of the soul and "watch it for fear of its being filled with the so-called pleasures of the body and thus becoming big and strong, and then not minding its own business, but attempting to enslave and rule what is not appropriately ruled by its class and subverting everyone's entire life" (442a-b)? Although injustice is unmistakably different from licentiousness, Socrates' account of injustice at 444d is virtually identical to that of licentiousness at 431a-b.; At 444d he says: "To produce injustice is to establish a relation of ruling, and being ruled by, one another that is contrary to nature"; and at 431a-b: "And when . . . the smaller and better part is mastered by the inferior multitude . . . the man in this condition is called weaker than himself and licentious (*akolaston*)." Even the notion of "by nature" that appears in connection with justice and injustice is found, too, in the initial consideration of moderation (431a).

35. Yet even in the *Gorgias* there is no doubt that the ordered soul is the moderate one (506e-507a).

in the *Gorgias*, Socrates takes it as his task to define the four virtues and to distinguish them from one another.[36] Finally—and this is the eighth way in which Socrates conflates justice and moderation—justice is called the "health" of the soul (444c). Yet the virtue that most readily comes to mind at the mention of the soul's health is surely moderation.[37]

Just as Socrates' surprising conception of moderation came without prior warning, so too does his near identification of justice with moderation. For Socrates leads us to expect that justice will be the fourth virtue of the soul, and hence distinct from all the others, including moderation, which is the third. At 427e-428a he sketches a plan to identify first "the other three," and then to discover the fourth in what remains. He begins by supposing that the correctly founded city is perfectly good, and, as such, is "plainly" (*dēlon*)[38] wise, courageous, moderate, and just.[39] He then asserts that whichever of these we happen to find will leave as the remainder what has not been found: as in the case of any other four things, he says, if we were seeking any one of them and recognized it first, that would suffice, but if we recognized the other three, that, too, would suffice, since—again, "plainly"—the fourth[40] could be nothing but "what is left over."[41] From

---

36. The *Republic* assigns the virtues to different parts of city and soul and defines them quite differently from one another—except in the case of justice and moderation. In this way it is unlike the *Protagoras*, for example, where Socrates argues that all the virtues are in some sense the same or closely related (or, at the very least, inter-entailing).

37. See 3.404e, where Socrates says: "And just as simplicity in music produced moderation in souls, does it in gymnastic produce health in bodies?" Here moderation—not justice—in the soul is the counterpart of health in the body. Later on as well health in the soul is aligned with moderation: see 9.571d, where Socrates speaks of a man who has a "healthy and moderate relationship to himself." In Book 6 the man who has a philosophic nature is said to have "a healthy and just disposition, which is also accompanied by moderation" (490c). Although healthy is paired here with just, the pair is joined immediately by moderation.

38. *Dēlon* ("clearly" or "clear") appears several times within the space of just a few lines, causing the reader to wonder whether it really is *dēlon* that the good city has precisely these four virtues.

39. Bloom points out (1968, 373) that the question of whether justice is a virtue has yet to be decided. One is right to suspect for this reason as well (in addition to the reason cited in note 38) that none of what has just been said is all that *dēlon*.

40. Socrates makes it sound as if it is a feature specifically of foursomes that the identity of the last member of a group may be discovered in what remains after all the others are accounted for. By placing emphasis on the number four Socrates certainly disposes the reader to be on the lookout for four distinct virtues, with justice being the fourth.

41. Although it has frequently been remarked that nothing is left over after the first three virtues are defined (see, e.g., Nichols 1987, 91; Bloom 1968, 374; Annas 1981, 119), it is less widely recognized that justice is given the same account that has already been given to moderation—though

the start, then, and even before he tries to identify any of the four virtues, Socrates anticipates that one of the four will prove difficult to find; one will have to be discovered by seeing what remains after the other three are found (427e–428a). There is never any real doubt as to which one of the four virtues the fourth, "left-over" one will be. For Socrates has just enumerated the virtues of the correctly structured and perfectly good city—wise, courageous, moderate, and just—and it is in precisely this order that he goes on to define them. Yet, even if justice is what is left over, we expect it—perhaps even expect it especially—to be a virtue in its own right, the fourth and last in a series of virtues, each of which is distinct from the others. Socrates indeed says, twice, that justice "rivals" the others in terms of its contribution to the overall virtue of the soul (433d). As such, it should surely be a separate and significantly different new virtue—not simply a duplicate of moderation.

Justice, then, the virtue that remains after the others are defined, ought to have sufficient substance to stand on its own and compete with the others. Indeed, Socrates says of it that, as the virtue remaining after wisdom, courage, and moderation have come to light, it is the power that gives rise to the others and sustains them once they have come into being (433b).[42] Not only does Socrates offer no support for this improbable claim but, having made justice the necessary condition of the other virtues' coming into being and persevering, he actually pretends to wonder—as if there can now be any question about it—which of the virtues is the most valuable to the city. Can there be any doubt that the virtue that gives rise to and sustains the others is the most important one?[43]

---

see Danzig 1988, 97; and Neu 1971, 240. Brann (2004, 132) thinks that it is moderation that is redundant. But moderation is the virtue defined first, making justice the one that is superfluous. Roochnik (2003, 25 n. 13) speaks of the "apparent overlap of moderation and justice."

42. Both Glaucon (358b) and Adeimantus (366e) had inquired about the "power" (*dunamis*) justice and injustice exert in the soul and what they do *to* the person who has them. See, too, 1.351e, where Socrates asks about the power injustice has, and 9.588b, where Socrates speaks of the "respective powers of doing injustice and doing just things."

43. See Wilson 1984, 42. According to Socrates' argument at the end of Book 9, licentiousness, the opposite of moderation, seems to be the cause of all vice. Even so, moderation need not be the cause of all virtue, although it may be unlikely for someone who lacks moderation to be virtuous in the other ways. In the *Gorgias* (at 507a-c), the moderate man is said necessarily to be also just, courageous, and pious, but, of course, there Socrates is addressing Callicles, the great champion of licentiousness.

Considering, then, that justice is supposed to be a fourth, distinct, vitally important virtue of the soul, it is profoundly unsettling that Socrates virtually effaces the line between it and moderation. Yet there can be little doubt that Socrates is well aware of his subterfuge. First, Socrates at 430d suddenly prefers to avoid defining moderation: "Well now, there are still two left that must be seen in the city, moderation, and that for the sake of which we are making the whole search, justice. . . . How could we find justice so we won't have to bother about moderation any further?" (430d). It is Glaucon who must insist that, in accordance with the procedure Socrates himself had outlined—whereby three of the virtues are to be discerned first and then the fourth in what is left over—they consider moderation first. What reason could Socrates have for proposing that they bypass moderation and proceed directly to justice other than that he knows full well that once he defines moderation, precious little will be left for justice? Note, too, that Socrates actually does eventually do what he had hoped to do, namely, skip moderation and head directly to justice. When he reviews the virtues in the individual soul and their likeness to their counterparts in the city (441c-442b), he speaks first of the private man who is wise in the same way the city is; next, of the city that is courageous in the same way the private man is; and third, of the man who "is just in the same manner that a city too was just"—namely, by having his two smaller parts, reason and spirit, set over his largest, appetite, and seeing to it that appetite not become filled with the pleasures of the body and, as a result, not mind its own business but attempt to enslave the other parts. There is no mention of moderation here: indeed, how could there be? And in the enumeration of the virtues that follows immediately (442c-d), where Socrates succinctly and distinctly rehearses the definitions of the other three virtues, including moderation, he avoids saying what justice is—note the circumlocution he employs with respect only to justice: "Now, of course, a man will be just because of that which we are so often saying, and in the same way. . . . Has our justice in any way been blunted so as to seem to be something other than what it came to light as in the city?" (442d). Tellingly, in the one place where Socrates does define all four virtues together, he changes their order—he defines moderation first, then courage, then wisdom, and finally justice—so as to separate moderation from justice as much as possible (433c-d). Socrates, it seems, does not dare to set the definitions of moderation and justice side by side lest their near identity be detected.[44]

Second, and perhaps even more disconcerting than Socrates' attempt to avoid defining moderation before defining justice, is his attempt even earlier, at 427d-e, to transfer the task of discovering justice to Glaucon, Adeimantus, Polemarchus, and the others. He tells Glaucon to find himself an "adequate light" somewhere and to look for it himself (427d), and here, too, it is Glaucon who holds him to his promise (427d-e). Why does Socrates, after going to such great lengths to found a city, all for the sake of finding justice (376c-d), try now to renege on his commitment to "bring help to her as I am able" (368c)?

By his conspicuous and clumsy attempts to dodge his responsibility Socrates indicates that he has no adequate and separate definition of justice that he is prepared to propose: his first choice is to offer no definition; his second is to define justice without first defining moderation. Since Glaucon denies him both options, he has no alternative but to define justice, and to do so after already having assigned to moderation the definition he wants to give to justice. The internal harmony and accord and friendship and acceptance of one's proper role and self-rule that he now associates with justice he has already connected with moderation.[45] Indeed, rather than confine moderation to the city's and soul's appetitive part, as he surely might have, he chose instead, as we have seen, to disperse it throughout the city and soul, making it the cause of their harmony or accord. Moderation thus in effect preempts justice's claim to an integrative role, rendering it all but redundant.

By failing to carve out for justice any distinctive role or definition, and by insisting nonetheless that justice is a fourth and distinct virtue, one that brings into being and preserves all the others, Socrates causes us to

---

44. See, too, 435b, where Socrates says that a city is just when each of its classes minds its own business, but then leaves the nature of the other virtues (including moderation) unarticulated: "and, again, moderate, courageous, and wise because of certain other affections and habits of these same classes."

45. See *Charm.* 161b, where Charmides suddenly recalls having heard from someone that "moderation is doing our own business." In the *Charmides*, however, the minding one's own business is not internal but external. That Socrates in the *Republic* uses for justice the same defining formula as is proposed in the *Charmides* for moderation is yet another way in which he brings justice and moderation together.

suspect that justice as it really is may actually be missing from the current discussion, and that we would therefore do well to look beyond it to find a justice that is both significantly different from moderation and all the other virtues, and arguably the most important one, rivaling the others for the title "most valuable virtue" (433c) inasmuch as it is the virtue that engenders and preserves the rest. The only justice that can satisfy these two criteria is one that is directed outward to one's fellow men, one that has regard for the interests of others.[46] Justice of this kind is clearly distinct from moderation;[47] moreover, it alone can anchor the other virtues. For only when wisdom, courage, and moderation are grounded in a virtue that accords value to someone other than oneself is their character as virtues assured.[48]

What Socrates has given us in *Rep.* 4, then, are distorted definitions of both moderation and justice. Socrates starts out with a definition of moderation as restraint of the bodily appetites, but shifts problematically to one according to which it is a matter of all the parts of the city and soul jointly holding the same opinion. And he makes justice virtually unrecognizable. For, despite Socrates' strained efforts to depict justice as the cordial relations among the parts of the soul, justice is in its essence a social or interpersonal virtue. Although it is not unrelated to moderation (as reasoned control of appetites[49])—indeed, no virtue is—it is not the same or nearly

---

46. See Aristotle, *EN* 5.1.1129b25–33: "Justice then in this sense is perfect virtue, though with this qualification, namely, that it is displayed towards others. This is why justice is often thought to be the chief of the virtues . . . because its possessor can practice his virtue towards others and not merely by himself."

47. As Benardete (1989, 86) observes, "Moderation is the only good of the city that does not concern itself with other cities."

48. Perhaps for this reason Polemarchus in Book 1 agrees that justice is human virtue (335c), and Thrasymachus accepts that justice is *the* virtue of the soul, the one that ensures that a man will have a good life, will "live well," and will be blessed and happy (353e-354a). See, however, *Meno* 73d-e, where Socrates corrects Meno's overhasty assertion that justice is virtue; he should have said it is *a* virtue.

49. Despite Socrates' insistence in the *Laches, Protagoras, Meno,* and *Euthydemus* that it is wisdom that keeps courage from becoming reckless confidence, a case could be made that it is in fact moderation that does so. There is a sense, of course, in which, as in the *Protagoras* (332a-333b), moderation and wisdom are the same: when they are both construed as the opposite of thoughtless imprudence (*aphrosunē*).

the same as moderation.[50] It concerns the way in which people regard and treat one another—not the way in which the internal parts of the soul do.[51]

As we have seen, Socrates betrays in many ways his recognition that his characterization of justice as internal makes it not a distinct virtue but a replication of moderation: (1) by expressing his preference to define justice without first defining moderation—even though such a procedure clearly violates his strategy of discovering justice in what remains after the other *three* virtues are defined; (2) by his reluctance to define justice at all; (3) by his using nearly identical language and nearly identical metaphors for both—musical metaphors such as *sumphonia* and *harmonia* and the high, low, and middle placement on the musical scale, as well as the metaphor of friendship; (4) by having both pervade the whole soul; (5) by explicitly characterizing the just man as moderate; (6) by defining justice in the end as he had defined moderation at the start (at 430–431)—that is, as the superior by nature mastering the inferior; and (7) by calling *justice* "health of the soul." Socrates has not, then, provided in Book 4 a new definition of justice; instead he has given moderation a second name. Yet justice, properly speaking, is the social and interpersonal virtue that disposes one to refrain from harming others, including refraining from depriving them of their due. It is closely connected to just acts.[52]

Socrates indeed acknowledges three times the tight tie between justice and just acts: (1) in his argument at 433e–434a, where he shamelessly links the new justice that involves a city's or soul's parts doing only their own job and not that of another to the kind of justice by which judges see to it that no one either has what belongs to someone else or is deprived of what

---

50. In the *Protagoras* (330c–332a), it is holiness that Socrates argues is identical—or nearly so—to justice.

51. Since moderation is so evidently an internal virtue Socrates looks first, in its case, not to the city but to the individual soul. From there he proceeds to make moderation, however improbably, a relationship among classes in the city, finally reading the city's moderation back into the soul. Only in the case of moderation does Socrates interpolate an observation about a virtue as it is in the soul in the midst of a consideration of the virtues of the city ("and in each one"—432a); only with respect to moderation is he not reluctant to define an individual virtue before it is established that the soul, like the city, has three parts.

52. See 444e–445a: "to do just things, practice fine ones, and be just."

belongs to him;[53] (2) at 442d-443a, where Socrates and his interlocutors seek to "reassure" themselves that the new justice indeed qualifies as justice by testing it in light of vulgar standards (*ta phortika*)—that is, in terms of the unjust acts that the man who is just in this new way would presumably be most unlikely to engage in; and (3) at 444c, where Socrates draws a comparison between just acts and healthy things and between unjust acts and sick things: just as healthy things and sick things produce health and sickness in a body, so do just actions and unjust actions produce justice and injustice in the soul; and just as health in the body is ruling and being ruled according to nature, and sickness in the body is ruling and being ruled not according to nature, so is justice in the soul the ruling and being ruled that are according to nature, and injustice the ruling and being ruled that are contrary to nature.

This third instance is, like the first (see note 53), not sustainable. It is not at all evident that just actions produce justice, and unjust actions injustice, in the same way that healthy things produce health, and sick things sickness. For, whereas healthy and sick things are so called precisely *because* they produce health and sickness—indeed, there is no other sense in which they may be said to be, respectively, healthy and sick—it is not true of just and unjust actions that they are so called because they produce justice and injustice in the soul; or that it is for that reason alone that they may be said to be, respectively, just and unjust. On the contrary, an action is ordinarily called just or unjust because of how it affects or is intended to affect *others*. If these actions do also produce a condition in the soul, that condition, one would think, is not justice or injustice but moderation or immoderation. The more unjust actions one performs—temple robberies, thefts, betrayals, and adultery; neglecting parents, failing to care for the gods, and all

---

53. Socrates willfully obscures the clear difference between, on the one hand, not having or not being permitted to have what is not one's own and, on the other, not *doing* or not being permitted to do what is not one's own. Moreover, although he has thus far stipulated only that justice is a matter of *not* having and *not* doing what is *not* one's own, he nevertheless proceeds to affirm the dubious proposition that justice is a matter of *having and doing* one's own and what belongs to one (433e-434a). And from here he goes on to "infer" the argument's startling conclusion that justice is doing one's own job in the city (434c). In this passage (433e-434a) Socrates illegitimately connects *dikas* as judgments to *dikaiosunē* as justice by way of *dikaiou* as just. Before Plato, the term *dikaiosunē* was used rarely; *dikē* was used both for judgment and for the justice of reciprocity and retribution. See Havelock 1969 and 1978.

other such things (442e-443a)—the more one enflames the baser desires and the more immoderate one becomes. And, of course, once one has become more immoderate, one is more likely to commit further acts of this kind—for all vice, all injustice, stems from *pleonexia*, the rapacious craving for and pursuit of more and more, and *pleonexia*, in turn, from appetites run amok.[54] This is so especially when one includes among the appetites not only those for food, drink, and sex, but also the desire for and love of money (as in Book 9).[55] If, as Socrates says at 443b, things commonly (or "vulgarly") regarded as injustices are particularly uncharacteristic of the just man on account of how the parts in him stand with respect to ruling and being ruled (and how they "mind their own business"), then isn't the reason the just man is unlikely to commit injustice that he tends to be moderate?

Justice in the soul is the disposition to treat others fairly and not to harm them. The just man, then, is properly said to be one who neither wishes to cause, nor intentionally causes, injury to others.[56] To be sure, only a moderate man—a man whose soul is not only harmonious but is governed by reason's moderate desires—could be so disposed.[57] Nevertheless, a distinction must be drawn between the disinclination to harm others and the moderation without which there could be no such disinclination. Rather than

---

54. Aristotle attributes injustice (in its narrower sense, that is, when it is not simply another word for vice) to *pleonexia*. See *EN* 5.2.1130a20–35.

55. At 580e Socrates brings together appetitiveness and love of money by noting that money is required to satisfy the appetites. See, too, 6.485e: "Money and the great expense that accompanies it are pursued for the sake of things [pleasures] that any other man rather than this one [the true philosopher] is likely to take seriously." Even earlier, at 442a, Socrates includes love of money among the appetites, but without drawing a connection between the desire for pleasure and the money required to satisfy that desire: the soul's desiring part is the largest in the soul "and by nature the most insatiable for money." The Phoenicians and Egyptians are called money-lovers at 436a (see, too, the "love of money" [*philarguron*] at 347b, which, along with love of honor, is worthy of reproach), and the appetitive class is called the moneymaking one at 441a. In the case of the oligarchic man, the soul's love of money and its appetitive lusts are at odds, even though such a man "puts the desiring and money-making part on the throne." His love of money leads him to be miserly, and so not to use his wealth to satisfy any desires beyond the "necessary"; he suppresses rather than indulges the unnecessary ones (554c-d).

56. On intentional injustice, see Chapter 4, note 39.

57. See 6.486b, where Socrates says that the orderly (i.e., moderate) man (here, the philosopher), who "is not a lover of money, or illiberal, or a boaster, or a coward," could not become "a hard-bargainer or unjust."

distinguish between the two, however, Socrates opts in *Rep.* 4 to define justice and moderation in the same way.[58]

IV. Resolution

All the puzzles, surprises, and difficulties noted above converge, in effect, on just two questions. The first is why Socrates defines moderation so oddly as shared opinion concerning who or what should rule—a definition that appears neither before nor after Book 4—rather than, conventionally, as controlled appetites; the second, why Socrates fails to offer a definition of justice that both is true to its nature and maintains its distinctness from moderation.

With respect to the first question—why moderation is defined in *Rep.* 4 as rulers and ruled "singing the same chant together"—the answer can only be that, thanks to this distraction, no one protests, no one even seems to notice, when Socrates finally assigns moderation's *usual* definition to justice. Socrates makes sure to interpolate the "shared opinion" definition of moderation between his original definition of moderation as self-control and his later identical definition of justice. Immediately after saying that the city in which "the desires in the common many are mastered by the desires and the prudence in the more decent few" (431c-d) is the one that "ought to be designated stronger than pleasures, desires, and itself . . . and moderate in these respects too" (431d), Socrates suddenly interjects: "And, moreover, if there is any city in which the rulers and the ruled have the same opinion about who should rule, then it's this one" (431e). Had Socrates held fast to his definition of moderation as self-mastery, he could hardly have gone on to assign that same definiens to justice.

With respect to the second question—why Socrates fails to accord justice its distinctive and more familiar sense—the answer must be, because there is no simple and straightforward way to defend justice, to show that an other-regarding social or interpersonal virtue is profitable for the agent.

---

58. Even if committing injustice is "more characteristic of every other kind of man" (443a) than a moderate one, moderation and justice are not the same. One might just as well argue that since dressing immodestly is more characteristic of every other kind of woman than a religious one, religiosity and modesty are the same.

If Socrates is not prepared to allow justice to falter, he must find a way to make justice self-regarding; he must obfuscate the difference between it and the virtue that *is* internal—moderation.[59] Since Glaucon had indeed at the start of Book 2 included being healthy among goods desirable in themselves (and for their consequences), it is to be expected that he will readily agree, as he in fact does at 445a-b, that having a healthy soul is desirable in itself, and that there can hardly be anything worse than life with a corrupted one. For Glaucon's sake Socrates praises the virtue of the soul that makes it healthy, namely, moderation—but he calls it justice.

Without the city-soul analogy Socrates could never have made the case that justice is an internal virtue. Had he suggested directly that justice is a matter of the better part of the soul ruling the worse, who would not have said (as Socrates himself does at 4.430e-431b) "But that is moderation!"? By looking to the city, however, where people or classes interact with one another, Socrates can plausibly make large-scale justice internal to the city, and, by analogy, individual justice internal to a man's soul. Nevertheless, justice at both levels is in fact a matter of how one entity regards and treats another: a city's justice concerns its relations with other cities and, perhaps, with its own people—not the relations of its people or classes with one another; an individual's justice concerns his relations with other people.[60]

To be sure, even if justice is defined, as it should be, as the social and interpersonal virtue of having regard for others, it is not impossible to defend its desirability or profitability in itself for oneself. Insofar as being concerned for others disposes one not to commit acts of injustice, and insofar as refraining from acts of injustice contributes to the health of one's soul (the moderation that Socrates is determined to call justice),[61] it does profit

---

59. See Nichols 1987, 59: Socrates must "locate justice in the soul" if he is to defend it as absolutely good. He cannot do so if he instead "locates justice in the proper relations among men."

60. Socrates lacks confidence in his definition of justice in the city ("Let's not assert it so positively just yet"—434d) and is not prepared to commit to it until he verifies that the same definition applies to the individual. If it does not, he says, political justice will have to be revisited and "perhaps, considering them [political and personal justice] side by side and rubbing them together like sticks, we would make justice burst into flame" (434e-435a). Socrates thus keeps alive the possibility that in the end it won't be justice in the city that illuminates personal justice but the reverse, and that as a result political justice will have to be redefined.

61. Glaucon and Adeimantus for the most part speak of the profitability of justice. Yet it is more natural to think in terms of *acts* being profitable, and states or powers being desirable: only once, at 445a, does Socrates speak of the profitability not only of performing just acts but also of *being* just.

a man to be just. But how circuitous is the path of such profit.[62] It might well also be the case—and no doubt this is what Socrates believes—that justice is, like eyesight and health, advantageous: to have the proper regard for other people is life-enhancing in itself, above and beyond the specific uses to which it may be put. Even so, however, the clear and immediate beneficiary of one man's concern for others is others: that is why it is justice whose profitability Socrates is asked to defend, and also why justice's defense is so difficult.[63] By contrast, the clear and immediate beneficiary of moderation is oneself, with others benefiting only indirectly. And indeed Glaucon values moderation in the soul; he even regards it as desirable in itself.[64] Glaucon is in this respect not at all like the *Gorgias*'s Callicles:[65] he may have been initially perturbed by the lack of luxury in the city of sows (372d), but he soon comes to appreciate the more modest censored, purged, and purified version of the luxurious or "feverish" city: "That's a sign of our moderation," he says proudly in Book 3 (399e). And in Book 4, Glaucon unhesitatingly proclaims that without moderation (now, of course, called justice) the soul would be confused and corrupted, making life not "worth living" (*biōton*—445a-b). In order to persuade Glaucon that justice is desirable in itself, then, all Socrates has to do is name the healthy state of the soul justice. In so doing he satisfies Glaucon's and Adeimantus's demand that he identify the power (*dunamis*) justice has when it is in the soul.[66]

---

62. D. Sachs's famous 1963 article notwithstanding, Socrates' point is a valid one: when a person commits injustice he enflames the baser appetites of his soul and thus disturbs his soul's health and creates in it a condition he finds undesirable—though the unhealthy and undesirable state of the soul is not, of course, as I argue, injustice but immoderation. See Socrates' image of the human being composed of a human being, a lion, and a many-headed beast at 9.588–89, discussed in addendum II. For further discussion of the relationship between interpersonal justice and psychic "justice," see Demos 1964 and Hall 1974.

63. See Chapter 4, section IX. In the *Theatetus* (177a) the unjust are "punished" by living a life "after their own likeness," as "bad men tied to bad company" (*kakoi kakois sunontes*).

64. Adeimantus raises no objection to the austere conditions of the healthy city of sows (it is Glaucon who protests its asceticism—372c), yet he is clearly displeased at the deprivations the guardians are to endure (4.419a-420a). Ferrari observes ([2003] 2005, 93) that "self-discipline is in effect the favourite virtue of Glaucon and Adeimantus." Yet, it is not quite accurate to say, as he does, that "their construal of justice as self-guardianship turns justice into a version of self-discipline, a care of the self." For it is not they but Socrates who construes justice in this way.

65. In this respect Glaucon is not like Thrasymachus either: when arguing with Thrasymachus Socrates could only make the point that injustice "within one man" makes him unable to accomplish his ends (352a); he could not simply say, as he can to Glaucon, that injustice (or vice) is "a sickness, ugliness, and weakness" in the soul (444d-e).

66. See note 42 above.

The reason it is so difficult for Socrates to make the case for the desirability in itself of justice is that those he addresses fail to see its attraction. The goodness of justice lies precisely in that it disposes a man to consider the interests of others—surely a noble thing. But to those who do not see that valuing others is noble and that disregarding their concerns and, a fortiori, mistreating them is shameful, or to those who do not see the noble as desirable in itself, what exactly is one to say?[67] Moderation's advantage over justice is that it can be defended as something desirable in itself for oneself—in the sense that it is good for one to be healthy or fit in both body and soul. But it is nevertheless likely that for Socrates the true worth even of moderation lies in that it keeps a person from committing injustice, that is, from visiting harm on others.

V. Conclusion

That the primary direct beneficiary of a person's justice is not the person himself but those with whom he associates is, of course, Thrasymachus's view, and it is the last thing Socrates can afford to broadcast when justice is under attack. Thrasymachus had said of the just man (1.343d-e) that when he holds a ruling office not only do his domestic affairs suffer from neglect but his justice prevents him from making up for that loss by helping himself to "the public store." Moreover, thanks to his being just he incurs the ill will of his relatives and acquaintances, since he is unwilling to commit injustice to profit them. And it is clear that Socrates does not disagree: as he describes the aristocratic father of the timocratic son in Book 8, he is someone "who is willing to be gotten the better of so as not to be bothered" (549c). When Socrates speaks to men who, like most, think that

---

67. See Aristotle, *EN* 8.13.1162b35-1163a1: "All men, or most, want what is noble, but choose what is profitable; whereas it is noble to do a good turn not for the sake of receiving one in return, it is profitable to be the receiver of good deeds." Not everyone can simply be virtuous, however: "It is necessary that the appropriate character—loving the noble and being disgusted by the base—somehow precede virtue" (*EN* 10.8.1179b29–31). In a sense Runciman (2010, 52) is right to complain that "Socrates continues to insist that the behaviour of a just person who is firmly and consistently disposed to be just is both good in itself and beneficial to the person so disposed. But he has not succeeded in demonstrating either." Yet, perhaps those who challenge Socrates to prove justice's benefit to the just man himself ask too much. For in seeking such a proof one reveals one's inability to appreciate the plain and simple good that benefiting others is.

if justice is in the first instance good for someone else it cannot but be one's own loss (see 343c, where Thrasymachus says that justice and the just "are really someone else's good, the advantage of the man who is stronger and rules, and *a personal harm* to the man who obeys and serves"), he wisely underplays justice's benefit to others. He thus forbids poets and prose writers to say "that many happy men are unjust, that many wretched men are just, that doing injustice is profitable if one gets away with it, and that *justice is someone else's good and one's own loss*" (3.392b-c). Nevertheless, as Socrates sees it, no matter what one gives up by being just, justice is nobody's loss. For him, what makes justice the supreme virtue is precisely that in being someone else's good it is simply good—good in itself—a reflection, one might say, of the highest of all Forms, the Form of the Good. But without having actually seen the Good, Socrates cannot adequately defend justice, cannot fully express its goodness. As he says, "the just and noble things . . . will not have gotten themselves a guardian who's worth very much" in the man who, in his ignorance of the Good, fails to know "in what way they are good" (506a).[68]

There are, to be sure, those who think Socrates sees no worth in virtue unless it is of direct and evident benefit to the man who has it. Allan Bloom (1968, 397), for example, argues that it is Socrates not Glaucon who cannot value any virtue, including justice, unless it has utility: whereas Glaucon wants to know why justice is desirable in itself, "the Socratic teaching" is that "virtue pursued for its own sake is without ground and has a tincture of folly." According to Bloom, "Socrates seems to deny the existence of the independent moral virtues . . . presented by Aristotle as ends in themselves, pursued only because they are noble. Socrates presents instead two kinds of virtues, one low and one high but both mercenary in the sense that they are pursued for the sake of some reward." It is left to "the great tradition from Aristotle to Kant," Bloom continues, to overturn the Socratic moral teaching.[69] Yet, as we have seen, Socrates on his own places justice in the category containing things desirable and likable

---

68. To see the Good is to know its effects (that it is the cause of all that is right and noble; that it provides truth and intelligence [517c]) just as to see the sun is to understand its powers (that it is responsible for the generation, growth, and nourishment of the visible things [509b]).

69. See Prichard's 1928 lecture (Prichard 2002). Prichard argues that Socrates' defense of justice in the *Republic* is based entirely on self-interest rather than on disinterested moral obligation.

in themselves; it is he who calls this category "noblest" (358a).[70] Moreover, in the *Phaedo* (98e-99a) he attributes his having remained in prison rather than escaping to Megara or Boeotia to his thinking it not only better and more just to endure his penalty but also more noble (*kallion*). And in the *Gorgias*, Socrates is at pains to prove to Polus that if committing injustice is less noble than suffering it, it is necessarily more shameful (*aischion*); that if suffering it is more noble it is also better (474c-475e); and in general "that all just things are noble to the extent that they are just" (476b). Even if justice is, on Socrates' account, to be liked not only for itself but also for its consequences, who is to say that the consequences he has in mind are limited to or are even primarily consequences for oneself? After all, Socrates prides himself on having received no wage at all for his labors on behalf of justice (*Ap.* 31b). Indeed, it is clear right from the start, in Socrates' early discussion of justice with Cephalus and Polemarchus, that he thinks justice is at its core a matter of having regard for others—indeed, for all others, whether friend or enemy. And Socrates' understanding of justice as what is advantageous simpliciter (337a),[71] rather than, as Thrasymachus would have it, what is advantageous "for the stronger" (338c), suggests that for Socrates justice is indeed profitable—but that it profits either everyone or, on occasion (that is, when associated with a ruling craft), specifically "the weaker" (342c-d, 346e). It is only when he is put in the position of having to defend justice's profitability that he feels constrained to emphasize its advantage for the just man himself.

Addendum I: Justice in *Rep.* 1

Socrates' first lesson about justice in *Rep.* 1, the single truth that gets right to the heart of the matter, is that the just man harms no one. Socrates

---

70. See 10.608e, where Socrates states simply that "what destroys and corrupts everything is bad, what saves and benefits is the good." Bad and good in this passage are not here bad and good for oneself.

71. Socrates is apparently known for regarding justice as advantageous; that must be why Thrasymachus forbids him to say that justice is the needed (*to deon*), the helpful (*to ōphelimon*), the profitable (*to lusiteloun*), the gainful (*to kerdaleon*), or the advantageous (*to sumpheron*) (336d). Note that in his dealings with Polemarchus Socrates as a matter of course substitutes good (*agathoi*) for useful (*chrēstoi*) (334c-335a) or uses the two terms together.

rejects unequivocally Polemarchus's conception of justice as a doling out of good to friends and harm to enemies: "It is not the work of a just man," Socrates says, "to harm either a friend or anyone else" (335d); "It is never just to harm anyone" (335e).[72] It is indeed because the just man never over-reaches, never seeks to prosper at the expense of another, that Thrasymachus holds justice in contempt.[73] It is Thrasymachus's view—one that is shared by many (348e) but trumpeted by him with particularly smug certainty—that injustice alone is profitable, and that the more perfect the injustice the more profitable.

In opposing Thrasymachus Socrates adopts the very strategy he will later employ in responding to Glaucon and Adeimantus: he considers what justice is in a city before turning to justice within the individual person (although he does not in *Rep.* 1 resort to the pretext that justice is easier to see when it is larger). Socrates contends, against Thrasymachus, that it is precisely the *perfectly* unjust who can accomplish nothing, for surely some measure of justice is needed if anything is to get done. Indeed, whereas injustice produces factions, hatreds, and quarrels among men, justice inspires the accord (*homonoia*) and friendship (*philia*) that make it possible for people to work together in any enterprise, just or unjust (351d-e). All groups, whether they are as large as a city or as small as two men (351e), will be hobbled by injustice and bolstered by justice. So, too, will the single man.

Despite the striking similarities between this early argument and the city-soul analogy Socrates uses later on,[74] the two are not the same. For Socrates does not say here that an entity is just or unjust on account of its internal accord or discord.[75] On the contrary, Socrates contends explicitly that a city is unjust when it commits injustices against other cities: "Would you say that a city is unjust (*adikon*) that tries to enslave other

---

72. For Glaucon, benefiting friends and harming enemies is something the *un*just man does (362b-c).

73. According to a common misreading of Thrasymachus's contention that justice is "the advantage of the stronger," Thrasymachus is thought to value justice. It is not, however, justice per se that he values; it is someone else's justice, that which the admirably unscrupulous can easily exploit. For Thrasymachus the road to success is paved with one's own injustice and the justice of others.

74. See Weiss 2007.

75. In Glaucon's account in Book 2 of the genesis of justice (358e-359b) there is likewise no suggestion that the agreement among the city's members to refrain from harming one another makes the *city* just.

cities unjustly, and has reduced them to slavery, and keeps many enslaved to itself?" (351b). (He makes the identical point at 10.615b.) It would seem that in *Rep.* 1 Socrates derives what injustice is in the city from what it is in an individual, namely, the mistreatment of others.[76] What marks bands of pirates and robbers—two of the groups Socrates cites in making his point—as unjust is not, to be sure, their internal dissent but the crimes they commit against outsiders. In fact, were it not for the justice their members exhibit toward one another—"honor among thieves," "thick as thieves"— these groups could not be effectively *un*just.

In *Rep.* 1's account the justice and injustice that are "in" the city or in the other groups are not the properties of groups but are instead the ways in which the groups' members are disposed to interact with one another: "Do you believe," Socrates asks Thrasymachus, "that either an army, or pirates, or robbers, or any other tribe that has some common unjust enterprise would be able to accomplish anything, if *its members* acted unjustly *to one another*? . . . It is injustice that produces factions, hatreds, and quarrels among themselves, and justice that produces unanimity and friendship. . . . Will injustice not also cause them *to hate one another* and to form factions, and to be unable to accomplish anything in common *with one another*?" (351c-e). When there is injustice *in* the group, hatred flares up between the group's members. The group itself, however, is not, at least at first, considered unjust on that account.

Where the argument veers off course, where Socrates muddies the waters, is when he permits himself—and persuades Thrasymachus—to regard the injustice *of the group* as diminished, as less than perfect, when its members treat each other justly: he contends that the *group*'s injustice is perfect or more perfect when not only the group commits injustice but its members also treat each other unjustly. Strictly speaking, however, the group's injustice is unaffected by the justice (or injustice) that arises among or between its members: the group is not more perfectly unjust if its members are unjust toward one another as well; it is only less cohesive and effective. Nevertheless, since Socrates' urgent business at the moment

---

76. Socrates says rather explicitly in a rarely cited passage (4.426b-c) that cities behave as individual men do. After describing men who indulge themselves so excessively that they are beyond cure, Socrates poses the following question to Adeimantus: "Or isn't it your impression that the very same thing these men do is done by all cities with bad regimes?"

is to defeat Thrasymachus's notion that the more complete and perfect the injustice, the more profitable, he cleverly highlights injustice's tendency to splinter, divide, and enflame enmity, and to hinder as a result the satisfactory execution of any project—and in particular any unjust project—undertaken by a group.

More than that is needed, however, if Socrates is to refute Thrasymachus decisively: he must show not only that men who treat each other unjustly will not be able together to execute any venture successfully, but also that the projects undertaken by an unjust individual working alone will fail. Socrates therefore now poses the question, What is the effect of injustice's "coming into being" within one man? (351e).[77] If injustice in a city, a clan, an army, "or whatever else" is crippling, making the unit unable to function and dividing it against itself so that it becomes its own enemy (as well as an enemy of the just), so, too, Socrates supposes, will injustice render the single man unable to act, "because he is at faction and is not of one mind with himself" and is "an enemy both to himself and to just men" (352a).[78]

As in the city-soul analogy, so, too, here, Socrates looks at the individual as a group writ small. Yet, it is not immediately obvious that a single man can have injustice "within" him in the way a group of men can: we recall that the injustice "within" the group actually disposes the group's members to treat each other badly; but who are the members within a single man whose cooperativeness can be impeded by injustice? An argument that began as a quite sensible analysis of justice and injustice in terms of how men within a group interact with one another, and how the nature of that interaction determines what the group is able and unable to accomplish,

---

77. It is clear from the discussion in *Rep.* 1 that Plato is not, as Runciman (2010, 27–28) charges, "wedded to a preconceived and empirically unsustainable belief that psychic harmony—or, as we might say, a well-adjusted personality—is attainable only by someone who is steadfastly and consistently disposed to behave in ways which, by his criteria, count as just." This discussion suggests, on the contrary, that psychic harmony aids those who undertake *unjust* endeavors. Nor is Runciman right to imply (52) that Socrates dismisses out of hand the possibility that men might, "as Thrasymachus expects them to do," "apply such wisdom, courage, and temperance as they have to the pursuit of their selfish ends." In *Rep.* 1 Socrates argues that it is people whose souls are in order who are best equipped to achieve their unjust ends.

78. We note that Socrates offers no justification for the riders he tacks on to his pronouncement about the effect of discord on the group. He introduces without warrant or support the idea that the group will be an enemy to its opposite and to the just (352a), and so, too, that the individual who experiences internal disharmony will be an enemy to just men and to the gods who are just (352a-b).

devolves into an arguably far less reasonable consideration of justice and injustice in terms of the inner workings of a solitary man. What makes the shift particularly suspicious is how subtly Socrates lays the groundwork for it: he begins at 351c with injustice as found in rather large groups (city, army), proceeds from these at 351e to somewhat smaller groups (pirates, robbers), and from there to an even smaller group of two. But rather than stop with the very smallest group there is, a group of two, Socrates moves on at 351e to a single individual, as if there is no difference between the very smallest group, on the one hand, and one man, on the other—as if one man is just an even smaller "group." But, of course, it is not the case that a group consisting of one man is just a smaller group than one consisting of two; a single man is not a group of men at all, not even a very tiny one. And if justice and injustice are features of relationships among and between men, as they were conceived to be at every stage of the transition from larger to ever smaller groups, then they do not apply to a single man's relationship with himself.

One could, of course, regard the parts of a man's soul, however improbably, as independent "men," as independent agents. Yet even so—even if a single person may be likened to a group consisting of parts that both act and interact—it will still be the case that the man who commits injustice toward others, like the group that does so, is unjust, regardless of how his parts treat one another; if anything, internal justice, whether in a man or in a group, only maximizes the entity's ability to commit injustice and thus to be unjust. When injustice comes into being "within one man," the man indeed suffers the experience of being at odds with himself, of suffering internal faction and disharmony—but that is because his "parts" are at war *with one another*. This unwelcome state of discord is not, however, what makes a man unjust any more than internal strife is what makes a group unjust. With his expression "injustice within one man," Socrates is able to conceal the fact that a man's being divided against himself is not responsible for *his* being unjust any more than that a group that is fractured from within is on that account an unjust group. On the contrary, in the case of both group and individual, internal fractiousness actually impedes the entity's ability to commit injustice and to be effectively unjust. Single men are unjust, as are cities, if they comport themselves unjustly with respect to others; so, too, their parts. Since the injustice of the parts hampers the ability of the whole to commit injustice, it cannot be the case that the whole is more unjust—or is more perfectly unjust—when its parts are unjust to one another.

Since injustice remains first and foremost the disposition of men (or groups of men or cities) to mistreat one another, the only way an individual man can be unjust is if he is inclined to wrong others. He can certainly, metaphorically speaking, be "his own enemy," but he isn't unjust until he is someone else's enemy.[79] Thus, if one is asked what injustice is when it "comes into being within one man," one would do well to distinguish between (1) the man's own injustice, which would dispose him to harm other men, and (2) the injustice of his parts toward one another, which would, on Socrates' account, make his own injustice (toward others) less efficient and hence more likely to fail. In case (1), the effect of injustice would be to make a man generally uncooperative and hence unable to get along well *with others*; it would indeed foster hatred *in him*—but not toward himself. In case (2), injustice would make the man's parts fight with one another. Either way, justice and injustice are oriented outward: a just or unjust man is just or unjust toward other men; a man's just or unjust parts are just or unjust toward other parts. All Socrates has added for the sake of disconcerting and discrediting Thrasymachus is the (mistaken) notion that an unjust entity whose parts are also unjust is more fully unjust (though surely less successful in executing its unjust projects) than one whose parts are just.

What Socrates shows in this argument, then, is that what he calls imperfect injustice—that is, injustice whose efficiency is boosted by internal justice—is more profitable than perfect injustice. What he does not show, however, is that it is not profitable for a group—or for a man—to be unjust. He establishes in the case of a group that it is less profitable to have men *in it* who are unjust toward one another, and by analogy, that it is less profitable for a man to have parts in him that are unjust toward one another—because both groups and individual men who experience internal conflict have difficulty accomplishing their own ends. To be sure, by contending that an entity's being completely unjust entails its harboring debilitating friction internally, Socrates is able to fend off the Thrasymachean

---

79. It is possible for a man to commit injustice against himself, by visiting on himself an undeserved harm. This is what Socrates refuses to do in the counterpenalty stage of his trial (*Ap.* 37b). Yet to commit injustice against oneself requires that one look on oneself as an "other." It is not the same as internal discord.

contention that perfect injustice is the most profitable condition of all. The fact remains, however, that since a man's injustice is not the enmity between him and himself any more than a group's injustice is its internal disharmony, injustice per se cannot be so handily dismissed as unprofitable.

Although up until the argument's summary Socrates maintains that a whole is imperfectly unjust when its parts are just toward one another, he appears in the summary at last to abandon that idea and to suggest instead that it is the men themselves—that is, the members of the group rather than the group itself—who are under these circumstances less than completely unjust. Those about whom we say that they "vigorously accomplished some common object *with one another* although *they* were unjust," he says, could not have been "completely unjust" because, were it not for "a certain justice *in them* that caused them at least not to do injustice *to one another*," they could not have pursued—with one another—their unjust goals, the injustice "they were seeking to do to others" (352c). The "certain justice in them" is no longer regarded as justice in the group but is now conceived of as being in each of the participating men: they are able to work together because *they* are "only half bad from injustice." In other words, since an unjust man is one who is so ill disposed toward others that he cannot accomplish anything that requires cooperation, a man must be at least somewhat just, somewhat well disposed toward others, if he is to bring to fruition any project that requires joint action.

It seems, then, that Socrates has said nothing thus far to support the contention that a person's own injustice toward others is not profitable. He has argued that injustice among an entity's parts hampers the efforts of the whole; he has made the case that a man's own injustice makes him unable to cooperate with others and thus obstructs *joint* ventures; but he has not offered any reason to think that a person who is unjust (as opposed to a person whose parts are unjust toward one another), a person who hates others, and so cannot work in concert with them, cannot successfully execute those projects he undertakes alone. In order to close this gap, Socrates next illegitimately drops the qualifications "with one another" and "some common object" (352b-c), declaring simply that "the wholly bad and perfectly unjust are also perfectly unable to accomplish anything" (352c-d). Suddenly his point is no longer that those who cannot restrain themselves from harming others are unable to work together to accomplish a common goal; he implies instead that such men are not able to realize their own private ends, good or bad. Yet Socrates has given us no reason to doubt that unjust men are quite able to accomplish their malevolent ends—so long as they either do not have to work with others or do not suffer internal turmoil.

Since groups, men, and men's parts are just or unjust on account of how they are disposed toward others—toward other groups, other men, other parts—one is tempted to suppose that the virtue that is the group's or individual's harmonious internal state is moderation (*sōphrosunē*), and its discordant internal state, licentiousness (*akolasia*). Insofar, however, as Book 1 does not arrange the members of its group or the parts of its souls hierarchically, with the best of them in charge—the accord within a band of pirates or robbers is not made to depend on there being a better man at the helm—the virtue described here is neither justice nor moderation. As we know from the portrayal of the oligarchic man in Book 8 (553d), it is possible for the worst part of a soul to dominate and yet for the soul to achieve a harmony of sorts: the soul's avaricious appetitive part can compel spirit to honor what it desires and coerce reason to further only its ends.[80] Moderation, however, requires more than that reason be the brains of the operation: a moderate soul is one in which reason, the soul's best part, rules, one in which reason's more temperate desires—the "simple and moderate desires, pleasures and pains, those led by calculation accompanied with intelligence and right opinion" (4.431c)—hold sway. Indeed, even when moderation is defined as shared opinion, it requires the recognition of better and worse elements in the city and soul, and an agreement among all elements that the better should rule (4.431d-432a, 442c-d).

Socrates' argument, then, successfully defends neither justice nor moderation—unless rhetorical effectiveness counts as success. Its aim is to disarm Thrasymachus, to make him doubt the one thing he is most sure of,

---

80. It is the tyrannic man whose soul is hopelessly disordered, and the democratic man whose soul is happily anarchic (9.577c-578a, 579c; 8.561a-e). As the image in Book 9 of the creature whose human exterior houses a many-headed beast, a lion, and a human being suggests, moderation requires not simply that one of the components be in charge, but specifically that "the human being within most be in control" (589a). It is noteworthy that the oligarchic *city*, unlike its corresponding man, is "not . . . one but of necessity two, the city of the poor and the city of the rich, dwelling together in the same place, ever plotting against one another" (551d). As Benardete astutely points out (1989, 197), Callipolis is no less divided into rich and poor—though in reverse, with the rulers being the poor. In Callipolis, however, the economic split does not result in a city divided against itself.

namely, that one's own injustice is profitable for oneself, one's own justice only for someone else. All Socrates establishes, however, is that it is beneficial even to the unjust man to have accord among his parts.[81]

In *Rep.* 4, too, Socrates seems deliberately to muddle the matter of what exactly justice is and who or what has it. At times he appears to hold that justice is a feature of wholes—a condition of harmony or accord within cities or human souls. Yet at other times, he speaks of justice as something one does—mind one's own business—which is, or should be in his scheme, a feature of parts, whether parts of a city (its classes) or parts of a soul.[82] And he even on occasion attributes minding one's own business, a feature of parts, to wholes.[83] Consider the following cases. (1) At 434c Socrates says that "each of them [the classes of the city] minding its own business in a city would *be* justice and would make the city just." Socrates appears to be saying that justice is both an attribute of classes (parts), insofar as they are the ones minding their own business, and of the city (the whole), *on account of* its classes minding their own business. (2) At 441d-e, Socrates says: "The one within whom each of the parts minds its own business will be just and mind *his* own business." Here Socrates evidently thinks that a person is just because his parts mind their own business—*and* because he minds his. And this despite his emphatic refusal at 443c-d to apply the name justice to a man's "minding his external business": "And in truth justice was, as it seems, something of this sort [namely, each craftsman practicing his own craft]; however, *not* with respect to a man's minding his external business but with respect to what is within" (443d). Indeed, Socrates makes it quite clear that until he and his interlocutors address the inner workings of the human soul they will not have yet confronted the justice that is in

---

81. Note Socrates' rather weak conclusion that in his "opinion" (*hōs ge moi dokei*), men who are just "do look as though" they are happier than men who aren't (352d).

82. If the justice of parts were their internal harmony an infinite regress would result: each part would have to have parts that would mind their own business, but these parts, too, would have to have such parts, and so on.

83. Minding one's business in a city is a virtue only when there is reciprocity. No matter how suited one is to making shoes, there is no virtue in making nothing but shoes if others are not producing the other things that are needed. There is also no virtue in being ruled if no one suitable is ruling. Socrates, therefore, defines justice in the city as a matter of "each" (i.e., all)—child, woman, slave, freeman, craftsman, ruler, and ruled—minding his own business (433d). Although minding one's own business is a virtue of parts, it is not a virtue of parts in isolation.

"human beings singly" (434d).[84] (3) At 9.586e, Socrates says that "when all the soul . . . is not factious, the result is that each part may . . . mind its own business and be just." In this passage it is not the harmonious soul but the soul's parts that are called just—when they mind their own business.[85]

As these examples show, Socrates wants justice to do double duty: to be both a matter of minding one's own business and a state of harmony or accord. It is no doubt tempting to suppose that for Socrates the state of *being* just is a condition of wholes but *acting* justly is something parts do to produce that state. Yet, if that were the case he surely would not speak, as he does, of parts *being* just (as in example [3]) and of wholes minding their own business (as in example [2]).

It is, of course, for good reason that Socrates makes justice a feature both of parts and of wholes, a matter both of what one does (mind one's own business) and of how one is (harmonious). For, if, on the one hand, Socrates is to sustain a connection between his conception of justice and its ordinary (vulgar) sense, the sense in which it requires that people refrain from encroaching on each other's person and property, he needs to hold on to the formula of "minding one's own business."[86] But if, on the other hand, he is to have any hope of making a case for the profitability of justice, he must

---

84. Heinaman (1998, 38) maintains that what makes individual members of classes personally just or unjust is whether they do their own job or meddle in the job of another. But personal or individual justice is not even considered until 434e, where Socrates explicitly makes the turn from what constitutes the city's justice to what individual justice is, "Let us apply what came to light there [with respect to the city] to a single man," and where he designates personal justice and injustice as matters solely of the internal workings of individual souls. Indeed, Socrates withholds approval from his own analysis of justice in the city until he sees it prove itself valid for the individual internally (434d).

85. Another instance of the deliberate confusing of parts and wholes occurs at 4.423d: "Each of the other citizens too must be brought to that which naturally suits him—one man, one job—so that each man, practicing his own, which is one, will not become many but one; and thus, you see, the whole city will naturally grow to be one and not many." Whereas it is presumably the case that if each man does his own job the city will become one, it is not the case either that (1) the man himself will become one, or (2) the city will become one *because* the man does. A man becomes one by his parts doing their own jobs, the city by its men (or classes) doing theirs.

86. At 433a-b Socrates observes that "we have both heard from many others and have often said ourselves" that "justice is the minding of one's own business and not being a busybody." What is regularly heard and said, of course, is that justice is not taking or having what is another's and not one's own—which Socrates counts on to be close enough to "minding one's own business and not being a busybody" that they seem about the same. See 433e-434a. See Dover 1974, 44: "Honest administration of money or property entrusted to one's safe-keeping is normally treated as a manifestation—almost the manifestation par excellence—of *dikaiosynē*."

maintain that cities and individuals are just, not because of anything they do or refrain from, but simply because they are internally well ordered. As we have seen, however, internal order is not justice but, at best—that is, when a city's or soul's rational part masters the others—moderation.[87]

Addendum II: Why Be Just? *Rep.* 8–10

In the final three books of the *Republic* Socrates defends justice in four ways. First, he maligns the tyrant; second, he extols the pleasures of philosophy; third, he praises moderation; and fourth, he enumerates the material rewards of justice that had been suppressed until now. (The second and third ways, as we shall see, are not unrelated to the first: the tyrant's pleasures are not philosophic, and so are not ultimately satisfying; moderation is the virtue in which the tyrant is most deficient.) Just as Socrates' defense of justice in Book 1 falls short—he shows only, as we have seen (in addendum I), that it is profitable for a group to have members who treat each other justly and profitable for an individual to have parts that get along, but not quite that it is profitable for a group to act justly toward other groups or for an individual working alone to act justly toward other individuals—so, too, do the *Republic*'s final books establish less than Socrates or we would like. These books offer good reasons for avoiding the life of tyranny, for pursuing philosophic pleasures, and for being moderate. But being just still is of no use to one who does not seem so; the only difference between these later books and *Rep.* 2 is that in the later books Socrates offers assurances that those who are just will also seem so— probably to men and certainly to gods.

The first defense of justice is actually an excoriation of the tyrant: since the tyrant is the worst man—worse even than the tyrannic man who does not actually become a tyrant (578c)—his opposite, the just man, is the best man; since the tyrant is most wretched, the just man is happiest (599b-c).

---

87. Vlastos (1971, 86) sees the shift from justice as a "relational predicate" to justice as a "one-place group predicate" as unwitting equivocation that vitiates (though not irreparably) Socrates' argument. The view argued for here is that for Socrates it is moderation that is the one-place group predicate and justice the relational one. The only reason Socrates conflates the two is in order to render justice "profitable."

The tyrant's soul is horribly disordered, and the tyrant himself, "while not having control of himself, attempts to rule others, just as if a man with a body that is sick and without control of itself were compelled to spend his life not in a private station but contesting and fighting with other bodies" (579c-d). The choice between the life of the tyrant and that of his polar opposite is thus simple and clear: the life of injustice that comes so highly recommended by Thrasymachus (545a) is to be avoided at all costs, and the just life pursued. Socrates' elaborate treatment of the intermediate regimes, those that lie between the best one, kingship or aristocracy,[88] and the worst one, tyranny, and of the men who are analogous to them (8.545b-562a), though fascinating and illuminating in its own right, is of only secondary importance as compared with the more pressing matter of the contrast between the two extremes of men: the best and the worst, the most unjust and the most just (544c, 545a, 576d-e, 580b-c, 618e).[89] The only decision in life that is of any real consequence is that between justice and injustice (618d-619a). Once the tyrant emerges as worst and most wretched and most unjust, it is not surprising that Glaucon chooses as happiest the man who, by contrast, is kingliest and king of himself, the man who is best and most just (580b-c).

In Socrates' second approach to establishing justice's superiority to its alternatives, he argues that philosophic pleasures are the best, purest, and indeed the only real pleasures; yet he says nothing to support his identification of philosophy with justice. In his first pleasure argument, he contends that the philosopher, having experienced all pleasures, is in the best position to judge which are best (581c-582d);[90] moreover, the philosopher is best at arguing, and so best at judging (582d-e). As he concludes this argument Socrates announces triumphantly, but without warrant: "Well then . . . the *just* man has been victorious over the unjust one" (583b).

---

88. Socrates twice (5.499a, 8.544a) qualifies his designation of Callipolis as best, saying "*if* this one is right."

89. Although Socrates asks Glaucon to rank the five types of men according to "who in your opinion is first in happiness, and who second, and the others in order, five in all," and although Glaucon complies, choosing them, "like choruses in the very order in which they came on stage," when Socrates repeats Glaucon's answer he announces: "Ariston's son has decided that the best and most just man is happiest . . . while the worst and most unjust man is most wretched"; the men in between drop out (580a-c).

90. Socrates adds, too, that only the philosopher would have gained his experience "in the company of prudence" (582d).

In the second of his pleasure arguments Socrates maintains that only the pleasures of learning are real pleasures—they alone are not, as other pleasures are, mere releases from pain (583b-586b); they alone are pure and unmixed with pain (586b); indeed, the pleasures of the soul's thinking part are, for each part of the soul, best, truest, and most "their own" (586c-587a). Socrates thus seeks to dispel the all-too-common delusion that the tyrannic man, despite his viciousness—or perhaps because of it—enjoys the most and best pleasure.[91] What emerges from Book 9's consideration of the tyrant's "soul as a whole" (*holēs psuchēs*—577a, 579e) is that the tyrannic man least does what he wants, that his desires get no real satisfaction, and that he is generally needy and "poor in truth" (577e). Speaking "boldly" (*tharrountes legōmen*—586d), Socrates asserts that the only way in which all the parts of the soul (or "all the soul," *hapasēs psuchēs*—586e) find fulfillment and reap "the best pleasures, and, to the greatest possible extent, the truest pleasures," those that are "most properly their own," is by following the wise (*phronimon*) or philosophic (*philosophōi*) part to its pleasures (586d-e).[92] By contrast, when the soul is controlled by either of

---

91. Socrates knows there are men who are like children (perhaps he has the *Gorgias's* Polus in mind—see *Gorg.* 466b-c, 468e, 470d-471d) who "look from outside" and are "overwhelmed by the tyrannic pomp set up as a façade" (577a).

92. This is what Socrates means when he says at 7.518c that the "instrument with which each [person] learns ... must be turned ... *together with the whole soul*" if it is to see what is brightest. Socrates' point at 586d-587a is that the dominant part of the soul determines how the whole soul is turned. See, too, 6.498b, where the budding young philosopher secures the body as a helper for philosophy before he tackles the "more intense gymnastic." A similar idea is found in Aristotle (*EN* 9.4.1166a): the good man desires the good of all the elements of his soul for the sake of the intellectual part of himself (*tou dianoētikou*); he seeks to preserve especially the part of him with which he thinks (*touto hōi phronei*), since the thinking part (*to nooun*) constitutes what he really is, or at any rate does so to a greater extent than anything else. Most translators render *exēgētai* "prescribe" or "ordain," taking Socrates to be saying that the desires of the two other parts of the soul—the gain-loving and victory-loving—find their own pleasures, their true pleasures, in those the rational part (*to phronimon*) prescribes for them. I follow Bloom (1968), however, in taking *exēgētai* to mean "leads." Socrates must then be understood to be saying that the two other parts get the pleasures that are properly their own, their pleasures that are truest—as much as they are able to partake of true ones—when their desires "follow knowledge and argument" and pursue with them the pleasures to which the rational part leads. Socrates had just said that the only true pleasures are those of thinking (*phronēseōs*) and virtue, and that no bodily pleasures are true ones (586a-b). (He repeats this point at 587b, where he says that "there are, as it seems, three pleasures—one genuine, and two bastard.") What follows from this conclusion, as Socrates now daringly asserts, is that the other parts can experience true pleasures, their own pleasures, only to the extent that they can share in the pleasures of *to phronimon*.

the other parts, what happens is that all the parts—both the dominant and the subservient ones—forfeit their own pleasure and pursue a pleasure that is "alien and untrue" (586d-587a).

The tyrant, then, it seems, no matter how much pleasure he attains, cannot be satisfied. The gain-loving part of his soul, though in a position of power and therefore able to compel the rest of the soul to do its bidding, indeed acquires pleasures, but they are false and foreign (587a). Since the tyrannic soul is most distant from law and order as well as from argument, and since the kingly and orderly soul is least distant, the tyrant will be farthest from a pleasure that is true and his own, and the king closest. The king's pleasure, according to Socrates' curious calculation, exceeds the tyrant's by a factor of 729. Since the king is just and the tyrant unjust, the happiness of the just man and just life must surpass that of the unjust by a similar margin. By identifying the king as the man who enjoys genuine pleasures and the tyrant as the man who experiences only false ones, Socrates can then join Glaucon in celebrating "the good and just man's victory in pleasure over the bad and unjust man's" (588a). By dividing men into three categories, the gain-loving, honor-loving, and wisdom-loving, and characterizing the tyrant as the gain-loving man, and his "opposite," the king, as both just and wisdom-loving, Socrates eases the (unjustified) assimilation of king to philosopher and philosopher to just man.[93]

Socrates' third tack is to laud moderation as if it were justice—just as he did in Book 4. The virtue that is diametrically opposed to the vice of the tyrannic man, to his licentiousness, to his erotic drive for pleasures no matter how shockingly indecent and lawless, is moderation. The injustices—that is, the unjust acts—to which the tyrant is prone are traceable to his internal disorder: he finds himself driven to commit ever more unspeakable crimes as he seeks to satisfy the insatiable and lascivious lusts that reign in his deeply disturbed soul.

If one reason the tyrant is less happy than the just man is that his soul, like the city to which it corresponds, is "filled with much slavery and

---

93. It is not the case, as Benardete (1989, 40), for example, supposes (citing 9.583b), that "the identification of justice and philosophy" is something "that Socrates comes finally round to." Indeed, in the *Theaetetus*'s "digression" (171d-177c), Socrates similarly begins by contrasting the philosopher with the non-philosopher, but the "two patterns set up in what is (*en tōi onti*)" are of the just man and the unjust. In the *Theaetetus*, Socrates makes no attempt to bridge the gap between them.

illiberality, and . . . those parts of it that are most decent are slaves while a small part, the most depraved and maddest, is master" (577d), then surely the just man's greater happiness is attributable to the greater orderliness in his soul. But is that greater orderliness justice? Is it not moderation? As if to reinforce the notion that it is the moderate man and life that are best, Socrates introduces the striking image of a human being who encompasses within himself a many-headed beast, a lion, and a human being. Indeed the whole of Socrates' case for the profitability of moderation is contained in this colorful image. It cannot be profitable, Socrates contends, for a man to commit injustice if as a result he enslaves the best, most divine, part of himself to the part that is most depraved, most godless, and most polluted, any more than it is worthwhile to enslave one's children to a savage and bad man for gold (589d-590a). The effect licentiousness has on a man is to give free rein to the many-formed beast within him and to suppress the human element. Yet surely it is best for a person to be guided by what is most human in him, that is, by the reasoning part of the soul—by his own reasoning part, if possible, but by someone else's, if not. To be ruled by someone else in this way is not, as Thrasymachus would have it, to one's detriment (590c-d), but is decidedly to one's benefit. Optimally, all people would be piloted by the same divine thing and be friends and alike in this way. The aim of law is to instill reasoned control; so, too, the aim of parents: they take charge of their children only until the children's own rational rule is activated (590e-591a).

The purpose of punishment, too, as explained in Book 9, is to restrain people's appetites so that their good sense can hold sway in their souls. As Socrates observes at 591b, what happens to the man who does not get away with doing injustice and is punished is that the bestial part of his soul is put to sleep and tamed, and the tamed part freed. Punishment brings the whole soul to its best nature,[94] so that it acquires "moderation and justice accompanied by prudence" (591a-b).[95] In the *Gorgias* as well punishment is said to release a soul from baseness: first, it prevents the soul from

---

94. See also 2.380b, where Socrates forbids the poets to say either that people punished by the gods don't profit from their penalty or that a god makes a person wretched by punishing him. It is permissible for them to say only that bad men are wretched because they are in need of punishment, so that the god benefits them by punishing them.

95. This is the only time the properly ordered state of the soul is called justice in Book 9. A discussion of this passage follows.

continuing to fester as if with sores underneath to the point that it becomes incurable (478a-b); second, it keeps the soul away from the things it desires, since feeding its base appetites will only make it worse (505b); third, it brings benefit by way of the infliction of pains and griefs,[96] the only way a soul can be freed of injustice (525b);[97] and fourth, it "moderates men and makes them more just and comes to be the medicine for baseness" (478d). In working directly on the irrational elements of the soul, on the many-headed beast and on the lion, punishment brings to the soul the kind of gentleness and discipline that prevents the recurrence of injustice. Pain is inflicted, then, not only so that the soul will recoil in fear from repeating its crimes, but also so that it will desist from injustice as a result of having become more moderate.[98]

Socrates surely could have offered up his tri-creatured image in Book 2 and brought the deliberation regarding which is better, justice or injustice, to an early and swift close—were it not for the fact that what the image shows is not that it is better to be just (or to have justice in one's soul) but that it is better to be moderate. Although the image provides a good reason for *acting* justly—indeed, it is introduced as a repudiation of the view expressed earlier "that *doing* injustice is profitable for the man who is perfectly unjust but has the reputation of being just" and as support for the agreement that had already been reached with respect to the powers of "doing injustice and doing just things" (588b)—it does not promote justice as the best and most profitable condition of the soul. Instead it teaches that the one thing that matters to the intelligent man is "becoming moderate" and achieving "accord in the soul" (591c-d); nothing else takes precedence over these ends—not health, strength, or beauty (591b). Such a man develops a "habit" (*hexis*—591b, 591c, 592a) in the soul more worthy of honor than its counterpart in the body, and is vigilant lest money or honor disturb

---

96. Aristotle, *EN* 2.3.1140b: "Another indication is the fact that pain is the medium of punishment; for punishment is a sort of medicine and it is the nature of medicine to work by means of opposites."

97. The soul's being "freed from injustice" means, in this context, that it is relieved of its desire to go on committing injustice.

98. The derogation of poetry in Book 10 as well as the recommendation that it be banished from the city are also ways of supporting and promoting moderation. Poetry enables the irrational part to gain dominance in the soul (606a), and enthrones pleasure and pain as kings in the city in place of law and argument.

it. His attention is focused exclusively on his soul—that is, on preserving its moderation.

That the ordered state of the soul commended here had earlier been called justice is by now all but forgotten. In Books 8 and 9, even though Socrates is supposed to be defending the life of justice, he frequently— at 8.555c, 559c, 560c, and at 9.571d, 573b, 575b, 591d—calls the properly ordered condition of the soul moderation and its disordered state immoderation or licentiousness. At 8.586e, where Socrates recommends intellectual pleasure over the other kinds—a passage discussed in the previous section—Socrates briefly speaks of the soul's *parts* being just by minding their own business, but he does not call the nonfactious soul, or the person who has such a soul, just. Only once does the term "justice" appear in connection with such a soul—at 9.591b, where Socrates says that when the bestial part of the man who is punished is put to sleep and the tamed part freed, his "whole soul" is "brought to its best nature, acquiring moderation and justice accompanied by prudence." But even here justice is paired with moderation. Moreover, when Socrates calls tyrants unjust it is because "they live their whole lives without ever being friends *of anyone*" (576a). Although Socrates immediately catches and "corrects" himself, remembering, as it were, that "if our previous agreement about what justice is was right" (576a-b), a man is unjust not because he never experiences "true friendship" (576a), but because he fails to "become *his own* friend" (*philon genomenon heautōi*—4.443d), he was right the first time.[99]

Glaucon suspects, and Socrates confirms, that a man whose overarching concern is to preserve his soul's internal accord, his moderation, would not be willing to "mind the political things" (592a)—at least not as political things are ordinarily understood. Socrates explains, however, that there is an alternate sense in which one can mind the political things, that is, by minding the affairs of one's own soul. The moderate man would thus mind the things "in his own city," but would not care for his fatherland "unless some divine chance coincidentally comes to pass" (592a). Nor, for that matter, would he care for the city Glaucon and Socrates have been founding in

---

99. The link between justice and friendship recalls something Socrates said in Book 1 about injustice: "It will make him ... an enemy both to himself and to just men. ... The unjust man will also be an enemy to the gods ... and the just man a friend" (352a-b). Socrates deliberately conflates internal discord with external. See note 78 above.

speech; Glaucon is wrong to think that it is this city that Socrates intends
by the phrase "in his own city." On the contrary,[100] the man whose eye is
trained on his soul will at best find a pattern in heaven[101] in accordance
with which to found *himself*.[102] He would then "mind the things of this city
[i.e., of his own soul] alone, and of no other" (592b), and it will be of no relevance to him whether the city in speech does or does not exist somewhere
(592b). Under ordinary circumstances, then, the moderate man does not
care for others. But at the same time, because of his disciplined soul, he is
least likely to cause anyone harm.

---

100. Socrates would not begin his response to Glaucon with *All'* unless he meant it to be ad-
versative, with the *All'* implying "not that, but . . ."

101. The *Republic* is careful not to confuse heaven with the realm of the Forms. It consistently
treats heaven as part of the visible realm, the part in which the sun reigns. (Socrates even draws attention at 6.509d to the phonetic connection between "of the heaven" [*ouranou*] and "visible" [*hora-
tou*]—if this is indeed the play on words to which he refers. Another possibility is that Socrates
avoids *ouranou* because it is too close to *nous* and hence to the intelligible. See Bloom 1968, 464 n.
35; Reeve 2004, 205 n. 38. *Crat.* 396c seems to combine both possible accounts.) See, too, the allegory of the Cave at 516a-b, as well as 596c and 596e, and the myth of Er at 614c-615a, 616b-c, and
619c-e. At 500c it is explicitly the orderly pattern of "what is" that the philosopher sees—not a pattern in the heavens (see Chapter 1, note 55). Indeed, even when the philosopher, in studying the
heavens as part of his intellectual training, directs his attention to their nonvisible patterns (529c-
530b), it is still the heavens, as distinct from the Forms, that are the subject of his investigation.

102. Some translate this passage "to found himself as its citizen," "to make himself its citizen"
(see Grube and Reeve 1997; Shorey 1963; Vegetti 2005). But Adam (1969) takes it as I do (as do
[more or less] Cornford 1945, Bloom 1968, Griffith 2000, Lee 1955, J. Sachs 2007, Reeve 2004, and
Allen 2006). Indeed, Plato prepares the reader to take the expression *heauton katoikizein* to refer
to founding himself—i.e., his soul—as one would found a city (and so, too, to take the expression
"his own city" at 592a to refer to his soul) by using similar expressions at 590e ("until we establish
a regime in them [*en autois . . . politeian katastēsōmen*] [i.e., in the children] as in a city") and at 591e
("he looks fixedly at the regime within him" [*pros tēn en hautōi politeian*]) (this passage is surely the
one that prompts Glaucon to venture that the moderate man will not be willing to mind the political things). See also 10.608b: "fearing for the regime in himself" (*peri tēs en hautōi politeias*). Only
at 7.540e is it clearly the polis the philosophers live in (rather than the one that lives in them) that
they will provide for. Vegetti (2005), believing that how one translates the passage at 592a-b determines whether the *Republic* is political or is concerned ultimately with individual justice, ten-
dentiously takes the passage to say that the just man, the philosopher, will relocate from his native
city to the city of the paradigm (the city whose pattern is "in heaven") and "take part in the practical affairs of that city and no other." In my view, this passage, no matter how it is read, is insufficient to resolve the question of whether the *Republic* is a political work or one that is exclusively
ethical. What it does show is that the man who is preoccupied with his soul will "mind the political things" only as concerns his own psychic condition. Cf. *Theaet.* 176e, where two patterns for
the soul are "set up in what is (*en tōi onti*)": the just which is divine and most happy, and the unjust
which is godless and most miserable.

Since neither Glaucon nor Adeimantus is philosophic by nature or likely to become philosophic by divine dispensation or coercive training, it is not surprising that in the *Republic*'s late books, philosophy takes a back seat. Books 8, 9, and 10 encourage not the life of philosophy but the more accessible life of *being* moderate and *acting* justly: by "practicing justice with prudence," we will be "friendly to ourselves and to the gods" (621c; cf. 351e-352b). Socrates' intricate and labored demonstrations of the superiority of philosophic pleasure to other forms of pleasure (Book 9's second and third arguments in support of justice—580c-583a, 583b-588a) are served up as endorsements of the just (or moderate) life—not of the philosophic.[103] For Glaucon and Adeimantus to do well they need to be kings not of cities but of themselves (612b). They need to refrain from injustice and keep their souls moderate. Since each of these ends tends to reinforce the other, even concentrating their efforts on just one of them is likely to produce both. The brothers will not, to be sure, become in this way the most just of men: they will not be like the good philosophers of Book 6 and certainly not like Socrates. But they will not be the least just either. They will care for their own souls, if not for the souls of others—and they will harm no one.

---

103. Bloom (1968, 435) thinks that the *Republic* teaches "nothing other than the necessity of philosophy and its purity and superiority to the political life." Yet this is certainly not the most sustained and most pronounced message of the *Republic*'s last three books, and so not the teaching with which Socrates leaves Glaucon and Adeimantus. Even in Book 10's myth of Er, where the man who is just *without philosophy* is seen foolishly choosing the life of the tyrant for his next life, philosophy is a bulwark against a life of extreme injustice rather than an end in itself. And what is said of the man who "philosophizes in a healthy way" (and whose luck does not fail him in the lottery) (619d-e) is that he is likely to journey through the heavens rather than beneath the earth—that is, to live the only life that culminates in ascent to the heavens: a just life. For further discussion, see the next chapter.

CONCLUSION

"In a Healthy Way"

Plato ends the *Republic* with the myth of Er (10.614b-621d). As the nightlong conversation in the home of Polemarchus and Cephalus winds down, Socrates recounts the tale of Er, a man who has recently died but returns to life to share with the living his observations of life after death. The myth is introduced, at least ostensibly, to bolster Socrates' assertion that in the long run the just will fare well and the unjust poorly: not only will the just and unjust experience, respectively, good and bad things in their lifetimes at the hands of men (613b-e), but the gods will bestow on them far greater premiums and penalties after they die.[1]

---

1. Socrates uses this occasion to rehabilitate the gods and to correct Adeimantus's earlier unflattering portrayal of them as (1) being as easily fooled by appearances as men are (363a, 366b), (2) allotting good things to bad men and bad to good (364b), and (3) being responsive to bribery (364e-365a, 365e; see, too, Glaucon's account at 362c). Socrates presents them instead, in Book 10, as astute, just, and fair. Nevertheless, some of the features of the way in which future lives are determined cannot but give us pause, though we are cautioned that whatever goes awry is the fault of the chooser and not of the god (617e).

Surprisingly, however, the myth provides few details about the after-life's rewards and punishments.[2] All we are told is that the souls of the just go up to the heavens and pass smoothly through them (614c-615c), and that when they complete their journey, they relay to the others "the inconceivable beauty of the experiences and the sights" they enjoyed while there; and that the unjust, "lamenting and crying, remember how much and what sort of things they had suffered and seen in the journey under the earth" (614e-615a). We do indeed hear of the terrible fate in store for "those whose badness is incurable"—of these, most are tyrants[3]; only a few are private men who have committed unspeakable evils—as well as for those "who had not paid a sufficient penalty" but nevertheless sought to "go up" (615e-616a). Er reports that the ascent of these men from under the earth is blocked, and that their very attempt to break through the barrier occasions a fearsome roar. Some are then simply led away; others, however, are bound and stripped of their skin, dragged along the wayside, "carded like wool on thorns," and thrown into Tartarus (616a). Yet we learn nothing about the nature of the punishments to which the less spectacularly wicked are subjected before they venture to ascend, for, Er says, "to go through the many things would take a long time" (615a). Nor are we made privy to the wondrous delights with which the righteous are feted. Concerning the latter all the text says is "The bounties were the antistrophes of these" (616a-b).

Not only is the myth disconcertingly reticent about the rewards and punishments visited on the righteous and wicked upon their death, but the bulk of it is devoted to another matter entirely: the way in which the souls of the dead go about choosing their next life (617d-621b).[4] How disappointed Glaucon must be, having anticipated a story that would be simply "pleasant" to hear (614b).[5] Among the more disturbing features of the process by which souls select their new life are the following: (1) that their choices are

---

2. See Ferrari 2008, 127.

3. See *Gorg.* 525e-526b, where Socrates tells Callicles that for the most part it is powerful men who become exceedingly base.

4. See Ferrari 2008, 126.

5. See Lampert (2010, 275), who observes that Glaucon and Adeimantus cannot really mean it when they "high-mindedly" ask Socrates not to consider rewards: "The goodness of justice must consist in a good that is good for them"; "They want to be just but they need it to pay" (277). This is why, as Bloom points out (1968, 435), Socrates must prove the immortality of the soul, as he attempts to do at 608d-611a: how else can he persuade Glaucon that justice will be fully rewarded?

said to be free (617e), yet it seems that the way they have lived their most recent life or the experiences they underwent in it go a long way toward determining their choice of the next; (2) that the souls tend to exchange a former good life for a new bad one, and vice versa (619d),[6] so that a person who was just in his last life may well choose for his next time around the least just—and most wretched—life there is, the life of a tyrant (619c-d); and (3) that a lottery determines which souls choose first and which last (617d-e, 619b, 619e, 620c-d), though it certainly seems that a lottery should have no place in a system of strict lex talionis. These aspects of the myth seem to undermine rather substantially its putative lesson that justice pays, that it is rewarded not only in this life but in death, that the "prizes, wages, and gifts coming to the just man while alive from gods and human beings, in addition to those good things that justice itself procured . . . are nothing in multitude or magnitude compared to those that await each when dead" (613e-614a). Indeed, these troubling elements inject into what should have been a process of equitable remuneration a measure of chance and uncertainty and arguably even of unfairness; they certainly appear to suggest that the life of injustice can yield greater rewards than at least some just lives—if not forever, then at least for the next incarnation.[7]

Socrates reneges, then, as it were, on his promise to deliver "the full measure of what the argument owed" (614a), namely, a straightforward and detailed account of justice's postmortem rewards. By inserting instead unexpected and perturbing oddities into his afterlife myth,[8] he intimates

---

6. Bloom (1968, 436) thus thinks that for all men other than the philosopher, "there is a constant change of fortune from happiness to misery and back." See, too, Ferrari 2008, 129.

7. According to Annas (1982, 139), the myth "contains no optimistic promise of final reward to induce us to be just"; it "presents no guarantee at all that those achievements [viz. the moral achievements of individuals] will 'in the end' get their due reward and not have been thrown away" (135). The myth of Er indeed differs in this way from the afterlife myths of the *Gorgias* (*Gorg.* 523a-527a), *Phaedo* (107d-114c), and *Phaedrus* (246a-250c).

8. In Lear's view (2006, 41) the myth is essentially comforting insofar as the one possibility it does not entertain is that of an "afterlife in which the just would be mocked and tortured by malevolent gods." But the myth could have been far more reassuring than it is: whereas it could simply have said that the just will be rewarded handsomely and the unjust severely punished, it instead makes souls choose their next life and includes a lottery that is most unsettling. Indeed, the myth renders even reward problematic: those who are rewarded first tend to make bad choices for their subsequent incarnation. Annas (1982, 125) calls the myth of Er "a confused and confusing myth" "whose message is blurred."

that justice's "prizes, wages, and gifts" are hardly the best reason to choose justice. Indeed, he notes that the only thing that really matters is having the good sense to distinguish the good life from the bad,[9] the just from the unjust:

> From all this he will be able to draw a conclusion and choose—in looking off toward the nature of the soul—between the worse and the better life, calling worse the one that leads it toward becoming more unjust, and better the one that leads it to becoming more just. He will let everything else go. For we have seen that this is the most important choice for him in life and death. (10.618d-619a)

If in some way the myth is supposed to "save us" (*hēmas an sōseien*), to keep us practicing the justice and prudence that will help us hew to the "upper road" (621b-c), how is it to be construed? What is its lesson?

Through his myth of Er Socrates appears to be teaching us, if not quite why we should be just, then at least which is best among the ways we might live and which not nearly as good. One less than ideal way to live is justly but thoughtlessly so. Er speaks of a man whose lot has placed him first in line to select his next life. Having "lived in an orderly regime in his former life, participating in virtue by habit, without philosophy," he "immediately chose the greatest tyranny . . . due to folly and gluttony" (619b-d). Being at the head of the queue gave this man little time to reflect and no opportunity to see how and what other souls chose; he thus made his selection far too hastily, not realizing, for example, that a tyrant might be so evil as to eat his own children. It is a choice he will quickly come to regret (619c).[10]

---

9. Specifically, one is to look at all the combinations that make up particular life patterns— beauty, poverty, wealth, various habits of soul, good and bad birth, private station and ruling office, strength and weakness, facility and difficulty in learning, etc.—and choose a just life, a life between extremes that avoids excess in either direction (618c-619b). It is likely that the man who was formerly just by habit and not by philosophy was simply ignorant of the extremes that tyranny entails; he failed to take up the most crucial study.

10. As Halliwell points out (2007, 452), the man who was just by habit without philosophy and hence not punished at all might as a tyrant "become eternally unredeemable." Indeed, this outcome is one about which Socrates had just cautioned Glaucon: each of us "must go to Hades adamantly holding to this opinion so that he won't be daunted by wealth and such evils there, and rush into tyrannies and other such deeds by which he would work many *irreparable* evils" (619a). In the *Phaedo*, those who are just by habit without philosophy (82a-b) fare much better after death than do their counterparts in the *Republic*. They are considered "happiest," becoming in their

Er proceeds to contrast with the man who was in his lifetime virtuous—just[11]—by habit the man who was unjust, the man who has come "from the earth" (619d).[12] This man, Er reports, both because he himself has labored and because he has seen the labors of others, is disposed to choose more carefully and more judiciously than the formerly just man—that is, he is likely to "exchange" evil for good (619d). This man, who "went up with the greatest delight" when his attempt to ascend from the lower realm triggered no roar (616c), is not about to risk a return.

A third type of man, distinguished both from the man who is just by habit and from the man who is simply unjust, is the man who "always philosophizes in a healthy way" (*hugiōs*—619d-e). If this third man's lot "does not fall out among the last," Er says, "it is likely" (*kinduneuei*)[13] that "he will not only be happy here but also that he will journey from this world to the other and back again not by the underground, rough road but by the smooth one, through the heavens" (619e). That this man will be happy *here* is not in doubt and does not seem to depend on his place in the lottery; that he will travel pleasantly afterward, however—that is, that the life he chooses will be a just one—appears to be somewhat less certain.[14] The lottery once again seems to play a critical role: if the healthy philoso-phizer does not get to choose until the end there may simply be no just lives left. To be sure, this predicament is only barely possible: not only is there little reason to think that all the decent lives would have already been chosen—after all, there are far more patterns of lives than there are souls

---

next life social and tame creatures like bees, wasps, or ants, or returning as "measured" (*metrious*) human beings.

11. This man could not have "come from heaven" (619c) unless he were just.

12. As was noted in Chapter 5, addendum II, despite the fact that Socrates discusses many types of men—and cities—in the *Republic*, the two that matter in the long run are the just and the unjust. See 618d-e.

13. Ferrari (2008, 130) takes *kinduneuei* as a "caveat" alerting the reader to the need to exercise "the appropriate level of caution in accepting *any* message that purports to be about the afterlife" (emphasis in original). Since, however, *kinduneuei* does not appear with respect to the first type of man or the second, its presence exclusively in the case of the third type may well signal that no such man was ever actually observed. In this case, therefore, the best the spokesman could do was venture a conjecture, "on the basis of what *is* reported from there" (*ek tōn ekeithen apangellomenōn*—619e).

14. What turns on whether this man's lot is or is not among the last is whether or not he will travel the smooth road. This I take to be the force of "not only," *ou monon*: his place in the lottery will affect this second consequence of healthily philosophizing.

(617e-618a)—but the "spokesman" had just issued an assurance at 619b that "even for a man who comes forward last, if he chooses intelligently and lives earnestly, a life to content him is laid up, not a bad one"; moreover, Odysseus, who in fact draws "the last lot of all," succeeds in finding among the remaining lives a life that is just or at least not unjust, "the life of a private man who minds his own business" (620c).

To what extent, then, are souls' choices affected by their character, their life experience, and their place in the lottery? It would appear that the fate of the souls is not quite predetermined by their past,[15] yet also that they do not make their choices in a vacuum.[16] On the one hand, that one chooses out of one's disposition and experience is clear both from 619b, where the choice of tyranny is "due to folly and gluttony," and from 619d, where the experience of having "labored," that is, of having been punished, is said to make one more inclined to choose carefully. And, of course, the choices made by Orpheus, Thamyras, Ajax, Agamemnon, Atalanta, Epeius, Odysseus, the swan, other musical animals, and various beasts reflect their past experiences as well as their habits and strong likes and dislikes (620a-d). On the other hand, according to Necessity's daughter Lachesis, the soul's choice is free: "Virtue is without a master; as he honors or dishonors her, each will have more or less of her. The blame belongs to him who chooses; god is blameless" (617e). Although character and life experiences thus surely predispose people to certain choices, they do not eradicate the freedom to honor or dishonor virtue, to choose a good life or a bad. Moreover, if, as we are told, the order (*taxin*) in one's soul is not a feature of the life patterns from among which one chooses (618b), but the soul necessarily changes in accordance with the pattern selected, then it must be the case that the soul, regardless of its current order, is sufficiently flexible to "become different" (*alloian gignesthai*) in response to its new life pattern (618b).

With respect to the effect of the lottery, Socrates is evidently determined to preserve the role of chance in the selection process, and for that reason

---

15. For this view, see Annas 1982, 132–33; also Halliwell 1988, 22. In Halliwell 2007, 464, the view is qualified: "Yet Socrates' comment [at 618b-619a], in keeping with the *Republic* as a whole, clearly presupposes that life is not ethically predestined from the outset. . . . Moral agency must be exercised at every moment to maintain the commitment of a life."

16. Thayer (1988) characterizes the choosing soul as "unqualified" (372) or as "unconstituted or qualityless" (373), though subject to influences: knowledge, anticipation of pleasure and happiness, habits of the previous life, and past experience.

insists (by way of Er and the spokesman he quotes) on the lottery's non-trivial ramifications: a man of the first type—one who lives justly by habit in a well-ordered regime—is seen to make a foolhardy choice that he will subsequently regret, in part because he is first to choose; and a man of the third type—one who always philosophizes in a healthy way—may be prevented from choosing his preferred life because he is among the last to choose. Even in the case of the man of the second type—one who was formerly unjust—the spokesman is careful to add: "and due to the chance of the lot" (619d).

If the myth teaches that the state of one's soul, the way one has lived, and one's place in the queue all affect, but do not fully determine, a dead man's choice of his next life, what does it tell us about the living? For surely the myth is best understood—and is most morally valuable—if taken not literally but metaphorically, that is, not as providing information about how the souls of the dead come to be reincarnated but rather as illuminating the nature of the living by asking what sorts of lives they would choose if they could.[17] Surely if a person can choose a life pattern and thereby alter the order of his soul once he is dead, he can do the same within the span of his lifetime.

Thus the first man, the one who lived justly by habit, is attracted to the life of injustice, though clearly not to a life as unjust as a tyrant's—at least once he becomes aware of what such a life entails. As we have seen, it is in part because he is the very first to choose and in part because he never lived under a tyranny that he seizes too quickly on the tyrannical life, which is an exaggerated version of the life he wants. For many men, the tyrant's life is so blindingly seductive that they can't see at first that it is also horribly destructive.

---

17. See Halliwell (2007, 469), who reads the myth as "an allegory of the life of the soul in *this* world" (emphasis in original), and Thayer (1988, 377), who argues: "Far from stressing the idea of our immortality . . . Plato is informing us that we have but one life to live and the supreme concern within the space between birth and death is our one and only chance to live well." Thayer is certainly right to think that the myth contains lessons for our present life—not for the hereafter: "The stakes are so high because we chance to have it only once" (379). But if he thinks the choice of life we make is fixed for life, he may be mistaken: punishment, for example, can effect a life-altering change within one's lifetime; catastrophic events may do so as well; even philosophic conversation can change a life's course. As Halliwell puts it (469–70), "The soul's salvation—at any and every point of its existence—is to be found nowhere else than inside its capacity to determine its own ethical self by choosing between good and evil." In Annas's view (1982, 133–34), by contrast, once one chooses a tyrant's life, one can do nothing but what a tyrant does.

Of the *Republic*'s protagonists, Glaucon and Adeimantus seem most closely to resemble this man.[18] They are virtuous—or just—by habit (or perhaps by education and breeding) without philosophy. To be sure, they support justice (2.358d, 367d-e), yet whereas they grasp intuitively why injustice is profitable, they are at a loss as to why justice is. When Glaucon in Book 2 sketches the genesis of justice he describes it as a compromise between the best and the worst, where *the best* "is doing injustice without paying the penalty" (359a). And neither brother has difficulty singing the praises of injustice. It is not unlikely, then, that somewhere in the inner recesses of their souls Glaucon and Adeimantus are attracted to tyranny.[19] Moreover, since the brothers, having lived justly, would not have experienced the misery the unjust suffer, they would remain all too susceptible to tyranny's appeal. As Er reports, a virtuous man who because of his virtue escapes the harsh "labors" endured by those who are wicked is more likely than they to choose their next life unwisely (619d).

The second man, the one who paid dearly for his injustice, comes to prefer justice; punishment actually effects a change in his desires. But here, too, the lottery is a factor: what lives are actually available to this man? We can imagine his choice of justice being adversely affected by, for example, being born into a badly disordered society, or finding himself very wealthy or exceedingly poor, conditions that would incline him to revert to his former unjust ways.

The third man, the one who philosophizes "healthily," wants to live justly. If such a man chooses a life of injustice it is only because no better life is available to him—perhaps the only lives from which he can choose are lives of excess or of extremes. It is true that the spokesman had predicted that no one, not even he who chooses last, would find himself in such a bind; but surely the spokesman spoke this way in order to stave off despair and to promote prudent decisions. As it turns out, however, the man who philosophizes healthily will travel by the smooth road through the heavens only "if his choice does not fall among the last" (619e): although

18. Bloom (1968, 436) thinks this man is like Cephalus. But Cephalus probably lived unjustly for most of his life, turning to justice only as death approached (1.330d-e).

19. Bloom (1968, 425) speaks of the brothers' "lust for tyranny"; Vegetti (200, 153) sees Glaucon and Adeimantus as potential tyrants; Dobbs (1964, 263) says of Glaucon that he "remains fascinated by the tyrannical or perfectly unjust life."

he fervently desires a life of justice, it might happen, however improbably, that no just life remains. One thing is quite clear, however: if such a man chooses injustice, it is not because injustice is what he has all along secretly craved. And if he chooses justice, it is not because he has sinned and suffered. What the myth makes manifest is that the man who always philosophizes in a healthy way would choose justice *if he could:* Socrates notes but does not dwell on the possibility that there might be no just life available to the healthy philosophizer, nor does he direct Glaucon's attention to it; after all, it is hardly salutary for Glaucon to believe that a just life might be unavailable to one who wishes to choose it. But the idea provokes Plato's readers to consider what they would do were they to face conditions that (seem to) make the choice of justice impossible.

As in Book 6, where Socrates' enumeration and explication of three philosophic types inevitably suggested a complementary fourth, so, too, do the three lives limned here hint at an additional one needed to round out the set. In Book 6 the trio of types—(1) the philosophic nature that matured into a philosopher, (2) the philosophic nature that was corrupted and thus prevented from becoming a philosopher, and (3) the nonphilosophic nature that was incapable of becoming a genuine philosopher—was completed by (4) the nonphilosophic nature that was forcibly transformed into a philosopher. And here in Book 10, there are similarly three men—(1) the man who in his most recent life was just by habit, (2) the man who was unjust, and (3) the man who philosophized always "in a healthy way"—and these, too, cry out for a fourth, namely, (4) the man who philosophizes in an *un*healthy way. If men of types (1) and (2) are just and unjust, respectively, but do not philosophize at all, and if type (3) is a healthy philosophizer, then surely the unhealthy philosophizer constitutes type (4). Since the man just by habit is distinguished not from a philosopher simpliciter but specifically from a healthy philosopher, our attention is ineluctably directed to the missing unhealthy philosopher: what sort of life, we wonder, would he choose?

We have already met men who philosophize in a healthy way: they are the philosophers of *Rep.* 6 who are just in their souls (486b, 487a) and who take care to preserve themselves from unjust and unholy deeds even if they must hide themselves away in order to do so (496d-e). Indeed, it is said of them that they have "a *healthy* and just disposition" (490c). And have we not encountered as well men who philosophize in an unhealthy way? Are they not the philosophers of *Rep.* 7, who, as we have seen (in Chapters 2 and 3), are nowhere said to be just (although Glaucon seems to assume they are—7.520e) and are never called healthy? They come to philosophy by way of coercion; they would initially have preferred to remain in the Cave. Moreover, as was argued in Chapter 2, these philosophers are appetitive by nature; they are moderate only because they were turned away by force from the material world, and their ties to it severed; their moderation is not of their choosing. Regardless of how they eventually come to live—contemplating the Forms and even the Form of the Good and committing no overt injustice—they do not live this way in accordance with their nature. Had they never been compelled to view the Forms, they would desire the goods of this world—not those of the transcendent one. And one shudders to think what they would choose if their lot were among the first.[20] If men of types (2) and (3) would choose a just life, would not men of type (4), like men of type (1), who were previously just by habit, choose the life of tyranny, foolishly and gluttonously pursuing what they craved but were denied? Those who are selected to be turned to philosophy, we recall, are not ordinary men but gifted ones: "The sharper it [their puny soul, their *psucharion*] sees, the more evil it accomplishes" (519a). Might then their choice of tyranny, unlike that of the man who is just by habit, be one they won't even come to regret?[21]

As in the description of the philosophers in Books 6 and 7, here, too, in Book 10, the type of philosopher Socrates represents is not explicitly considered; we are not told what kind of life he or someone like him (if there were such a one) would choose after death. Nevertheless, there can be no doubt that of the four men we have considered the one to whom Socrates is most akin is (3), the man who philosophizes in a healthy way and chooses, so long as he can, a life of justice. One suspects, however, that just as Socrates is very much like the philosophers of Book 6 among whom he includes himself (6.496c) but is still not simply one of them, so, too, does he closely resemble but also differ from the man of Book 10 who

---

20. Going off to dwell permanently on the Isles of the Blessed, which was the fate of these philosophers in Book 7 at 540b, is apparently no longer on the table in Book 10.

21. It is left to the reader to notice the missing fourth type. Socrates prefers to leave Glaucon with the favorable impression he had of the philosophers who will rule *kallipolis*; he wants Glaucon to like philosophers. Plato, however, must hope his readers will be drawn only to the philosophers by nature of *Rep.* 6.

philosophizes in a healthy way. The possibility in Book 10 of there being no just life available is the mythical counterpart to the condition in Book 6 of being surrounded by corruption and having no ally with whom to come to the aid of justice. When the philosophers of *Rep.* 6 are isolated and unwelcome, when the political arena is a den of beasts, they withdraw into themselves, preserving the purity of their souls by steering clear of unjust or unholy deeds (496d-e). *Rep.* 10 invites us to imagine a comparable but even worse predicament, one in which no just life is available.[22] In such a situation, even the man who always philosophizes in a healthy way will have no choice but to forgo justice; he will have to "journey from this world to the other and back again . . . by the underground, rough road" (619e). Nevertheless, just as Socrates does not "stand aside under a little wall" (496d) when spurned by his fellow citizens in a city awash in vice but, despite it all, finds a way—his "private" way—to be politically engaged, so surely, too, would he manage somehow to live a life of justice even if no such life is available. Just as Socrates cares for the souls of others despite discouraging conditions, thereby exceeding in his goodness even the just philosophers of *Rep.* 6, so would he also choose justice when there is no justice to be chosen, thereby surpassing even *Rep.* 10's healthy philosophizer. By ingenuity and by sheer force of will, and most of all by dint of an absolute and unwavering commitment to justice, Socrates would turn even an unjust life into a just one.

---

22. This even worse situation may well obtain in *Rep.* 6 as well: "Seeing others filled full of lawlessness, he is content *if somehow* (*ei pēi*) he can live his life here pure of injustice and unholy deeds" (496d-e). The "if somehow" seems to imply that living justly may not be possible for this philosopher either.

WORKS CITED

Adam, James. 1969. *The Republic of Plato*. 2 vols. Cambridge: Cambridge University Press.

Allen, R. E., trans. 2006. *Plato: The Republic*. New Haven, CT: Yale University Press.

Altman, William H. F. 2009. "Altruism and the Art of Writing: Plato, Cicero, and Leo Strauss." *Humanitas* 22:69–98.

Annas, Julia. 1981. *An Introduction to Plato's Republic*. Oxford: Oxford University Press.

———. 1982. "Plato's Myths of Judgement." *Phronesis* 27:119–43.

Aquinas, Thomas. 1947. *Summa Theologica*. Fathers of the English Dominican Province. New York: Benziger Bros.

Bambrough, Renford. 1956. "Plato's Political Analogies." In *Philosophy, Politics, and Society*, edited by Peter Laslett, 98–115. Oxford: Macmillan.

Barker, Ernest. 1959. *The Political Thought of Plato and Aristotle*. New York: Dover.

Barney, Rachel. 2008. "*Eros* and Necessity in the Ascent from the Cave." *Ancient Philosophy* 28:357–72.

Benardete, Seth. 1989. *Socrates' Second Sailing: On Plato's Republic*. Chicago: University of Chicago Press.

Blondell, Ruby. 2002. *The Play of Character in Plato's Dialogues*. Cambridge: Cambridge University Press.

Bloom, Allan, trans. 1968. *The Republic of Plato, with Notes and Interpretive Essay*. New York: Basic Books.

Brann, Eva. 2004. *The Music of the Republic: Essays on Socrates' Conversations and Plato's Writings*. Philadelphia: Paul Dry Books.

Brickhouse, Thomas C. 1981. "The Paradox of the Philosophers' Rule." *Apeiron* 15:1–9.

Brickhouse, Thomas C., and Nicholas D. Smith. 1994. *Plato's Socrates*. Oxford: Oxford University Press.

Brown, Eric. 2000. "Justice and Compulsion for Plato's Philosopher-Rulers." *Ancient Philosophy* 20:1–17.

———. 2004. "Minding the Gap in Plato's *Republic*." *Philosophical Studies* 117:275–302.

Brown, Lesley. 1998. "How Totalitarian Is Plato's *Republic*?" In *Essays on Plato's Republic,* edited by E. N. Ostenfeld, 13–27. Aarhus: Aarhus University Press.

Burnet, John. 1902. *Platonis Opera*. Vol. 4. Oxford: Clarendon Press.

———. 1914. *Greek Philosophy: Thales to Plato*. London: Macmillan.

Burnyeat, Myles. 1985. "Sphinx without a Secret: Review of Leo Strauss, *Studies in Platonic Political Philosophy*." *New York Review of Books* 32.9 (May 30):30–36.

———. 1990. *The Theaetetus of Plato*, translated by M. J. Levett. Indianapolis: Hackett.

Cicero, Marcus Tullius. 1913. *De Officiis* [*On Duties*]. Vol. 21, edited and translated by Walter Miller. Loeb Classical Library no. 30. Cambridge, MA: Harvard University Press.

———. 1914. *De Finibus* [*On Ends*]. Vol. 17, edited and translated by H. Rackham. Loeb Classical Library no. 40. Cambridge, MA: Harvard University Press.

———. 1923. *De Senectute, De Amicitia, De Divinatione* [*On Old Age, On Friendship, On Divination*]. Vol. 20, edited and translated by William Armistead Falconer. Loeb Classical Library no. 154. Cambridge, MA: Harvard University Press.

Clay, Diskin. 1988. "Reading the *Republic*." In *Platonic Writings/Platonic Readings*, edited by Charles L. Griswold, Jr., 19–33, 269–72. London: Routledge and Kegan Paul.

Cohen, Getzel M. 1983. "Colonization and Population Transfer in the Hellenistic World." In *Egypt and the Hellenistic World*, edited by E. Van't Dack, 63–74. Louvain: Studia Hellenistica.

Cooper, John. 1977. "The Psychology of Justice in Plato." *American Philosophical Quarterly* 14:151–57.

———. 1984. "Plato's Theory of Human Motivation." *History of Philosophy Quarterly* 1:3–21.

———. 2000. "Two Theories of Justice." *Proceedings and Addresses of the American Philosophical Association* 74(2): 5–27.

Cornford, Francis MacDonald, trans. 1945. *The Republic of Plato*. Oxford: Oxford University Press.

Craig, Leon Harold. 1994. *The War-Lover: A Study of Plato's Republic*. Toronto: University of Toronto Press.

Cross, R. C., and A. D. Woozley. 1964. *Plato's Republic: A Philosophical Commentary*. London: St. Martin's Press.

Danzig, Gabriel. 1998. "True Justice in the *Republic*." *Illinois Classical Studies* 23:85–99.

Davies, J. C. 1968. "A Note on the Philosopher's Descent into the Cave." *Philologus* 112:121–26.

Dawson, Doyne. 1992. *Cities of the Gods: Communist Utopias in Greek Thought*. Oxford: Oxford University Press.

Demos, Raphael. 1964. "A Fallacy in Plato's *Republic?*" *The Philosophical Review* 73:395–98.

Denyer, Nicholas. 1986. "Ethics in Plato's *Republic*." In *Philosophers Ancient and Modern*, *Philosophy*, suppl. vol. 20., edited by Renford Bambrough, 19–32.

Dobbs, Darrell. 1985. "The Justice of Socrates' Philosopher Kings." *American Journal of Political Science* 29:809–26.

———. 1994. "Choosing Justice: Socrates' Model City and the Practice of Dialectic." *American Political Science Review* 88:263–77.

Dorter, Kenneth. 2006. *The Transformation of Plato's Republic*. Lanham, MD: Lexington Books.

Dover, Kenneth J. 1974. *Greek Popular Morality in the Time of Plato and Aristotle*. Oxford: Oxford University Press.

Evans, J. D. G. 2010. *A Plato Primer*. Ithaca, NY: Cornell University Press.

Ferrari, G. R. F. [2003] 2005. *City and Soul in Plato's Republic*. Sankt Augustin: Academia Verlag. Reprint, Chicago: University of Chicago Press.

———. 2007. "The Three-Part Soul." In *The Cambridge Companion to Plato's Republic*, edited by G. R. F. Ferrari, 165–201. Cambridge: Cambridge University Press.

———. 2008. "Glaucon's Reward, Philosophy's Debt: The Myth of Er." In *Plato's Myths*, edited by C. Partenie, 116–33. Cambridge: Cambridge University Press.

Gosling, J. C. B. 1973. *Plato*. London: Routledge and Kegan Paul.

Griffith, Tom, trans. 2000. *Plato: The Republic*. Cambridge: Cambridge University Press.

Grube, G. M. A., trans. 1981. *Phaedo*. In *Plato, Five Dialogues: 'Euthyphro,' 'Apology,' 'Crito,' 'Meno,' 'Phaedo.'* Indianapolis: Hackett.

———, trans., and rev. C. D. C. Reeve. 1997. *Republic*. In *Plato: Complete Works*, edited by John M. Cooper, 971–1223. Indianapolis: Hackett.

Hall, Robert. 1974. "Plato's Political Analogy: Fallacy or Analogy?" *Journal of the History of Philosophy* 12:419–35.

Halliwell, Stephen. 1988. *Plato: Republic 10*. Warminster: Aris and Phillips.

———. 2007. "The Life-and-Death Journey of the Soul: Interpreting the Myth of Er." In *The Cambridge Companion to Plato's Republic*, edited by G. R. F. Ferrari, 445–73. Cambridge: Cambridge University Press.

Havelock, Eric A. 1969. "*Dikaiosune*: An Essay in Greek Intellectual History." *Phoenix* 23:49–70.

———. 1978. *The Greek Concept of Justice*. Cambridge, MA: Harvard University Press.

Heinaman, R. 1998. "Social Justice in Plato's *Republic*." *Polis* 15:23–43.

———. 2004. "Why Justice Does Not Pay in Plato's *Republic*." *Classical Quarterly* 54:379–93.

Hitz, Zena. 2011. "Degenerate Regimes in Plato's *Republic*." In *Plato's Republic: A Critical Guide*, edited by Mark McPherran, 103–31. Cambridge: Cambridge University Press.

Howland, Jacob. 2004. *The Republic: The Odyssey of Philosophy*. Philadelphia: Paul Dry Books.

Irwin, Terence. 1977. *Plato's Moral Theory: The Early and Middle Dialogues*. Oxford: Clarendon Press.

———. 1995. *Plato's Ethics*. Oxford: Oxford University Press.

Kahn, Charles. 1987. "Plato's Theory of Desire." *Review of Metaphysics* 41:77–103.

Kamtekar, Rachana. 2004. "What's the Good of Agreeing? *Homonoia* in Platonic Politics." *Oxford Studies in Ancient Philosophy* 26:131–70.

Keyt, David. 2006. "Plato and the Ship of State." In *The Blackwell Guide to Plato's Republic*, edited by Gerasimos Santas, 189–213. Oxford: Blackwell.

Klosko, George. 1986. *The Development of Plato's Political Theory*. New York: Methuen.

Kraut, Richard. 1973. "Egoism, Love, and Political Office." *Philosophical Review* 82:330–44.

———. 1997. "The Defense of Justice in Plato's *Republic*." In *Plato's Republic: Critical Essays*, edited by Richard Kraut, 197–221. Lanham, MD: Rowman and Littlefield.

———. 1999. "Return to the Cave." In *Plato*, edited by Gail Fine, 2:235–54. Oxford: Oxford University Press. Reprint and revision of *Proceedings of the Boston Area Colloquium in Ancient Philosophy* 7 (1991):43–61.

Lampert, Laurence. 2010. *How Philosophy Became Socratic: A Study of Plato's Protagoras, Charmides, and Republic*. Chicago: University of Chicago Press.

Lane, Melissa. 2007. "Virtue as the Love of Knowledge." In *Maieusis: Essays on Ancient Philosophy in Honour of Myles Burnyeat*, edited by Dominic Scott, 44–67. Oxford: Oxford University Press.

Lear, Jonathan. 2006. "Myth and Allegory in Plato's *Republic*." In *The Blackwell Guide to Plato's Republic*, edited by Gerasimos Santas, 25–43. Oxford: Blackwell.

Lee, Desmond, trans. 1955. *Plato: The Republic*. New York: Penguin Books.

Lombardo, Stanley, and Karen Bell, trans. 1992. *Plato: Protagoras*. Indianapolis: Hackett.

Mahoney, Timothy. 1992. "Do Plato's Philosopher-Rulers Sacrifice Self-Interest to Justice?" *Phronesis* 37:265–82.

Mara, Gerald M. 1997. *Socrates' Discursive Democracy: Logos and Ergon in Platonic Political Philosophy*. Albany: SUNY Press.

McCoy, Marina. 2008. *Plato on the Rhetoric of Philosophers and Sophists*. Cambridge: Cambridge University Press.

McPherran, Mark. 1991. "Socratic Reason and Socratic Revelation." *Journal of the History of Philosophy* 29:345–73.

Miller, Mitchell. 1986. "Platonic Provocations: Reflections on the Soul and the Good in the *Republic*." In *Platonic Investigations*, edited by Dominic J. O'Meara, 163–93. Washington, DC: Catholic University Press.

———. 2007. "Beginning the 'Longer Way.'" In *The Cambridge Companion to Plato's Republic*, edited by G. R. F. Ferrari, 310–44. Cambridge: Cambridge University Press.

Morrison, Donald. 2001. "The Happiness of the City and the Happiness of the Individual in Plato's *Republic*." *Ancient Philosophy* 21:1–24.

Nehamas, Alexander. 1992. "What Did Socrates Teach and to Whom Did He Teach It?" *Review of Metaphysics* 46:279–306.

Nehamas, Alexander, and Paul Woodruff, trans. 1989. *Plato: Symposium*. Indianapolis: Hackett.

Nettleship, Richard Lewis. 1955. *Lectures on the Republic of Plato*. London: Macmillan.

Neu, Jerome. 1971. "Plato's Analogy of State and Individual: *The Republic* and the Organic Theory of the State." *Philosophy* 46:238–54.

Nichols, James H., Jr., trans. 1987. *Laches*. In *The Roots of Political Philosophy: Ten Forgotten Socratic Dialogues*, edited by Thomas L. Pangle, 240–68. Ithaca, NY: Cornell University Press.

———. 1998. *Plato: Gorgias, with Introduction, Notes, and Interpretive Essay*. Ithaca, NY: Cornell University Press.

Nichols, Mary P. 1984. "The *Republic*'s Two Alternatives: Philosopher-Kings and Socrates." *Political Theory* 12:252–74.

———. 1987. *Socrates and the Political Community: An Ancient Debate*. Albany: SUNY Press.

Nussbaum, Martha C. 1986. *The Fragility of Goodness: Luck and Ethics in Greek Tragedy and Philosophy*. Cambridge: Cambridge University Press.

Pangle, Thomas L., trans. 1980. *The Laws of Plato*. Chicago: University of Chicago Press.

Plotinus. 1975. *The Essential Plotinus*, edited by Elmer O'Brien. 2nd ed. Indianapolis: Hackett.

Popper, Karl. 1945. *The Open Society and Its Enemies*. 2 vols. London: Routledge.

Prichard, H. A. 2002. "Duty and Interest." In *Moral Writings*, edited by Jim MacAdam, 21–49. Oxford: Clarendon Press. Inaugural lecture delivered before the University of Oxford on October 29, 1928.

Ranasinghe, Nalin. 2000. *The Soul of Socrates*. Ithaca, NY: Cornell University Press.

Reeve, C. D. C. 1988. *Philosopher-Kings: The Argument of Plato's Republic*. Princeton, NJ: Princeton University Press.

———. 1989. *Socrates in the Apology*. Indianapolis: Hackett.

———, trans. 2004. *Plato: Republic*. Indianapolis: Hackett.

Robinson, Thomas M. 1970. *Plato's Psychology*. Toronto: University of Toronto Press.

Roochnik, David. 1996. *Of Art and Wisdom: Plato's Understanding of Techne*. State College, PA: Penn State University Press.

———. 2003. *Beautiful City: The Dialectical Character of Plato's Republic*. Ithaca, NY: Cornell University Press.

Rosen, Stanley. 2005. *Plato's Republic: A Study*. New Haven, CT: Yale University Press.

Runciman, Walter G. 2010. *Great Books, Bad Arguments*. Princeton, NJ: Princeton University Press.

Sachs, David. 1963. "A Fallacy in Plato's *Republic*." *Philosophical Review* 72:141–58.

Sachs, Joe, trans. 2004. *Plato: Theaetetus*. Newburyport, MA: Focus Publishing.

———, trans. 2007. *Plato: Republic*. Newburyport, MA: Focus Publishing.

Sallis, John D. 1975. *Being and Logos: The Way of Platonic Dialogue*. Pittsburgh: Duquesne University Press.

Saxonhouse, Arlene. 1978. "Comedy in Callipolis: Animal Imagery in the *Republic*." *American Political Science Review* 72:888–901.

———. 1992. *Fear of Diversity: The Birth of Political Science in Ancient Greek Thought*. Chicago: University of Chicago Press.

Schleiermacher, Friedrich. 1855–62. *Platons Werke*. 3 vols. Berlin: G. Reimer.

Scott, Dominic. 2000. "Metaphysics and the Defence of Justice in the *Republic*." *Proceedings of the Boston Area Colloquium in Ancient Philosophy* 16:1–19.

———. 2007. "*Erōs*, Philosophy, and Tyranny." In *Maieusis: Essays on Ancient Philosophy in Honour of Myles Burnyeat*, edited by Dominic Scott, 136–53. Oxford: Oxford University Press.

Sedley, David. 2007. "Philosophy, the Forms, and the Art of Ruling." In *The Cambridge Companion to Plato's Republic*, edited by G. R. F. Ferrari, 256–83. Cambridge: Cambridge University Press.

Sharples, R. W., trans. 1985. *Plato: Meno*. Warminster: Aris & Phillips.

Shields, Christopher. 2007. "Forcing Goodness in Plato's *Republic*." *Social Philosophy and Policy* 24:21–39.

Shorey, Paul, trans. 1963. *Republic*. In *The Collected Dialogues of Plato*, edited by Edith Hamilton and Huntington Cairns, 575–844. Princeton, NJ: Princeton University Press.

Slings, Simon, ed. 2003. *Platonis: Rempublicam*. Oxford: Oxford University Press.

Smith, Nicholas D. 1999. "Plato's Analogy of Soul and State." *The Journal of Ethics* 3:31–49.

———. 2010. "Return to the Cave." In *Plato's Republic: A Critical Guide*, edited by Mark McPherran, 83–102. Cambridge: Cambridge University Press.

Stallbaum, G. 1881. *Platonis Omnia Opera*. Leipzig: O. Holtze.

Steinberger, Peter. 1989. "Ruling: Guardians and Philosopher-Kings." *American Political Science Review* 83:1207–25.

Strauss, Leo. 1952. *Persecution and the Art of Writing*. Chicago: University of Chicago Press.

———. 1964. *The City and Man*. Chicago: University of Chicago Press.

———. 2001. *Gesammelte Schriften*, vol. 3, edited by Heinrich Meier and Wiebke Meier. Stuttgart and Weimar: J. B. Metzler.

Taft, Richard. 1982. "The Role of Compulsion in the Education of Plato's Philosopher-Kings." *Auslegung* 9:311–32.

Thayer, H. S. 1988. "The Myth of Er." *History of Philosophy Quarterly* 5:369–84.

Thesleff, Holger. 1997. "The Early Version of Plato's *Republic*." *Arctos* 31:149–74.

Vegetti, Mario, ed. 1998–2007. *La Repubblica / Platone: Traduzione e commento*. 7 vols. Naples: Bibliopolis.

———. 2000. *La Repubblica / Platone: Traduzione e commento*. Vol. 2. Naples: Bibliopolis.

———. 2005. "Il tempo, la storia, l'utopia." In *La Repubblica / Platone: Traduzione e commento*, 6:156–62. Naples: Bibliopolis.

Vernezze, Peter. 1992. "The Philosophers' Interest." *Ancient Philosophy* 12:331–49.

Versényi, Laszlo. 1982. *Holiness and Justice: An Interpretation of Plato's Euthyphro*. Lanham, MD: University Press of America.

Vlastos, Gregory. 1971. "Justice and Happiness in the *Republic*." In *Plato: A Collection of Critical Essays*, edited by Gregory Vlastos, 2:66–95. New York: Doubleday.

———. 1973. "The Theory of Social Justice in the *Polis* in Plato's *Republic*." In *Interpretations of Plato: A Swarthmore Symposium*, *Mnemosyne* suppl. vol. 50, edited by Helen North, 1–40. Leiden: E. J. Brill.

———. 1985. "Socrates' Disavowal of Knowledge." *Philosophical Quarterly* 35:1–31.

——. 1991. *Socrates: Ironist and Moral Philosopher*. Ithaca, NY: Cornell University Press.

Voegelin, Eric. 1966. *Plato*. Baton Rouge: Louisiana State University Press.

Walzer, Michael. 1983. *Spheres of Justice*. New York: Basic Books.

Waterlow, Sarah. 1972–73. "The Good of Others in Plato's *Republic*." *Proceedings of the Aristotelian Society* 72:19–36.

Weiss, Roslyn. 1994. "Virtue without Knowledge: Socrates' Conception of Holiness in Plato's *Euthyphro*." *Ancient Philosophy* 14:263-82.

——. 1998. *Socrates Dissatisfied: An Analysis of Plato's Crito*. Oxford: Oxford University Press.

——. 2005. "For Whom the *Daimonion* Tolls." In *Socrates' Divine Sign: Religion, Practice, and Value in Socratic Philosophy*, edited by Pierre Destrée and Nicholas D. Smith, 81–96. Kelowna, BC: Academic Printing and Publishing.

——. 2006. *The Socratic Paradox and Its Enemies*. Chicago: University of Chicago Press.

——. 2007. "Wise Guys and Smart Alecks in *Republic* 1 and 2." In *The Cambridge Companion to Plato's Republic*, edited by G. R. F. Ferrari, 90–115. Cambridge: Cambridge University Press.

——. 2012. "The Unjust Philosophers of *Rep*. VII." *Proceedings of the Boston Area Colloquium in Ancient Philosophy* 27.

West, Thomas G., and Grace Starry West, trans. 1984. *Plato and Aristophanes, Four Texts on Socrates: Plato's 'Euthyphro,' 'Apology,' and 'Crito,' and Aristophanes' 'Clouds.'* Ithaca, NY: Cornell University Press.

White, Nicholas P. 1978. *A Companion to Plato's Republic*. Indianapolis: Hackett.

Wildberg, Christian. 2003. "The Rise and Fall of the Socratic Notion of Piety," *Proceedings of the Boston Area Colloquium in Ancient Philosophy* 18:1–28.

Wilson, John F. 1984. *The Politics of Moderation: An Interpretation of Plato's Republic*. Lanham, MD: University Press of America.

Woods, Cathal. 2009. "The Last Temptation of the Philosopher-Rulers." *Journal of Ancient Philosophy* 3 http://www.filosofiaantiga.com/documents/lasttemptation-May2009.pdf.

Yu, Jiyuan. 2000. "Justice in the *Republic*: An Evolving Paradox." *History of Philosophy Quarterly* 17:121–41.

INDEX

Adeimantus, 3–5; as attracted to
tyranny, 215; berates Socrates for
misleading questions, 20n27; on
city of sows, 4n8, 186n84; on first
two waves, 42; on the gods, 208n1;
on guardians deprived of good life,
115n61; and happiness of producers,
98; hides behind others while criticizing philosophers, 21n8; on justice
and divine nature, 66; and justice as
moderation, 7, 10; on law favoring
particular classes, 95; needs to be
king of himself, 207; as not having
seen the Good, 159; on philosophers
as useless or vicious, 4, 21, 22, 25n41,
33, 34; and philosopher-warriors, 44;
on philosophic rule, 20–22; on power
of justice and injustice, 177n42, 186;
and profitability of justice, 168–69,
185n61, 209n5, 215; on self-protective
philosophers, 140; Socrates attempts
to transfer task of discovering justice
to, 179; Socrates' engagement with,
6–8; and Socrates' laudation of philosophers of *Rep.* Book 7, 80; Socrates
reminds him of longer road, 84;
style of, 4; on where justice might be
found, 166–67; on why justice is better than injustice, 166, 166n6
afterlife, 146n41, 208–10
Alcibiades, 161
Altman, William, 70n44
anankazein (to compel, to necessitate),
107–12
Annas, Julia, 87n8, 133n7, 134n12,
210nn7–8, 214n17

Apology (Plato): on craftsmen, 25n43; on divine and human wisdom, 156n53, 158; on divine source of Socrates' mission, 136–37; on doing injustice, 147, 151; on effects of Socrates' elenctic activity, 160n63; on hatred of Socrates, 143; Meletus on Socrates as corrupter, 38n73; on minding one's own business, 138–39; on one who really fights for justice, 140; oracle on wisdom of Socrates, 10n21, 161n65; on philosophic examination, 142; on Socrates as father or older brother to Athenians, 154, 162n66; on Socrates frequenting public places, 9; on Socrates held back from politics, 131–32; on Socrates never taking compensation, 127, 142, 189; on Socrates' self-conception, 141n31; on Socrates' troubles, 142–43; on Socrates' wandering, 136, 136n17

Aristophanes, 13n4

Aristotle: on friendship of kings, 123n74; on justice, 146n40, 180n46, 183n54; on punishment, 204n96, on virtues, 65n32, 167n10, 187n67, 188

Benardete, Seth, 23n33, 30n58, 50n5, 170n21, 180n47, 196n80, 202n93

best natures: affected by chance, 32; change in meaning of, 67, 67n39; distinguished from rest of us, 62–63; education of, 63–64, 81–82; how can avoid ending up twisted and changed, 28; of *Rep.* Book 4 rulers, 12

Bloom, Allan: on Adeimantus, 4n8, 215n18; on cardinal virtues, 133n7; on change of fortune in non-philosophers, 210n6; on first two waves, 13n4; on Glaucon, 4n8, 5n10, 209n5, 215n18; on justice, 36n8, 167n9, 176n39; on philosopher-rulers, 51n9; on philosophers looking at the Good, 60n25; on philosophers of *Rep.* Book 7

as compelled to rule, 89n13, 105n43; on Socrates on virtue for its own sake, 188; on wage earner's art, 123n76

Brann, Eva, 132n4, 177n40

Brickhouse, Thomas C., 102, 106n44

Brown, Eric, 104n41, 106n44

Brown, Lesley, 96n29

Burnyeat, Myles, 90n16, 115n61

Callicles, 4n9, 21n29, 25n43, 145, 186

Callipolis: characteristics of, 8; coercion in, 8, 70, 153; as intended for Glaucon, 8–9; philosophers of, 8–9, 10, 42–43, 50, 61–62, 107; Popper's criticism of, 121n73

Cave allegory, 55–60; aim of, 62; bonds that hold the prisoners in the Cave, 68; philosophers of *Rep.* Book 7 compelled to go into the Cave, 70–76, 83, 87, 89, 100, 105–6, 112; philosophers of *Rep.* Book 7 likened to prisoners released from the Cave, 60–61, 75, 85; Socrates descends willingly into the Cave, 86, 89; some discern shadows more sharply than others in the Cave, 64; soul's journey to intelligible place likened to, 85

Cephalus: on decent men, 21n31; and founders' argument in *Rep.* Book 7, 99; as living unjustly, 215n18; on moderation, 170n22; on piety, 133–34, 135; *Republic*'s discussion of justice in home of, 134n11, 189; on Socrates as having come down, 139n27; Socrates compared with, 146, 146n41

chance: city of, 9, 10, 32–33, 42, 43, 62; education by, 81–82; in myth of Er, 213–14; necessity by, 110

Charmides (Plato), 26n45, 141n31, 179n45

children, sequestering of, 37n70, 45–46, 117, 118–20

Cicero, 6n14, 121–22, 136n17, 154

city of sows, 1n1, 4, 4n8, 167, 186, 186n64

city-soul analogy, 1n1, 84, 165, 168, 185, 190, 192

cooling/wetting analogy, 114

Cooper, John, 87n8

courage: applied to selfish ends, 192n77; in auxiliary class, 170; as easy to discover, 167; of guardians, 173; as mark of perfectly good city, 132; moderation contrasted with, 172; spiritedness associated with, 47n87; wisdom keeps it from being reckless, 180n49

craftsmen: do not beg to exercise their crafts, 24; do the business of others, 26n45; *erōs* lacking in, 69n44; and happiness of the city, 95, 97, 98; as not held in high esteem, 25n43; philosophers who start out as, 25; roles assigned to, 72n49; rulers compared with, 122–24; unwilling to use their craft to benefit others, 93

Craig, Leon Harold, 14n9, 54n17, 97n32

Crito (Plato): on big natures, 35n67; on choosing arguments that seem best, 144; on living well, 165n5; on in no way committing injustice, 147; on repaying debts, 101n37, 104n39; on Socrates' refusal to escape, 114n59; on Socrates' serenity before his death, 143; on spending money on nurture of children, 154n48

death, 19, 19n24, 27n47

decency: Adeimantus on even decent philosophers as useless, 21–22; Cephalus on, 21n31; decent but useless philosophers in *Rep.* Book 6, 22, 25–28, 29, 33, 130–32, 140, 156; good and decent men of *Rep.* Book 1, 122–28; justice and, 148–49; philosophers not moved by considerations that sway, 87; philosophers of *Rep.* Book 7 as not decent, 66, 66n35, 81, 156

Delphic oracle, 136

democracy, permissiveness in, 111

dialectic, 75, 77–78, 80, 81, 82

Dobbs, Darrell, 6n15

Dorter, Kenneth, 24n38, 106, 108n50, 165n5

Dover, Kenneth J., 198n86

Ecclesiazusae (Aristophanes), 13n4

education: of best natures, 63–64, 81–82; of guardians, 53–55, 73–74, 83–84; of philosophers of *Rep.* Book 7, 81–83, 100, 101

epistēmē (knowledge), 12, 63, 63n27

Er, myth of, 146n42, 206n101, 207n103, 208–18

erōs (passionate love), 69n44, 69–70, 71, 71n45, 78, 81, 161

erōtikoi (lovers), 14, 18, 71n47

eusebeia (reverence, piety), 156n53

Euthydemus (Plato), 36n68, 36n69, 139n28, 168n13, 180n49

Euthyphro (Plato), 133, 134n13, 150–51, 156–58

Ferrari, G. R. F, 50n7, 76, 186n64, 212n13

Forms: hydraulic effect and philosopher's orientation to, 19n22; philosopher shapes his soul in accordance with, 29n55, 29–30; philosophers of *Rep.* Book 7 see, 71, 72, 73, 217; pilot consults sky as philosopher consults, 23n35; *Republic* on heaven and, 206n101. *See also* Good, the

geometry, 54, 81, 82

Glaucon, 3–5; asks Socrates to lead, 13, 13n8, 130n1; as attracted to tyranny, 215; on banishment of the old, 120; begs Socrates to not abandon argument, 143, 152n47; Callipolis constructed for, 8–9, 42; on city of sows, 4, 4n8, 167, 186, 186n64; on compelling philosophers to rule, 88, 93, 94, 107, 113n58; on compulsion required for justice, 112; on disobedience by philosophers, 110; on education of

Glaucon *(continued)*
  guardians, 53, 54, 82n67, 83; on hap-
    piest type of man, 200, 200n89; and
    happiness of producers, 98; hides
    behind others while criticizing phi-
    losophers, 21n8; injustice defended
    by, 163; on justice as drudgery,
    114–15; and justice as moderation,
    7–8, 10, 178; on just man, 130, 146,
    166; on law favoring particular
    classes, 95; on medicine, 124n77; on
    men with good nature, 77, 78; on
    moderation, 171–72, 186; and myth
    of Er, 209, 215, 216; needs to be king
    of himself, 207; as not having seen
    the Good, 159; on one-man, one- job
    principle, 51; on philosophers as just,
    106, 113; and philosopher-warriors,
    41, 44, 50; on piety, 134; on power of
    justice and injustice, 177n42, 186; on
    prisoners of the Cave, 56–57; on prof-
    itability of justice, 168–69, 185n61,
    188, 209n5, 215; on rule by guardians,
    50–51; on rule by philosophers, 4, 7,
    12 13, 16 17, 20, 21, 31, 51, on rul-
    ers not wishing to rule, 91; Socrates
    as more sharp-sighted than, 64; on
    Socrates as naïve, 130; Socrates at-
    tempts to transfer task of discovering
    justice to, 179; and Socrates' claim
    about good and decent men, 128;
    Socrates' engagement with, 6–8;
    Socrates' laudation of philosophers
    of *Rep.* Book 7 designed to appeal to,
    78–79, 80; on Socrates persuading
    philosophers of *Rep.* Book 7 to rule,
    106, 153; and Socrates' resolution of
    problem of justice, 185; Socrates will
    take him no farther, 159–60; on soul's
    internal accord and politics, 205–6;
    style of, 4–5; Thrasymachus likened
    to, 128, 186n65; on three types of
    goods, 71n47; on why justice is better
    than injustice, 166, 166n6; on will-
    ingly doing injustice, 148

Good, the: in Cave allegory, 55, 56; *erōs*
    and, 69–70; philosophers of *Rep.*
    Book 7 and, 61, 68, 70–76, 83–87,
    103, 106, 109, 112, 114, 122, 159; piety
    and seeing Form of, 162; Socrates as
    not having seen, 159, 188; Socrates on
    it as being out of range, 159; turning
    knowing part of soul toward, 63, 69;
    unwillingness to rule after seeing, 85
Gorgias (Plato): on craftsmen, 25n43; on
    flattery, 157n54; on the incurably evil,
    119n69; on indulging in philosophy
    beyond youth, 21n29; on injustice,
    136n15, 189; on justice, 146n43, 147,
    148, 175–76; on living piously and in
    truth, 139n22, 151n46; on living well,
    165n5; on moderation, 177n43, 186;
    on painful but beneficial things, 7n17;
    on philosopher's task, 145; on piety,
    133; on political science, 31; Polus as
    like a child, 201n91; on proper role
    of citizen-statesman, 139; on punish-
    ment, 203–4; on Socrates as in love,
    161; Socrates compared with doctor
    in, 160; on Socrates' self-conception,
    141n31; on sophists, 166n7; on work
    of good citizen, 149
great soul, 25, 66n34
guardians: acquire virtues through
    training, 36n69; avoidance of gold
    and silver by, 12n3, 74; best among,
    67; demoted to military class, 43; edu-
    cation of, 53–55, 73–74, 83–84; en-
    suring happiness of city as task of, 95;
    fear of death of, 19n24; Glaucon on
    rule by, 50–51; happiness of, 97–98;
    as makers of new law, 30n57; "most
    precise," 53; as not being made happy,
    4, 4n8; philosophers contrasted with,
    6, 31; philosophers of *Rep.* Book 7
    compared with, 52n12; philosopher-
    warriors derived from, 44, 53; and
    philosophic dogs, 12, 45–48; sharp-
    sightedness needed by, 17; Socrates'
    praise for, 92n20; virtues of, 173

Gyges' ring, 108n49, 146, 169, 169n17
gymnastic: future guardians trained in, 47, 55, 67, 73; philosophy contrasted with, 53, 77, 78, 83; of the soul, 69; study of dialectic preceded by, 81, 82

Halliwell, Stephen, 211n10, 213n15, 214n17
happiness: Glaucon on happiest type of man, 200, 200n89; of the guardians, 4, 4n8, 97n33, 97–98; of the philosophers, 88, 93, 103; of the producers, 98; securing the city's, 94–98
Heinaman, Robert, 88n10, 97n31, 198n84
Hippias Minor (Plato), 130n1
Hitz, Zena, 23n38
Homer, 30
Howland, Jacob, 84n71
hupēretikē (service), 156–57
hydraulic model, 19, 19n22, 69, 72n50, 78n61

Irwin, Terence, 86n8, 99, 108n50, 126n84

justice: accord and friendship promoted by, 190, 191; in the city, 165–69, 190; and desirability of ruling, 86–87; elasticity of, 172; in founders' argument, 98–107; among four virtues of perfectly good city, 132; Glaucon on, 112, 130, 146, 166; as good in itself, 121, 169, 185–87, 188, 207n103; group injustice, 191–96; guardians not distinguished by, 187n67, 173; as health of the soul, 5, 7, 10, 182, 186; as internal, 164, 165, 168, 181, 185; just man harms no one, 189–90; levels of, 145–49; as minding one's own business, 174, 197–99; and moderation, 7–8, 10, 174–84, 185, 205; in moral virtues of philosophers, 36n68; musical metaphors for, 175, 181; in

myth of Er, 208–18; perfect injustice, 191, 192, 194, 195, 204; philosophers of *Rep.* Book 6 and, 138, 152, 153; philosophers of *Rep.* Book 7 and, 81, 113–21, 153–54, 217; piety as species of, 149–52; Polemarchus's definition of, 46; profitability of, 6–7, 127n88, 160n61, 166n7, 168, 169, 184–87, 189, 190, 195, 210–11, 215; as regard for others, 148–49, 152, 185, 186, 189; in *Rep.* Book 1, 6, 46, 99, 104, 113–14, 133–34, 165–66, 189–99; in *Rep.* Book 4, 5, 18n18, 164–65, 167, 168, 173–74, 180, 181, 184, 197; in *Rep.* Books 8–10, 199–207; repaying one's debts, 99–102, 104, 106, 114, 119, 120; resolution of Socrates' problem regarding, 184–87; of Socrates, 10, 130; Socrates attempts to transfer task of discovering to others, 179–80; Socrates' definition of, 5, 10, 173–84; Socrates devotes his life to fight for, 138; Socrates' engages Glaucon regarding, 6–8; Socrates on impiety of not coming to defense of, 134, 135, 163; Thrasymachus on, 123, 124, 126n86, 147, 180n48, 187–88, 189, 190, 191–92, 194–97; unselfishness of, 10

Kamtekar, Rachana, 96n28
Keyt, David, 22n32, 23n36
knowledge (*epistēmē*), 12, 63, 63n27
Kraut, Richard, 87n8, 102, 107n46

Laches (Plato), 133, 139–40, 156n52, 180n49
Lachesis, 213
Lampert, Laurence, 109n51, 126n87, 209n5
Lane, Melissa, 19, 72n50
Laws (Plato), 119n69
Lear, Jonathan, 210n8
love of wisdom: intelligence contrasted with, 65; philosophers associated

love of wisdom *(continued)*
with, 9, 12, 20, 27, 34n65, 35, 44, 49,
65; philosophers of *Rep.* Book 7 lack
natural, 72, 80–81; of Socrates, 162;
virtues associated with, 35
Lysis (Plato), 96n30

Mara, Gerald M., 134n10, 138n20,
142n33, 155n50
mathematics, 64n29, 82, 82n70
McCoy, Marina, 37n72
measure, 12, 16, 17, 17n14, 19, 20, 44, 67,
212n10
Meno (Plato), 36nn68–69, 64n29, 125n81,
137n18, 139n24, 160n61, 180n49
Miller, Mitchell, 88
moderation (*sōphrosunē;* temperance):
as aim of punishment, 203–4; applied
to selfish ends, 192n77; beneficiary
of, 186; as easy to discover, 167; of
groups, 196; of guardians, 173; as
internal, 181n51; justice and, 7–8, 10,
174–84, 185, 205; musical metaphors
for, 175, 181; and omission of piety
in *Republic,* 133, 134; of philosophers
of *Rep.* Book 7, 75, 81, 83, 103n38;
profitability of, 203; in *Rep.* Book
4, 12, 21n31, 103n38, 180, 184, 186;
as self-mastery, 170n23, 171, 184; as
shared opinion of who should rule,
172, 184; Socrates on, 169–73; and tri-
creatured image, 204
music, 19, 47, 53, 54, 67, 82, 83

necessity, 110–11, 116–17, 213
Nichols, Mary P., 70n45, 134n12,
161n65, 185n59
Nussbaum, Martha, 69n44

Odysseus, 130n1, 136n17, 213
oligarchic men, 67n37, 72n51, 75,
183n55, 196
one-man, one-job principle, 51, 51n9,
198n85

Pericles, 135–36
Phaedo (Plato): on dream state, 15n12;
oddities in, 2; on opinion, 160n61; on
philosopher's orientation to the Forms,
19n22; on philosopher's soul, 58n22;
on Socrates' imprisonment and death,
143, 189; on suicide, 158n57; on the
virtuous by habit, 146n42
philein (to love), 14, 14n11, 34n65, 71
philosophers: in Callipolis, 8–9, 10,
42–43, 50, 70, 107, 153; in Cave allegory, 58–59; by chance, 9, 10;
contrast in *Rep.* Books 5 and 6, 16,
34; convergence of political power
and, 109; disinclination to rule of,
85; as distinguished by what they
love, 14–16, 32; *erōtikoi* compared
with, 14, 18; four philosophic types in
Rep. Book 6, 9, 10, 11, 27, 38, 40, 44;
frivolity attributed to, 28; humility
unavailable to, 158; hybrids, 51–55;
as kings, 13, 33, 33n63, 53, 54, 61n26,
99, 118, 131n3; leadership qualities of,
17; love of wisdom associated with, 9,
12, 20, 27, 34n65, 35, 44, 49, 65; making of, 49–84; new type introduced at
502e, 11, 44, 50; "philosophic" dogs of
Book 2, 11–12, 44–48, 50; philosophic
nature gone bad, 33–38; philosophic
rule, 4, 6, 7, 16–17, 20–22, 28–29, 32,
34, 41–42, 44, 50, 86, 109, 119n70, 140,
153; Platonic dialogues display philosophic life, 1–2; pseudo-philosophers,
38–40; *Republic*'s two portrayals of, 1,
3, 8; as saviors of the city, 49; and ship
image, 20–24, 33n63; Socrates as in
love with philosophy, 161; Socrates as
left-out philosopher, 135; Socrates as
third paradigm of, 9–10, 156, 217–18;
Socrates' divine mission, 135–43;
Socrates engages Glaucon regarding, 6, 7–8; take back seat in later
books, 207; uselessness attributed to,
4, 21n29, 21n31, 22, 24, 24n38, 26, 80,

125n82; viciousness attributed to, 4, 21, 22, 24n38, 25, 25n41, 34–35, 39; virtues of, 16–20, 35–36, 36n68, 52

philosophers of *Rep.* Book 6, 16–33; cannot be manufactured, 61–62; in Cave allegory, 58–59; as decent but useless, 22, 25–28, 29, 33, 130–32, 140, 156; initial appearance of, 9, 11, 44; and justice, 138, 152, 153; as orderly and divine, 31, 65, 160; philosophers of *Rep.* Book 7 contrasted with, 9, 61–62, 65–68, 69, 76–77, 78, 90, 91, 109, 111–12, 118–21; philosophic natures that do not mature into philosophers, 20, 50; as rare, 62; rule by, 28–33; Socrates compared with, 136, 137–38, 140, 152, 160, 217–18; types of men from myth of Er compared with, 216–18; virtues of, 52; and war, 14, 78; willingness to rule of, 112, 121

philosophers of *Rep.* Book 7, 60–84; appetitive nature of, 68–69, 78, 112, 217; Cicero's criticism of, 121–22; as compatible with vice as well as virtue, 65; compelled to return to the Cave, 70–76, 83, 89, 100, 105–6, 107–12; as created to rule Callipolis, 61–62; decency lacking in, 66, 66n35, 81, 156; education of, 81–83, 100, 101; as either very good or very bad, 66–67; founders' argument for compelling rule by, 98–107; and the Good, 61, 68, 70–76, 83–87, 103, 106, 109, 112, 114, 122, 159; good and decent men of *Rep.* Book 1 compared with, 122; guardians of Book 3 compared with, 52n12; and justice, 81, 113–21, 153–54, 217; lack natural love of wisdom, 72, 80–81; making rulers of, 85–128; moderation of, 75, 81, 83, 103n38; natural philosophers of Book 6 contrasted with, 9, 61–62, 65–68, 69, 76–77, 78, 90, 91, 109, 111–12, 118–21; roles assigned in accordance with their natural

aptitudes, 72n49; Socrates attributes qualities of *Rep.* Book 6 philosophers to, 77–81; Socrates contrasted with, 88–89, 152–56; Socrates' opinion of, 120; as true philosophers, 67n40; unwillingness to rule of, 85, 86–94; as warriors, 54, 68n43

philosopher-warriors, 41–44; as "best natures," 12n1; and the Cave allegory, 55–60; love of wisdom as no part of, 53; merged to appeal to Glaucon, 7; as not necessarily spirited, 74n55; philosophers of *Rep.* Book 7 given attributes of, 78–79, 81; as philosophic hybrids, 51–55; piety absent in, 135; and Popper's criticism of the *Republic,* 121n73; as rare, 25n41; in typology of philosophers in *Rep.* Book 6, 11, 50

phronēsai (to think), 64n30, 64–65, 65n32, 66, 68, 201n92

piety: as absent in *Republic,* 10, 133–35, 162–63; the humility factor, 156–62; the risk factor, 149–52, 162–63; Socrates' god, 143–45; Socrates on trial for impiety, 133, 144n38; as species of justice, 149–52; versus wisdom, 158, 162

Plato: and decent but useless philosophers of Book 6, 131n3; dialogues of, 1–3. See also *Apology; Crito; Gorgias; Phaedo; Republic; Theaetetus; and other works by name*

pleonexia (desire for more and more), 183, 183n54

Polemarchus: philosophic dogs compared with, 46; on rule of the wise, 12; and Socrates' argument about justice, 113, 147, 189; Socrates attempts to transfer task of discovering justice to, 179; Socrates rejects his conception of justice, 114n59, 190; whispers question to Adeimantus, 4, 42

politicians: convergence of philosophy and political power, 109; decent but

politicians *(continued)*
  useless philosophers barred from
    politics, 131, 132; Glaucon on soul's
    internal accord and politics, 205–6;
    Gorgias on political science, 31; in ship
    image, 22–24; Socrates avoids politics,
    131, 135–36, 144; Socrates finds way to
    be politically engaged, 218
Popper, Karl, 59n24, 121n73, 131n3
Prichard, H. A., 188n69
Protagoras (Plato), 125n81, 133, 134n13,
    139n24, 176n36, 180n49
punishment, 203–4, 208–9, 215

Reeve, C. D.C., 37n72, 69n44, 96n28,
    105n42, 106n44, 146n41, 169n17
repaying one's debts, 99–102, 104, 106,
    114, 119, 120
Republic (Plato): on cardinal virtues, 10;
    city divided into three classes in, 43;
    city-soul analogy, 1n1, 84, 165, 168,
    185, 190, 192; comparisons of people
    and animals in, 44; on divine nature,
    66n33; division into books, 8n20,
    11; on doing whatever one wants,
    108n49; Glaucon and Adeimantus
    as addressees of, 3–5; Gyges' ring,
    108n49, 146, 169, 169n17; on levels
    of justice, 145–49; on minding one's
    own business, 26, 26n45, 138–39;
    myth of Er, 146n42, 206n101,
    207n103, 208–18; one-man, one-job
    principle, 51; opens with prayer to
    goddess, 134n11; piety as absent from,
    133–35, 162–63; "rolling around" in,
    168n12; sharp-sightedness as recur-
    ring theme in, 17, 17n15, 63n28, 68,
    71, 165; ship allegory, 20–24, 26,
    33n63, 91, 131n3, 137; on Socrates
    going down to Piraeus, 139, 152;
    Socrates' two tasks in, 6–8; statue-
    image, 96; tri-creatured image,
    186n62, 204; two portrayals of the phi-
    losopher in, 1, 3, 8; on unification of
    the city, 95n27. *See also* Cave allegory

Robinson, Thomas M., 165n5
Roochnik, David, 5, 123n76
rulers: compelling, 107–12; doctors
    compared with, 91, 91n17; founders'
    argument regarding, 98–107; mod-
    eration defined as shared opinion of
    who should rule, 172, 184; philoso-
    phers as kings, 13, 33, 33n63, 53, 54,
    61n26, 99, 118, 131n3; philosophic
    rule, 4, 6, 7, 16–17, 20–22, 28–29, 32,
    34, 41–42, 44, 50, 86, 109, 119n70, 140,
    153; responding to justice, 113–21;
    rule of the wise, 12–13, 44n81; in
    securing city's happiness, 94–98; in
    three-part division of city in *Rep.*
    Book 4, 43; unwillingness to rule,
    86–94. *See also* guardians
Runciman, Walter G., 121n73, 187n67,
    192n77

Sachs, David, 186n62
Sachs, Joe, 3n6, 133n7
Saxonhouse, Arlene, 139n26
Schleiermacher, Friedrich, 28n52
Scott, Dominic, 86n2, 109n52
Sedley, David, 87n9
sharp-sightedness, 17, 17n15, 63n28, 68,
    71, 165
Shields, Christopher, 74, 84n72, 108, 110
ship allegory, 20–24, 26, 33n63, 91,
    131n3, 137
Smith, Nicholas D., 106n44, 165n5
Socrates: attempts to transfer discover-
    ing justice, 179; on Callipolis, 8–9;
    on Cave allegory, 55–60; on city's
    happiness, 94–98; on compatibility
    of opposing qualities, 18; on crafts-
    men, 25n43; *daimonion* of, 25, 25n44,
    132n5, 136, 137, 140, 144; descends
    into the Cave willingly, 86, 89; de-
    votes his life to fight for justice, 138;
    divine mission of, 135–43; on educa-
    tion of guardians, 53–55, 81–84; as
    erotic man, 161; finds way to be po-
    litically engaged, 218; as founder, 152,

159; four approaches to defending justice, 199–207; Glaucon asks him to lead, 13, 13n8, 130n1; Glaucon's intelligence disparaged by, 5; god of, 143–45; and the gods, 156n52, 208n1; goes down to Piraeus, 139, 152; on the Good as out of range, 159; on himself, 130–33; humility of, 156–62; ignorance professed by, 158–59; justice as defined by, 5, 10, 173–84; as just man, 10, 130; as left-out philosopher, 135; on longer road, 84, 84n71; love of wisdom of, 162; on minding one's own business, 26, 26n45, 138–39; on moderation, 169–73; as naïve, 129–30; as never taking money for his efforts, 127–28, 141–42, 189; none of his close associates find fault with him, 161n64; as not having seen the Good, 159, 188; on opinion, 160; on piety as species of justice, 149–52; Plato's message distinguished from that of, 2–3; politics avoided by, 131, 135–36, 144; resolution of problem of justice, 184–87; says little about himself, 129; searches for justice in the city, 165–69; sharp-sightedness of, 64; on sophists, 37n72, 37–38, 39; as street philosopher, 155; tailors method to needs of his interlocutors, 2; as third paradigm of philosopher, 9–10, 156, 217–18; Thrasymachus complains about methods of, 21n27, 129; Thrasymachus's view of justice opposed by, 190, 191–92, 194–97; two tasks in *Republic*, 6–8; on unwillingness to rule, 85–94; on useful lies, 31–32; on virtue for its own sake, 188; on virtues of philosophers, 16–20; will take Glaucon no farther, 159–60

sophists, 37n72, 37–38, 39, 116, 117, 166n7

Sophocles, 19

sōphrosunē. See moderation (*sōphrosunē; temperance*)

soul: city-soul analogy, 1n1, 84, 165, 168, 185, 190, 192; gymnastic of, 69; philosopher's, 58n22; two patterns for, 206n102; virtues of, 64–65

statue-image, 96

Strauss, Leo, 2n3, 3n6, 4n8, 7n18, 69n44, 108n48, 109n51

Symposium (Plato), 34n65, 86n2, 155n50, 161

temperance. *See* moderation (*sōphrosunē; temperance*)

Thayer, H. S., 213n16, 214n17

Theaetetus (Plato): on becoming like a god, 158n59; on blending of character qualities, 52n13; on giving an account "in private," 139n23; on mathematics as preparation for philosophy, 82n70; philosopher and non-philosopher contrasted in, 202n93; on popular disparagement of philosophers, 130n1; on the small-souled, 67n36; on Socrates' *erōs* for sparring in speech, 161; on truth being "at our feet," 168n12; on two patterns for the soul, 206n102

Theages, 25

therapeia, 156–57

Thrasymachus: on being ruled by someone else, 203; callous and uncharitable behavior of, 126–27; complains of Socrates' methods, 21n27, 129; Glaucon likened to, 128, 186n65; on injustice as superior, 6, 130, 165–66; on justice, 123, 124, 126n86, 147, 180n48, 187–88, 189, 190, 191–92, 194–97; philosophers of *Rep.* Book 7 compared with, 154; rulers and doctors compared by, 91n17; on rulers considering only how to benefit themselves, 125; on rulers ruling willingly, 122–23; on Socrates, 129–30, 143; Socrates on his failing to care, 102–3, 149; on those who desire to rule, 91; on virtue of the eyes, 63n28

thumos (spirit, emotion, anger), 74, 74n56, 80
timocracy, 82n69
tri-creatured image, 186n62, 204
tyrannic man, 111, 196n80, 199–203, 205, 209, 210, 211, 213, 214, 199–203; disordered soul of, 196n80; as without friends, 205; in myth of Er, 210, 211, 213, 214; philosophers of *Rep.* Book 7 contrasted with, 111; terrible fates of, 209

Vegetti, Mario, 206n102, 215n19
virtues: assigned to different parts of the city, 176n36; cardinal, 10, 133, 133n7; four virtues of perfectly good city, 132–33; freely choosing virtue, 213; of guardians, 173; of philosophers, 16–20; philosophers of *Rep.* Book 7 lack full complement of, 72; pursued for their own sake, 188; of the soul, 64–65; virtuousness by habit, 212
Vlastos, Gregory, 96n28, 155, 199n87
Voegelin, Eric, 69n11

Wagner, Ellen, 74
war: in education of philosophers of *Rep.* Book 7, 82; philosophers of *Rep.* Book 6 and, 14, 78, 81; in *Rep.* Book 7, 54. *See also* philosopher-warriors
Waterlow, Sarah, 87n8
Weiss, Roslyn, 145n39
White, Nicholas P., 84n71, 87n8
Wilson, John F., 89n15, 104n39
wisdom: applied to selfish ends, 192n77; and courage, 180n49; divine versus human, 156n53, 158; as easy to discover, 167; location in the city, 169–70, 172; as mark of perfectly good city, 132; oracle on Socrates', 10n21, 161n65; versus piety, 158, 162; rule of the wise, 12–13, 44n81. *See also* love of wisdom
Woods, Cathal, 109

Xenophanes, 145
Xenophon, 7n18

Yu, Jiyuan, 114n60